David Burke is a freelance historian. His published works include *The Spy Who Came In From The Co-op: Melita Norwood and The Ending of Cold War Espionage* (2008) and *The Lawn Road Flats: Spies, Writers and Artists* (2014). He has taught at the universities of Cambridge, Salford and Leeds. He holds a PhD from the University of Greenwich.

'The contribution of Russian political émigrés to the development of the British communist tradition has finally been given the attention it deserves. Through his long-standing interest in Theodore Rothstein, and by making extensive use of security service files, David Burke has deepened our understanding of British responses to the Russian Revolution.'

Geoff Andrews, author of *The Shadow Man*

'Excellent ... really well written and delves very deep into the Rothsteins' lives ... the archival basis of the study makes it genuinely original. The book is well conceived, neatly structured and astute in its analysis.'

Matthew Worley, Professor of History,
University of Reading

RUSSIA AND THE BRITISH LEFT

From the 1848 Revolutions to the
General Strike

DAVID BURKE

BLOOMSBURY ACADEMIC
LONDON • NEW YORK • OXFORD • NEW DELHI • SYDNEY

BLOOMSBURY ACADEMIC
Bloomsbury Publishing Plc
50 Bedford Square, London, WC1B 3DP, UK
1385 Broadway, New York, NY 10018, USA

BLOOMSBURY, BLOOMSBURY ACADEMIC and the Diana logo
are trademarks of Bloomsbury Publishing Plc

First published 2018 by I.B. Tauris & Co. Ltd.
Paperback edition first published by Bloomsbury Academic in 2020

ISBN: HB: 978-1-7883-1064-2
PB: 978-1-8386-0212-3
ePDF: 978-1-7867-3324-5
ePub: 978-1-7867-2324-6

Typeset by OKS Prepress Services, Chennai, India

To find out more about our authors and books visit
www.bloomsbury.com and sign up for our newsletters.

For Züleyha

'Strong men have run for miles and miles,
When one from Cherry Hinton smiles'
Rupert Brooke, *Grantchester.*

'listen: there's a hell
Of a good universe next door; let's go'
e.e. cummings, *pity this busy monster, manunkind*

CONTENTS

LIST OF PLATES

Plate 12 Grigori Zinoviev. Public domain.

Plate 13 Maxim Litvinov. Public domain.

Plate 14 Georgi Chicherin. Public domain.

Plate 15 General Strike 1926. Clockwise from left to right: Workers' demonstration; Oxford University student volunteers armed with wooden staves; Clashes between strikers and volunteer workers outside Kings Cross Station; Special Constables collecting their truncheons. Public domain.

Plate 16 Ivan Maisky. Courtesy of the National Portrait Gallery.

Plate 17 Mikhail Tomsky. Public domain.

ACKNOWLEDGEMENTS

This book has a long history, and the number of people who have made this book possible are too numerous to mention. First and foremost I would like to thank Professor Fred Lindop for introducing me to Theodore Rothstein and the Jewish labour movement in London's East End and Dr Lewis Johnman for his encouragement and expertise in the field of labour history. Secondly, I would like to thank Professors Julian Cooper and Johnathan Haslam for encouraging me to broaden this research to include the Russian political emigration, and Professor Bob Davies for inspiring an interest in the history of the Soviet Union. I would also like to thank Professor Christopher Andrew and the Cambridge Intelligence Seminar for introducing me to 'the missing dimension' – the role played by intelligence in shaping our perceptions of the 'real world'. Professor Andrew's knowledge of the intelligence world is unparalleled. I would also like to thank fellow students and staff from the University of Greenwich and the Centre for Russian and East European Studies, University of Birmingham, who both 'thrilled over' and, no doubt, occasionally groaned over yet another Rothstein story. Jane Austen summed it up best: 'Think only of the past as its remembrance gives you pleasure.'

Finally, I would like to thank Olga Kimkhai for her untiring efforts in teaching an exceedingly bad pupil Russian and I.B.Tauris's Lester Crook, Jo Godfrey and Arub Ahmed for their patience and skill in preparing the text for publication.

LIST OF ABBREVIATIONS

ARCOS	All-Russian Co-operative Society
ASE	Amalgamated Society of Engineers
BF	British Fascisti
BSP	British Socialist Party
CID	Criminal Investigation Department
CORSGL	Committee of Russian Socialist Groups in London
CPGB	Communist Party of Great Britain
CPSU	Communist Party of the Soviet Union
CWC	Clyde Workers' Committee
DNI	Director of National Intelligence
DORA	Defence of the Realm Act
ECCI	Executive Committee of the Communist International
FJPC	Foreign Jews Protection Committee against Deportation to Russia and Compulsion
FPA	Federated Press of America
GC&CS	Government Code and Cypher School
GDC	Glasgow District Council (BSP)
HOW	Home Office Warrant
IFTU	International Federation of Trade Unions
IIB	Industrial Intelligence Bureau
ILP	Independent Labour Party
ISDA	International Social-Democratic Association
IWW	International Workers of The World

LRC	Labour Representation Committee
NKID	People's Commissariat for Foreign Affairs (Narkomindel)
NMM	National Minority Movement
OGPU	*Obyesinennoye Gosudarstvennoye Politicheskoye Upravleniye* (Soviet Security and Intelligence Service 1923–34)
OMS	Organisation for the Maintenance of Supplies
RFPF	Russian Free Press Fund
RILU	Red International of Labour Unions (Profintern)
ROP	Russian Oil Products
ROSTA	Russian Telegraph Agency
RPPEF	Russian Political Prisoners' and Exiles' Fund
RPPERC	Russian Political Prisoners and Exiles Relief Committee
RSDLP	Russian Social-Democratic Labour Party
SAPREPA	*Societe des amis du people russe et des peoples annexes*
SDF	Social Democratic Federation
SDP	Social Democratic Party
SFRF	Society of Friends of Russian Freedom
SIB	Special Intelligence Bureau
SLP	Socialist Labour Party
SPD	German Social-Democratic Party
SSSR	Union of Socialist Soviet Republics
SRs	Socialist-Revolutionaries
SSB	Secret Service Bureau
TASS	Telegraph Agency of the Soviet Union
TUC	Trades Union Congress
USSR	Union of Socialist Soviet Republics
VDA	Vigilance Detective Agency
VKP(b)	London cell of the Russian Communist Party
WSF	Workers Socialist Federation

Introduction

Stuart MacIntyre's book *Marxism in Britain: A Proletarian Science 1917–1933* is probably not on the modern-day intelligence officer's bookshelf but if the Cold War is to be understood without confusion it should be. The study of native 'Marxisms', often a neglected topic in Cold War studies, throws light on what many historians have referred to as 'the enemy within'. Too often, communism in Britain, and the secret war to defeat it, has been written in terms of foreign or 'alien' influence on British institutions, whether that be the trade unions, the Foreign Office, the universities or a political party. *Russia) and the British Left: From the 1848 Revolutions to the General Strike* is an attempt to address that problem by looking at the activities of the Russian political emigration in Britain, and the role of one Russian-Jewish political émigré family in particular. Theodore Rothstein and his son Andrew, along with his sister-in-law Zelda Kahan and her husband W. P. Coates, played an important part in the formative years of British communism, which was closely) monitored by the British secret service. This led to claims that British communism was effectively a Russian creation, with Theodore Rothstein acting as the *éminence grise*, the hidden hand of Moscow controlling the British Left.

This book explores Henry Pelling's compelling statement 'that there can be few topics more worthy of exploration than the problem of how it came to pass, that a band of British citizens could sacrifice themselves so completely [...] to the service of a dictatorship in another country'.[1] The case of the Cambridge Five – not discussed in this book – has often been the starting point for those interested in solving Pelling's conundrum. But an examination of the Russian political emigration between 1848 and 1928, viewed mainly through the lens of the Rothstein family and the British labour movement, demonstrates quite clearly that the history of Russian and Soviet intelligence activity in Britain goes back much further than the 1930s, when the Cambridge Five were recruited by the Russian Intelligence Service.

The relationship between the British left and Russia throughout this period was a two-way affair. Rothstein studied his Marxism in Britain and applied it to Russian conditions; he became a Bolshevik in 1902 but remained wedded to independent labour representation in Parliament. He was tutored in the anti-imperialist struggle by the English aristocrat Wilfrid Scawen Blunt, whose reputation as a radical later influenced his younger kinsman, the art historian and Cambridge spy Anthony Blunt. In the years leading up to World War I, Rothstein played a prominent part in the anti-militarist movement, consistently playing down the 'German menace' while challenging Britain's national imperialism. His arguments that British imperialism and jingoism were to blame for the deteriorating relations between the British Empire and their German rival struck a chord on the left. Back in Moscow he played a major role in undermining British imperial interests in Persia and the East.

The development of a British intelligence service capable of responding to these threats to the British Empire forms an important backdrop to this book, and the security service's monitoring of Theodore Rothstein before World War I sheds light on that service's ability not only to contain 'the enemy within' but also to identify and act against threats originating from 'alien' sources. In this respect, Rothstein's Russo-Jewish origins were regarded with some distaste by both Special Branch and MI5; anti-Semitism simmered beneath the surface of British society throughout the period under discussion.

During the war itself many 'enemy aliens' were interned. Rothstein was warned by friends that he was in danger of being detained, resigned his membership of the openly Marxist British Socialist Party (BSP), then affiliated with the Labour Party, and joined British intelligence's MI7. Even before the October Revolution this was an astonishing event. Special Branch had opened a file on him as early as 1899 owing to his opposition to the Boer War; while MI5 followed suit in 1911 because of his strong anti-British views expressed during the Agadir Crisis. But, after the Russian Revolutions of March and October 1917, Rothstein's British Marxist background and his knowledge of the German and Russian socialist movements proved to be too valuable an intelligence asset for the security and intelligence services to ignore. Moreover, he was exceptionally good at his job – so much so that the author John Buchan, among other notables in the business of propaganda, regarded him very highly.

Throughout his career with British intelligence Rothstein continued to work clandestinely for the BSP, both in its opposition to the war and in support of the international socialist movement. Between 1917 and 1920 he channelled the much maligned 'Moscow Gold' to those sympathetic to Soviet communism in the labour movement, and brought the disparate British Marxist groups together to form the Communist Party of Great Britain (CPGB) in 1920. To what extent Rothstein was acting as a native Marxist as opposed to a tool of the Communist International is an interesting question in the light of Pelling's statement and the reorientation of British Marxism in the 1920s. He was effectively debarred from Britain in 1920 and his clandestine activities passed to his son, Andrew.

Russia and the British Left, therefore, encompasses two periods. The first, 1848–1920, looks at the contribution of the Russian political emigration to British Marxism and the response of the British intelligence services, Special Branch and MI5, to what they regarded as a serious threat to British security. The second part, 1920–8, probes Pelling's conundrum and looks at four main incidents: the formation of the Anglo-Russian Committee and the Zinoviev Letter in 1924, the General Strike of 1926 and the ARCOS Raid of 1927. It concludes with the Comintern's strategy of 'Class against Class' and looks briefly at the events that led to Andrew Rothstein joining his father in Moscow in 1930, when, in many respects, the utopian idealism that had characterized the activities of father and son from 1890–1930 was subsumed by a more dystopian reality.

Both sections rely heavily, although not exclusively, on documents released by the security service MI5. This has its own dangers, not least the reliability of documents produced by a secret service; but this is a danger inherent in most documents. As a safeguard the research has been guided by the advice given to the author in 1981 by Andrew Rothstein, one of the subjects of this book:

> Speaking generally, anyone who seeks to interpret the struggle of the internationalists in the Social-Democratic movement, from say 1911 to 1920, in terms of conspiracy instead of politics, sows confusion instead of history at best, and at worst becomes a tool of unscrupulous falsification. You might find it useful to look up Marx's letter to Kugelmann after the Paris Commune, about the "police-tinged bourgeois mind" seeing the work of the International as "organising explosions" in various countries. It is on a par with the mind that sees British Communism as the work of "Russian Bolsheviks".[2]

Sound advice; conspiracy theory is never far away from politics, nor, of course, is bias a stranger to history. However, the 'police-tinged bourgeois mind' seeing 'organised explosions' everywhere has, thankfully, become more sophisticated since the days of Marx's First International and the Paris Commune. I have sought to strike a balance between the needs of state security and the activities, 'organised explosions' if you will, of a revolutionary party in a democracy. The release of security service documents has encouraged a growing historiography of intelligence studies; the following is intended as a small contribution to this subject, albeit from the point of view of the 'watched' as opposed to the 'watchers'.

1

The Russian Political Emigration

We've had enough of being carried away by our enthusiasms. It's high time we grew sensible. And all this, all this life abroad, and all this Europe of yours is just a delusion, and all of us abroad are a delusion. Mark my words, you'll see it for yourself.

Fyodor Dostoevsky, *The Idiot* (1869)[1]

The last decades of Tsarism gave rise to levels of political violence that both shocked liberals abroad and won their admiration. The female terrorists Vera Zasulich, Vera Figner and Sophia Perekovskaya inspired a number of literary works by Western writers on Russian nihilism and the darker aspects of the Russian secret police, among them *The Princess Casamassima* (1886) by Henry James and Oscar Wilde's *Vera, or the Nihilists* (1883) and *Lord Arthur Savile's Crime* (1891).[2] The most prolific English spy novelist of the late nineteenth and early twentieth centuries, William Le Quex, wrote four novels on nihilism and the Russian secret service, *Guilty Bonds* (1891), *Strange Tales of a Nihilist* (1892, republished in 1896 under the title *A Secret Service*), *The Czar's Spy* (1905) and *The Great Plot* (1907). Joseph Conrad's *The Secret Agent* (1907), set in the year 1886, brought to life Britain's anarchist cells and their covert dealings with foreign governments in late nineteenth century London. Conrad's *Under Western Eyes* (1911), a scathing attack upon the historical failures of European revolutionary ideals and movements, took place against an atmospheric backdrop of fog-bound St Petersburg and the conspiracies of the Russian political émigrés in Geneva.

Throughout this period Russia's ubiquitous secret police, the Third Department, set about detecting and persecuting all forms of sedition in act, word, or thought within the Russian empire and abroad. Established in the wake of the Decembrist conspiracy,[3] the Third Department targeted all manifestations of Russian idealism, democracy and utopian thought. Five of the Decembrists were hanged and over 100 sent in chains to the Siberian mines. Their heroic martyrdom inspired generations of revolutionaries and, paradoxically, the secret policemen recruited to oppose them.

The Third (civilian) Section of His Imperial Majesty's Chancellery, to give it its full title, comprised a small nucleus of professional detectives and a mass of poorly paid agents, spies and informers, it created the illusion of an all-seeing, all-knowing entity feasting on the vagaries of Russian law which decreed that 'non-denunciation of a crime, of an intended crime, or even of a suspected crime, was punishable just as severely as the crime itself'.[4] In this way an entire army of informers was created across all sections of Russian society, not least amongst that resolute group of *dvorniki* (caretakers), which to this day continue to grace most, if not all, of Russia's cities and towns. Their role had a devastating effect on the aristocratic 'salons' of St Petersburg and Moscow society that offered a toxic mixture of pleasure-seeking, literary criticism and political discussion:

> The *dvorniki* – each town house in Russia had one and he was on duty sixteen hours a day – were required to report to the police any suspicious conversations or movements.[5]

During the 1840s the centre of philosophical debate in Russia centred upon the 'Moscow Circles' which had first made their appearance in the 1820s in response to the Enlightenment only to be suppressed after the Decembrist rising. There were a great many of these circles; loose associations of gifted, imaginative intellectuals, each circle boasting its own individual character. The three principle circles were the Slavophil Circles that met at Madame Elagina's; the circles graced by Mikhail Bakunin; and the circles led by Alexander Herzen, the first to study the doctrines of the French precursors of socialism, and of Saint-Simonianism.[6] These circles, known to the Third Section as 'gangs of liberal bandits', recruited most of their members from the University of Moscow, which was also known as 'the University of secret Hegelism'.[7]

Herzen had been arrested in 1834 and had been charged with 'Opposition to the spirit of the Government, and revolutionary opinions imbued with the pernicious doctrines of Saint-Simon.' He was sent to Perm and then to Vyatka and Vladimir, 'where he was to live under the supervision of the local police authorities.'[8] At the beginning of 1840 he was returned to Moscow, but was soon re-arrested and accused of 'spreading rumours injurious to the Government.' He was again banished, this time to Novgorod.[9] In 1842 he was permitted to reside in Moscow under police supervision, and in 1847 he was granted an exit permit to go abroad and left Russia on the eve of the French Revolution of 1848.

The Second Republic, a democratic provisional government based on male universal suffrage, which replaced the regime of the French monarch Louis Phillipe, was welcomed by Herzen 'as a kind of Second Coming.' The liberal revolutions that now swept across Europe were a turning point in the history of the Russian intelligentsia, and set out in strong relief the rival philosophical and ideological claims of pan-Slavism and liberalism. While the Slavophils spoke of the 'decline of Europe' and of Russia's mission 'to save the soul of Europe', Herzen and his followers believed that Russia's true salvation would come from the revolutionary ideals of the West. The autocracy's fear of France in 1848 triggered considerable alarm in Russia. 'Napoleon's bid for mastery in Europe lay only thirty years behind' and it was generally supposed that France would 'renew the attempt'.[10] 'The Holy Alliance' of Austria, Prussia and Russia against the French-inspired revolutions was brought into force and the Russian Army was called upon to crush the liberal uprising in Hungary. Increased repression at home, supervised by the Third Section, led to a tightening of censorship and the literary output of the 'Circles' was severely curtailed.

The Second Republic, however, failed to live up to Herzen's Saint-Simonian dreams and the massacre of over 10,000 workers during the 'June Days'[11] led him to revise his attitude towards liberal democracy and the West. His letter to the French historian Jules Michelet, entitled 'The Russian People and Socialism', marked his spiritual return to Russia: 'In the midst of this chaos [...] in the midst of this world, disintegrating into ashes, [...] eyes involuntarily turn to the East [...] [Russia] is a people having Communism as its basic principle'[12] and would now 'show the world the path to socialism and thus to salvation'.[13] He regarded the free development of the *mir*, the village commune, which combined a common tenure of land with individual cultivation, and the *artel*, a union of workmen collectively entering into free agreements to work in various trades for a specific period of time, as Russia's challenge to western bourgeois society. Russia, owing to the existence of the Russian village commune and the *artel* would successfully bypass the 'dreaded stage of western European capitalism' and would reject the belief 'that only private enterprise or self-interest is socially creative, and that men in all their social actions are self-regarding'.[14]

Herzen's romanticised vision of the Russian peasantry and communal life stood in marked contrast to his life in the West. In 1852 he moved to London, where he experienced the *anomie* of the exile. 'There is no town in the world', Herzen wrote, 'which is more adapted for training one away from people and training one into solitude than London.'[15] He did, however, enjoy the city's relative tranquillity, where revolutionary violence and secret policemen were almost unknown:

> Until I came to England the appearance of a police officer in a house where I was living always produced an indefinable disagreeable feeling, and I was at once morally on my guard against an enemy. In England a policeman at your door merely adds to your sense of security.[16]

This sense of security helped Herzen cope with the isolation he felt living in London, where he lived for 12 years. London was then home to a number of prominent revolutionary exiles, including Karl Marx and from 1861 Mikhail Bakunin. He set up the Free Russian Printing Press and produced a number of pamphlets critical of Tsardom, which were then smuggled across the Russian border.[17] Between 1857 and 1867 he oversaw publication of *Kolokol* (*The Bell*), a popular weekly that poured 'clandestinely into Russia in numerous copies'.[18] Its success was staggering. 'It was read by everyone and became the mainspring of inspiration for the younger intelligentsia; it found its way even into Ministerial cabinets and the Winter Palace, and, more surprisingly still, [...] it reached the peasants, or at any rate some of the leaders of peasant revolts. In fact, for the space of about five years *The Bell* exercised the function of a dominant political force and served as the originator and promoter of public opinion in Russia – a case unique in modern history, considering the political and geographical circumstances of the whole venture.'[19]

The articles, written mainly by Herzen himself, 'were ultra-revolutionary, anarchistic and Bakunist in character.'[20] A trend that would become more pronounced following the shooting of demonstrators by Russian troops in Warsaw in 1861. The Polish uprising marked Herzen's final break with the Westernising liberals of his own generation. Following the emancipation of the serfs in the same year, many liberals made their peace with their Tsar and were determined to uphold Russian interests in Poland. Following the arrival of Bakunin in London in 1861 strong anarchistic tendencies in Herzen's thought vied with quasi-Slavophil and populist socialism to produce a specifically Russian spiritual and cultural philosophy. Herzen, however, remained a revolutionary and in 1869 he broke with Bakunin and sided with Marx's First International despite having previously described the *Communist Manifesto* of 1848 as 'Russian autocracy turned upside down.'[21] The next generation of Russian political émigrés continued this Marxist trend; detaching themselves more completely from the remnants of quasi-Slavophilism to grapple with the competing Western doctrines of liberalism and socialism. The experience of the Russian nihilist, Sergei Mikhailovich Kravchinski (better known to contemporaries by the pseudonym Stepniak) at a demonstration of British workmen in London's Hyde Park in 1885 not only identified the growing tensions unfolding between liberalism and socialism within British society; but also the nascent ideological aspirations of the Russian intelligentsia soon to be confronted by a Russian working class in the making:

> Here, in the centre of London, were hundreds and thousands of people, with banners, red flags, caps of liberty and even coffins on poles, surrounding a dozen platforms from which men were making recklessly seditious speeches, and circulating reams of tracts and leaflets, the mildest sentiments of which would have meant Siberia to the most highly privileged persons in Russia. Would the government do nothing? Would the vast crowd, apparently the nucleus of a revolution only buy a pennyworth of acidulated drops to give tone to its hoots for Lord Salisbury and Lord Randolph Churchill, and then go home unmolested and unconcerned?[22]

This apparent tolerance of the British Government towards sedition and political dissent, incredible to Stepniak, would shape the liberal democratic views of prominent Russian political émigrés in Britain as the nineteenth century drew to a close. However, in Hyde Park on that day Stepniak identified another group of demonstrators, 'a hardly imperceptible spot upon the vast expanse of the sea of heads', who would come to dominate Russian political émigré thinking in the early years of the new century:

> It was in 1885 – just eight years ago. The Conservatives were in power, and the Liberals organised an enormous mass meeting in support of the Franchise Bill. The meeting was an imposing one [...] A long line of platforms [...] stretched in a huge curve

from the Marble Arch to Hyde Park Corner. A dense crowd passed around each of the vans at which, like so many attractive magnates, stood the notabilities of Liberalism.

On the western ridge of the surging, restless human river there was another very small platform, overshadowed by a few red banners. It drew no crowd, and was but a hardly perceptible spot upon the vast sea of heads [. . .] When the meeting was over and the meeting broke up, the Socialists began their speeches [. . .] But the crowd was so out of touch and sympathy with the men who stood upon the solitary van, that when John Burns used a rather disrespectful expression with reference to John Bright, the crowd wanted to silence him, as he would not be silenced they rushed towards the van, broke and tore to pieces all the banners, pulled down the obstinate speaker, and wanted to throw him in the Serpentine [. . .] the crowd which attacked the platform on that occasion was as much a *bona fide* workman's crowd as that which flows to Hyde Park to the May Day demonstrations. I can say this because I saw it, having just arrived in England. This was my first experience of English political life.[23]

In his last speech before his death in December 1895, delivered before contributors to the Independent Labour Party's newspaper *Labour Leader*, Stepniak could remark upon – 'The great advance which Socialism has made in England [. . .] In ten years, I may say, the face of England has been changed in this respect.'[24]

Over the course of those ten years significant changes had indeed taken place in the world of organised labour, in Russia as well as in England. When he arrived in Britain in 1885 Stepniak had personified that period of Russian history associated with the individual acts of terrorism of the *Narodnaya Volya* (*People's Will*), by the time of his death he was a socialist of the William Morris type.

Born in the south of Russia on 14 July 1852 (O.S. 2 July),[25] of noble birth, Stepniak had been educated at the Aleksandrov Military Academy in St Petersburg. Spurning a military career, on graduation he left the army and enrolled at the St Petersburg Agricultural Institute. In the spring of 1872 he joined the Chaikovskii Circle, a revolutionary organisation affiliated to the *People's Will* that toured the Russian countryside seeking converts. 'Going to the People' became their slogan and Stepniak joined their campaign in Tver province. In 1875 he toured Europe, fought briefly in the Herzegovinia peasant uprising, and was imprisoned in Austrian Italy in 1877 as a result. On 13 August 1878 (O.S. 1 August), following his release and return to Russia he stabbed to death in broad daylight the St Petersburg police chief, Adjutant-General Mezentsev. The murder was an attempt to revive the flagging spirits of the *People's Will* by emulating Vera Zasulich's earlier unsuccessful attempt on the life of the St Petersburg police chief Colonel Trepov, which had resulted in a general wave of sympathy for the terrorists. He immediately fled Russia, living first in Switzerland and then in Italy, where he wrote for the Italian newspaper *Il Pungolo*. He produced a series of sketches for this paper on the Russian revolutionary movement, which were published in book form in 1882 under the title *La Rossia Sotterranea*. The work was translated into English in 1883 as *Underground Russia*, and immediately received high praise from, among others, Mark Twain and William Morris. The purpose of this book, Stepniak wrote, was to 'reconcile Europe to the bloody measures of the Russian revolutionaries, to show on the one hand their inevitability in Russian conditions, on the other to depict the terrorists as they are in reality, i.e. not as cannibals, but as human people, highly moral, having a deep aversion to violence, to which they are only forced by government measures.'[26]

His reputation went ahead of him with the book and he moved to England in 1884 because of the great popular success that *Underground Russia* had enjoyed there, entertaining the hope of enlisting the support of Western public opinion in the fight against the Russian autocracy. In England, as stated, his first experience of political life was at the great Franchise demonstration in Hyde Park. Soon afterwards he gave his first English lecture in 1886 to the Hammersmith Branch of William Morris's Socialist League, at

Kelmscott House. This lecture was chaired by Morris, and was attended by George Bernard Shaw, who later claimed that it was this experience which convinced Stepniak that 'the effusive rallyings round him of the little handful of toy revolutionists who called themselves "revolutionary social democrats", Anarchists, Fellows of the New Life, and so on,' would 'do his cause a great deal of harm and no good whatsoever.'[27] Stepniak, however, was certainly not averse to cultivating a wider audience for his views. In the same year he met the orthodox Tory MP W. Earl Hodgson, who after dispelling his initial suspicions concerning the curious taste of the tea (which he initially thought was poisoned), concluded that 'the Nihilists are aglow with the same spirit that would send the British Tories into rebellion were our fatherland suddenly to come under the absolute rule of the soulless and self-seeking caucus that lives to do the behests of Mr. Chamberlain.'[28]

However, despite introducing Hodgson to the delights of the Russian samovar, in his first five years in England, Stepniak remained closest to the socialists, although he would become increasingly dissatisfied with their internal disagreements, and their inability to offer anything in the way of practical help. Particularly damaging was the schism within the Social Democratic Federation (SDF), Britain's first avowedly Marxist organisation founded in 1884 by the Eton-educated, top-hatted stockbroker and Sussex county cricketer Henry Hyndman,[29] that led to the creation of William Morris's Socialist League in 1885.[30] The reasons behind this schism were many, but largely concerned differences of opinion over socialist tactics and the competing personalities of Hyndman and Morris. Accusations were made that Hyndman's position as editor of the SDF's newspaper, *Justice*, and as chairman of the SDF had allowed him to obtain dictatorial powers. Matters came to a head when charges were laid at Hyndman's door that he was guilty of absolutism and political opportunism.

The charges carried some weight. In 1884 Hyndman had assumed control of the socialist monthly, *To-Day*, which had previously been edited by the historian, and ally of William Morris, Belfort Bax. Hyndman had also expressed his approval of

General Gordon's despatch to Khartoum to supress the Sudanese revolt, which condemned him in the eyes of Morris and the anti-imperialist left. On 23 December 1884 an executive meeting discussed a vote of no confidence in Hyndman's leadership before adjourning for four days, finally carrying the motion by 10 votes to 8. The ten executive members then resigned from the SDF *en masse*, founded the Socialist League and launched a new socialist newspaper, the *Commonweal*.

The *Commonweal* was a far more attractive paper than *Justice*, and was dismissed by the SDF as being looser in its political judgement. It was certainly less theoretical concentrating more on what Morris referred to as 'the propaganda' as opposed to Marxian scientific socialism. The paper attracted a great deal of support from foreign revolutionaries including Stepniak, who contributed one of the first articles to the newspaper when Morris started it in 1885.[31] The theorist of the *People's Will*, Piotr Lavrov, then in exile in France and Lev Tikhomirov,[32] a member of the Executive Committee of the Narodnoya Volya living in exile in Switzerland, also sent a message of goodwill. Both Lavrov and Tikhomirov were 'Morrisian' in their vision, denying the relevance of capitalism to Russia's political development and engaging in polemics with the father of Russian Marxism, Georgi Plekhanov, who regarded the development of capitalism in agrarian Russia as a necessary first step in Russia's evolution towards socialism. In 1883 Plekhanov, who had been in emigration in Switzerland since 1880, had broken with the *People's Will* and had joined with Pavel Axelrod, Lev Deutsch, Vasily Ignatiev and Vera Zasulich to form the first Russian-language Marxist political organisation, the *Gruppa Ozvobozhdenie Truda* (the *Emancipation of Labour Group*), in Geneva to popularise the economic ideas and philosophy of Karl Marx. The group attracted a number of eminent intellectuals among them Peter Struve, Vladimir Ulianov (Lenin), Iulii Martov, and Alexander Potresov laying the foundations for a Social-Democratic Labour Party in Russia based upon the Social-Democratic movement of Western Europe. It was not accidental, therefore, that the old representatives of the *People's Will*, Lavrov, Stepniak and Tikhomirov, should be invited to write for the *Commonweal*; while the *Emancipation of Labour Group* published material in the more avowedly Marxist journals of the social-democratic SDF. It was, however, the great literary output of Stepniak in these years, which included articles in *The Times* on education and censorship in Russia, and on 'Russian Political Prisons' in Hyndman's *To-Day*, that determined the attitude of British Socialists, Liberals and Radicals towards the Russian revolutionaries.[33]

Stepniak's second major work to be published in Britain was *Russia Under The Tsars*, reviewed in the *Commonweal* for June 1885. This work explored the history of the *mir* (peasant commune) of the Russian village, the *veche* (popular assemblies) in medieval Russian towns and the evolution of despotism out of free institutions.[34] The whole tone of the book was one of looking backwards to a golden age, to a medieval period before tyranny had imposed itself on the people. 'In this idealised description of early Russia', one historian has observed, 'the reader recognises Stepniak's aspirations for the future of Russia.'[35] Such an approach, however, served merely to reinforce the agrarian-based socialism of Lavrov and Tikhomirov centred upon the Russian peasantry, which relied upon a simple propping up of the *mir* and the further development of *kustar* (small domestic industry). It also appealed to the romanticism inherent in Morris's thought with his looking back to monasteries, church fraternities and guilds. It was evident, therefore, that Stepniak, as a publicist, sought to maximise both the views of his old friends among the *People's Will* and his new friends in the Socialist League. This was not to be without significance. In 1882, the year before the formation of the Emancipation of Labour Group, Plekhanov had sought to merge his Marxist group – Deutsch, Zasulich, Axelrod and Ignatiev – with the *People's Will*. The new organisation was to publish a journal abroad entitled *Vestnik Narodnoi Voli* (*Courier of the People's Will*). Stepniak along with Lavrov and Plekhanov were to become its editors. The project broke down, however, owing to what Plekhanov saw as a lack of theoretical clarity among the *People's Will*, and in particular from Stepniak. In the spring of 1882 he voiced his fears in a letter to Lavrov:

You know my way of thinking, and I can assure you that it has not changed since I left Paris [...] we hoped and hope still to turn *Narodovolism* [the *populism* of the *People's Will*] on to the right road [...] In case of failure on our side, we shall have to go into opposition again; would that be fitting for me, as an editor of *Vestnik Narodnoi Voli?* Furthermore, there exists between me and Serg. Mikh. [Stepniak], it seems to me, a significant difference in views: he is a sort of Proudhonist,[36] I don't understand Proudhon; our characters are not alike; he is a person who is extremely tolerant of every variant of socialist thought, I am ready to make of *Capital* a Procrustean bed for all the collaborators of *Vestnik Narodnoi Voli.*[37]

Yet what Plekhanov did not realise at the time of writing was Lavrov's own closeness to the views of Stepniak and Tikhomirov. Indeed, Lavrov was to turn against his old friend Plekhanov, reproaching him for choosing to fight against other revolutionaries rather than against the common enemy – autocracy. European socialists were asked to play their part in this quarrel. *Commonweal*, if not directly employed by the *People's Will*, was certainly a vehicle for its message; publishing their views and ignoring completely those of the Emancipation of Labour Group. Moreover, censure of Plekhanov came from surprising quarters. Having based his claims for the applicability of Marxism to Russia on the 'Europeanisation' of that country by capitalism, Plekhanov devised his tactics accordingly. The future political development of Russia was to be based upon two revolutionary episodes of Western European history: France 1789 and Germany 1848. That is to say, a political revolution carried out by the liberal bourgeoisie, that is, France 1789, to be followed by revisionist or reformist, as opposed to revolutionary, tactics not unlike those adopted by the German Social-Democratic Party (SPD) post-1848. Western European socialists, however, could see little further than 1789 playing itself out again in late nineteenth-century Russia. Friedrich Engels, in a letter to Vera Zasulich, argued that 'Russia was approaching her 1789 [...] and it mattered not under what banner the revolution began.'[38] To Engels, as to many European socialists, the *People's Will* was to be the vanguard of revolution in Russia. It was ironic, however, that the self-sacrificing idealism of the *People's Will* should triumph over the minds of many Western European socialists at the very time when, according to Plekhanov, they had visibly declared their weakness. The assassination of Alexander II in March 1881, greeted enthusiastically by reformers throughout Europe, was dismissed as a futile act by Plekhanov. The failure of the *People's Will* to follow up assassination with a popular rising demonstrated their inability to move Russia forward without an organised political force in the country. At a time when Plekhanov was identifying the embryonic industrial working class as a potential revolutionary force in Russia, Western socialists, courted by émigré members of the *People's Will*, could see little further than the need for isolated acts of terrorism in support of a romanticised lost past. The *Commonweal*, by opening its pages to the *People's Will* and ignoring the growth of Social-Democracy within Russia contributed to this general attitude.

That this was the dominant position of the time was borne out by the disappointing coverage of the Russian revolutionary movement by the SDF in their newspaper, *Justice*. Throughout the 1880s the SDF concentrated their energies on domestic affairs, and did not cultivate the Russian political émigré community as assiduously as the Socialist League. This was undoubtedly a reflection of the SDF's parochialism when it came to the international socialist movement. As a result articles in *Justice* concerning the activities of the Russian revolutionary movement ignored developments taking place inside Russia, and merely reported the more sensationalist aspects of the Nihilist movement. The SDF in the first decade of its existence exhibited a chauvinism which served only to alienate the leading members of the Russian émigré community in Britain. Ideologically, the SDF should have arraigned itself alongside Plekhanov's Emancipation of Labour Group and in opposition to the *People's Will* but it was not until the founding conference of the Second International, an organization of socialist and labour parties formed in Paris on

14 July 1889, that the Russian revolutionary movement forced itself upon the attentions of the British Marxist movement. However, disagreements between the Russian delegates – Lavrov, Plekhanov, Beck and Kranz (the last from London) – convinced Stepniak, who had originally been invited to attend as a delegate from the Socialist League before protests from Hyndman caused him to withdraw, that in-fighting among the socialists was damaging the Russian revolutionary cause. Stepniak now changed direction and he began to forge contacts between the emigration and Radical elements within the Liberal Party. On 9 November 1889 he received a letter from Robert Spence Watson, President of the National Liberal Federation, offering his assistance in publishing and disseminating pamphlets on the Russian situation, with the aim of awakening public sympathy. The two men met in London in November 1889 and conducted further meetings throughout December with sympathetic friends. The result of these meetings was the formation of the Society of Friends of Russian Freedom (SFRF), a group dominated by Liberal sympathisers, who held views in direct opposition to Stepniak's former friends among the socialists.[39] Indeed, British socialists seeing in Liberal radicalism a bigger threat to their existence than that posed by Toryism were effectively, if not directly, snubbed. Stepniak continued to address socialist meetings, but he now did so on a very irregular basis. The Russian political émigrés in 1890 were being wooed by what Herzen in the 1850s had dismissed as 'mediocre rubbish', and the émigré 'socialist-narodnik' Nikolai Chaikovskii,[40] founder of the notorious Chaikovskii Circle in St Petersburg, had more politely referred to as 'the English tradition of moderation.'[41]

In September 1890 the SFRF tightened its organisation by setting up a General Committee of the Society consisting of 37 members, 13 of whom were also to serve on a smaller Executive Committee. The latter group consisted of such Liberal notables as W. P. Byles, J. Allanson Picton, G. H. Perris, Joshua Rowntree and T. Fisher Unwin. The SFRF published a journal entitled *Free Russia*, which first appeared in June 1890 and was issued monthly from September 1890, until its demise in January 1915. A number of Russians were associated with the group including Chaikovskii, who had emigrated to America in 1875 before arriving in England in May 1878, and Felix Volkhovskii, who had had been sentenced to life exile in Siberia at the famous 'Trial of the 193' in 1878.[42] In Tomsk he had been befriended by the American explorer George Kennan who, in 1889 had helped him escape by way of the Amur River, Vladivostock and Japan. In June 1890 he arrived in London where he began editing *Free Russia*. Like Chaikovskii and Stepniak he remained essentially an agrarian socialist and while in emigration developed views similar to Stepniak's – that the political revolution would precede economic emancipation.

The SFRF adopted the political programme for a new Russia worked out by Stepniak in 1891, established the Russian Free Press Fund (RFPF) and began publishing a Russian-language journal, *Letuchie Listki* (*Flying Leaflet*). Its first publication, written by Stepniak, was entitled *Chevo Nam Nuzhno?* (*What is to be Done?*) and called for a united attack upon the autocracy by all the opponents of Tsarism. However, in the course of this essay, Stepniak narrowed the opposition down to include only the educated class, the intelligentsia. By doing so he rejected both the peasantry and the working class as a revolutionary force. The revolutionaries, he argued, having alienated the peasantry as a result of the failure of their 'Going to the People' campaign, could no longer seriously approach the peasantry again; while to see the working class as 'the chief lever by which the autocracy can be overthrown is to abandon through theorizing any grasp of Russian realities.'[43] The Russian working class, he continued, could play no independent role owing to its relatively small size, its lack of education, and the complete want of any class-consciousness. Stepniak, who had formed a close friendship with the German prophet of 'evolutionary socialism', Edouard Bernstein,[44] linked his faith in the intelligentsia as a revolutionary force with Bernstein's belief that class antagonisms were decreasing in Western European democracies. Thus, Stepniak concluded, Russia would develop along the lines followed by

Liberal radicalism in England and by Bernstein and the evolutionary socialists of the German SPD; Plekhanov's application of Marxism to Russian conditions, therefore, was an anachronism:

> The violent actions we are now forced to employ are only temporary measures which will give way to peaceful cultural work just as soon as the present absolutism is replaced by popular representation. We absolutely and categorically distinguish between our tactics in the political arena and in the economic. In politics we are revolutionists. But regarding the introduction of socialism we are evolutionists – gradualists on the foreign model.[45]

Nor to Stepniak, with one eye on Russia and the other on England, was there a time more propitious for propagating these views. Constitutionalism in Russia was gaining ground as a result of the disastrous famine of 1891–2. With the socialists no longer a force in the countryside the liberal intelligentsia, shocked at the prospect of millions of peasants starving to death, were dismayed by the Russian Government's refusal to curtail grain exports, and joined with the *zemstvo* (the elective district councils in Russia) in providing whatever relief they could. In the area of relief provision the central Government proved woefully inadequate, and as a result pressures began to mount for the government to yield to the public some measure of authority in the formulation and execution of policy. Official Russia 'was held responsible for the plight of the peasants, and in the famine crisis they [the liberal intelligentsia] saw an opportunity to mount an offensive against the Tsarist government.'[46] In Britain both the SFRF and the RFPF, in reacting to the crisis were put at the disposal of the Russian liberal opposition.

While the Liberal radicals were consolidating their position in Britain as spokespersons for the democratic opposition developing in Russia, the Russian Social-Democracy began courting British working-class opinion. Although there were no Russian delegates at the Brussels Congress of the Second International[47] held in

August 1891, delegates there received a report from Plekhanov and Zasulich on the progress of social-democracy in Russia. This event, reported in *Free Russia* as 'a message [...] that the workers were organising in spite of their Tsar' received fuller treatment in the columns of *Justice*.[48] In an article entitled 'Social-Democracy in Eastern Europe', the SDF's treasurer, J. Hunter Watts, drew attention to Plekhanov's assertion that a reliance upon the communistic ideals of the peasantry would not save Russia from the painful experience of bourgeois rule, a proletariat, class antagonisms and class struggle. Citing Plekhanov, he made the point that the Government itself had actively, since defeat in the Crimean War, cultivated a capitalist class and had thereby created a proletariat:

> Now an industrial proletariat has entered the field, and it will no longer be the person seated on the throne of the Czars who will be menaced, the system itself will be assailed.[49]

This was a direct challenge to the attitudes held by leading Russian political émigrés in Britain since the days of Herzen. In 1891 Russian liberalism did not countenance an attack upon the system, but remained convinced that a constitution would be granted from above, as opposed to being taken from below by revolutionary action. This view gained traction after the death of Alexander III and the accession of Nicholas II to the throne in 1894. Nicholas II, widely regarded as more liberal in outlook than his father, was expected to introduce extensive reforms. These hopes, however, were soon to be shattered. In a famous speech delivered to a meeting of nobles at the beginning of 1895, Nicholas II referred to the wish of the *zemstvo* representatives for participation in the affairs of state as 'senseless dreams.'[50] In *Free Russia* Stepniak wrote:

> There is an end to all illusions and roseate hopes. The liberalism of Nicholas II was like the flower of the fern in which people obstinately believe though there were and are no tokens of its

real existence; but the mystic St. John's night is over, and everyone understands and realises that it would be idle any longer to expect the enchanted flower.[51]

Despite Stepniak's attempts to turn the RFPF's Russian-language newspaper, *Letuchi Listki*, into an exclusively Liberal enterprise, the failure of the 'enchanted flower' to bloom on Ivan Koupalo night[52] helped elevate social-democracy above liberal-constitutionalism as the dominant political philosophy among Britain's Russian political émigré community. The driving force behind these developments was the Russian Jewish immigrant population crammed into London's East End. In April 1891 the International Social-Democratic Association (ISDA) was formed 'for the purpose of advocating the principles of Social-Democracy among the Jewish workers of the East End of London.'[53] This venture proved so successful that in January 1892 ISDA moved to larger premises in Christian Street, Whitechapel; and the following September 'two hundred [...] Jewish comrades gathered to take part in a substantial repast, spread in their Hall, at Christian Street, Whitechapel, to celebrate the re-union in one society of two sections of Jewish workers'.[54] Among the speakers were Karl Marx's daughter, Eleanor Marx-Aveling, who spoke in Yiddish, and Stepniak, who spoke in Russian.

Past differences among the socialists were now buried; *Commonweal* fell into the hands of the anarchists and William Morris, Eleanor Marx-Aveling and others re-joined the SDF in 1893. The influential Whitechapel Branch of the SDF was formed soon after the Christian Street celebrations, and in May 1895 Stepniak, writing in the *Labour Leader* on the spread of Social-Democratic ideas in Russia, concluded:

The Russian Revolution is passing through a period of preparation. It does not sleep, but gathers strength. The day when the trumpet sounds, the Russian Social-Democracy will come upon the stage of history, and is sure to play one of the most important, if not the most important, part.[55]

Unfortunately, Stepniak would not live to see his prophecy come true; his life was cut short on 23 December 1895 when one fog-bound night he was struck by a train on a level crossing in London and killed instantly. With his death the SFRF and the FRPF became cut off from the new direction Russian politics was taking and new personalities came to the fore, in particular a young, newly arrived Jewish émigré from Lithuania, Fedor Aronovich Rotshtein (Theodore Rothstein).

2

East End Jewish Marxist

Now is the psychological moment for which many of us have
been on the look-out for the last ten or fifteen years; now is the
time to get into line with the continental Socialists whose good
fortune it is to have become the sole keepers of and champions
of Right a quarter of a century ago. The great obstacle in our
way has been forcibly removed by the war; there is not one left
to take the wind out of our sails any longer: Liberalism is dead
and rotting in its grave.

Theodore Rothstein, Justice, 7 April 1900.

Fedor Aronovich Rotshtein (1871–1953) was born into an
unorthodox Jewish family in Kovno, now Kaunas, in Lithuania,
on 26 February 1871 (O. S. 14 February). His father, an
apothecary, was an infrequent attender at the local synagogue and
nurtured ambitions for his son to become a physician. At a time
when the number of Jews permitted to attend university was
limited Aaron moved his entire family, his wife and three of his
four sons, to Poltava in the Ukraine so that Fedor Aronovich could
gain access to higher education.[1] At Poltava he became drawn into
student politics and joined a local underground reading circle of
the *People's Will* where he was introduced to the works of the
English utilitarians, the Russian anti-capitalists Chernishevskii
and Dobroliubov,[2] before reading the few Marxist texts that were
then circulating underground in Russia: the *Communist Manifesto*,
parts of the first volume of *Capital*, Friedrich Engels' *Development of
Socialism from Utopia to Science, The Condition of The Working Class in*

England and Marx's *Poverty of Philosophy*, which, somewhat surprisingly, booksellers had been granted permission in 1848 to import on the grounds that it was not applicable to Russian conditions and, therefore, could not pose a threat. The activities of the reading circle came to the attention of the authorities and after an 'anonymous tip-off' that he 'had better get out' Fedor Aronovich fled to Britain with his family in 1891 and anglicised his name, changing it to Theodore Rothstein.[3]

The Rothstein family had travelled initially to Germany where an older brother Phoebus was living in Danzig, before settling in the British northern industrial city of Leeds. On their arrival Rothstein's father leased an apothecary shop in Chapeltown, a predominantly Jewish district of the city where Theodore played an active part in Russian political émigré politics joining Stepniak and Robert Spence Watson's Society of Friends of Russian Freedom (SFRF), and publishing several articles in *Letuchie Listki* before being appointed the Society's honorary secretary. He also worked as an assistant editor on their English-language paper *Free Russia*, edited by the influential Liberal radical MP J. Frederick Green, and in this capacity he worked closely with Alexander Kerensky's future secretary, David Soskice.[4]

In 1893 Theodore Rothstein moved to London to write a Marxist history of Rome. He worked on this project for two years, studying mostly in the British Museum while being supported by his family who remained in Leeds. Although this work was never finished he published articles on Plato, Socrates, Alexander the Great, Julius Caeser, Demosthenes and Cicero in the Russian journal *Zhizn zamechatel'nikh lyudei* (*Lives of Famous People*). He also published an article on Roman poetry under the *nom de plume* E. Orlov in the journal *Zhizn'* (*Life*).[5] In London he settled initially in the predominantly Jewish area of Whitechapel and began editing two Yiddish socialist newspapers. He joined the Whitechapel branch of the SDF in 1895 where he met Anna Kahan, who he married soon after. That same year a Special Branch file was opened on Rothstein owing to his dealings with Stepniak and a number of other suspected 'nihilists' including

Anna's brother, Boris Kahan, who was then sharing an apartment on the Commercial Road with the notorious anarchist and founder of the Free Russian Library in Whitechapel, Aleksei Teplov. A far from successful terrorist, Teplov had been arrested in Paris in 1893 after an explosive device he was testing blew up prematurely, wounding him in the leg. The 'Plot' received widespread coverage in the British Press,[6] which reported that Teplov had been the victim of an act of provocation by an Okhrana agent; he was sentenced to three years imprisonment and in 1893 he came to London where he set up the Free Russian Library with the financial assistance of Nikolai Chaikovskii, Vladimir Burtsev and Vladimir Chertkov, Tolstoy's literary agent. A French police agent who visited Teplov's Library produced some 'alarming news when he described how the Library was offering courses in practical chemistry and giving instruction in complex substances, including formulas for nitro-glycerine.'[7] He also commented on the group's plans to organize Sunday trips to the countryside which, he believed, gave 'to those revolutionaries following a higher calling, the opportunity to perfect their skills in the manipulation of chemical compounds by carrying out open-air experiments'.[8] In 1897 the Rothsteins moved to Hackney where their sons Andrew and Eugene were born in 1898 and 1901 respectively, and their daughter Natalie in 1902.

In October 1896 Rothstein wrote his first article for *Justice* outlining a Social-Democratic philosophy which sought to establish a *modus vivendi* between the 'evolutionary "common-sensical" trade unionist and "practical" Fabian on the one hand, and the extreme revolutionists among the Anarchists and the French Allemanists[9] on the other.'[10] In addressing the twin doctrines of evolution and revolution, Rothstein argued that the two concepts were not necessarily opposed to one another:

we, at least the Social-Democrats, have outgrown to a very great extent this crude conception of revolution being a negation of evolution [. . .] To our mind a revolution is as much a legitimate movement in the evolutionary process of development of an organism as that piecemeal slow, and often imperceptible change with which the idea of evolution is generally associated.[11]

Rothstein's first article on the Russian revolutionary movement appeared in *Justice* in March 1897 and denounced Chaikovskii's attempt to demonstrate the proletarian nature of the People's Will arguing that class and class conflict in a true Marxist sense was purely an urban phenomenon. Vigorously attacking those disciples of Herzen, who believed that Russia could wed 'the most progressive ideas of Western Europe' with the 'antiquated conditions of Russian economic life' and pass into a Socialist society without first having to pass through the Capitalist stage of development, Rothstein lamented the lack of Socialism among the Narodniki abroad.[12] His first article devoted purely to British labour affairs, entitled 'Caveant Consules', appeared in *Justice* on 18 December 1897 and to some extent borrowed from his writings on the Russian revolutionary movement to lament the lack of Socialism among British trade unionists. His views were in keeping with Hyndman's. Following the great Dock Strike of 1889 and the subsequent growth in trade union membership, the SDF's attitude towards trade unions had been determined by Hyndman's denunciation of trade unionism as a distraction from socialist agitation.[13] Despite the efforts of Harry Quelch, an active trade unionist and editor of *Justice*, to counter these views the SDF had found it almost impossible to surmount the inherent conservatism dominating trade unionism, which relied upon sectionalism and ignored class organization. Quelch had earlier argued that while 'there is no necessary affinity between trade unionism and socialism [...] the place of the Social-Democrat is by the side of the trade unionist. [...] The trade unions', he concluded, 'offer a splendid field for propaganda, a propaganda which can be better carried on among them by example than by precept'.[14]

Over the next seven months, during the Engineers' Lock-Out (July 1897 – January 1898), socialists fiercely debated the respective merits of these two forms of propaganda. This dispute highlighted the divisions between the supporters of economic and political forms of organisation within the British labour movement. The Marxists of the SDF, wedded to the idea of political action – which coupled a commitment to electoral politics with a vague notion of revolution – sought to win the Amalgamated Society of Engineers (ASE) over to the notion of independent working-class political action; while the engineers themselves believed their dispute to be primarily one between the skilled men of the union and their employers over the maintenance of differentials and the Eight Hour Day. By the end of the dispute, with the ASE defeated, it was clear that for many skilled trade unionists future political action would be a further extension of their struggle in the workplace for control over management and the maintenance of craft skills and differentials. In these circumstances the politics of the ASE, and the skilled worker in general, were drawn away from the revolutionary rhetoric of the SDF towards the more pragmatic approach of the ILP. It was indicative of the SDF's ignorance of trade union affairs that during the lock-out *Justice*'s coverage of the dispute ignored the question of differentials and centred upon the wider issue of the Eight Hours Movement. Yet, if the SDF drew back from antagonising the engineers directly over the advisability of mounting purely sectional, craft disputes, it did not draw back from criticising their support for industrial over political forms of struggle:

> Suppose the engineers win this fight, as we seriously hope they may, it only means the partial adoption of an eight hours working day for a well-organised, highly skilled and, comparatively, well-paid body of men. It will not affect, except indirectly, the millions of workers whose want of organization makes it impossible for them to use the same means the engineers are now adopting, and whose poverty, while it prevents them from organizing, makes them an easy prey of capitalism, and condemns them to long hours and short

pay. Yet the engineers' struggle has already lasted nine weeks,
[...] here we have a net expenditure of £135,000. Why, for a
hundred and thirty-five thousand pounds, if the trade unionists
so desired it, they could completely transform the House of
Commons, and carry a Bill which could secure an eight-hour
day for all workers [...] all the loss and suffering inseparable
from a strike would be avoided.[15]

Instead of offering practical support the SDF was preparing to sit
back and wait for the engineers to learn their lesson: 'many a
lesson as severe as that now being learned by the engineers will be
enforced before the trade unions will recognize the duty and the
necessity of adopting political action for class purposes'.[16] The
Executive Council of the SDF passed the following resolution
summing up their position:

We therefore urge on the Amalgamated Society of Engineers
and all other labour organisations the necessity of devoting their
energies and their funds to political action, to the running,
returning, and maintaining as members of Parliament, and
other representative bodies, those who are neither hangers on of
the Tory nor the Liberal Party, but are pledged to the only
possible labour programme, the international programme of the
abolition of private property in the means of private property
and exchange.[17]

It is impossible to ignore here the enormous gulf that existed
between the SDF and the ASE. While the ASE was involved in the
day-to-day activities of overseeing strike action, the SDF had
opted solely for reliance upon moral instruction. In December
1897, towards the end of the strike, Rothstein poured scorn on the
SDF's shortcomings; pointing out that throughout the strike the
Liberal radical bourgeoisie had offered a defence of the engineers,
in marked contrast to the socialists who had failed to do so. In this
respect, he emphasised the campaign by the *Daily Chronicle* to get
'the employers to renounce the ideas of smashing the unions and

to recognize the elementary right of Labour to an organized existence and collective policy'.[18] What this demonstrated, he argued, was that a section of the bourgeoisie, predominantly Liberal radical in outlook, accepted that 'trades unionism as it exists today does not only not constitute to him any danger, but what little disadvantage it still possesses is amply repaid by its repudiation of political and revolutionary action and its confining itself to a policy of peaceful compromising usually called "collective bargaining."'[19] But while this had been appreciated by progressive sections of the bourgeoisie, there was little evidence to show that the same lessons had been learnt by Britain's trade unionists:

> During the last two or three decades they have shown a remarkable want of appreciation of their class position, and now on seeing so many smooth tongued and open-handed middle class men coming to their rescue they will still more deeply plunge into their stupid self-contentment, [...] They will persist in their ossified trade union policy, and repudiate all political action independent of the programme of either of the two bourgeois parties. Thus a great lesson which some of us have expected from the manifest inability of trade unionism to grapple with large issues will be lost, and the working man of this country, flattered by the modern Circes, will be, as heretofore, a ready prey to their masters.[20]

Drawing upon Quelch's earlier position on the correct relationship to be struck between the SDF and the trade unions Rothstein argued that socialists within the trade union movement must raise the political aspects of the Engineers' Lock-Out at the forthcoming National Conference of the trade unionists: 'many Socialists of the SDF and the ILP will undoubtedly be present, and on them devolves the duty to present our case. Let them spare no efforts to put the present fight and the attitude assumed towards it by the middle class, in their proper light. Otherwise we in England shall have to do our work over again.'[21] Rothstein had identified a changing socialist response towards the practice of trade unionism but he had done so merely as a 'duty to present our case'. The central problem remained; there was still an assumption that trade unionists once made aware of the political realities of their class position would renounce the practical support they had received from sections of the middle class, and experience a major shift in their political allegiance. It was a reading of trade unionism, shared with other socialists that put the primacy of politics and political theory above the economic attachment of leading sections of the organized working class to sympathetic elements within the middle class.[22] Moreover, there was little evidence to suggest that Rothstein's call for more socialist involvement in the trade union movement had altered the general outlook of the SDF National Executive:

> Trade unionism, when it forms an aristocracy of labour, as in England, so far from helping on the general cause of the workers, heads that cause back. The old trade unionism is, in fact, nowadays a reactionary force [. . .] When *will* Englishmen learn a little wisdom and throw their weight into politics for their own advantage?[23]

It was a valid question. During the recent York by-election – an event which followed immediately upon the defeat of the ASE – the Conservative Party candidate had been gaining political advantage from the fact that the Liberal candidate, Sir Charles Furness, was also a member of the Engineering Employers' Federation. Furness, claiming to be the working engineer's friend, promised a number of concessions to the engineers and had secured the support of both the Trades Council and the north-eastern organiser of the ASE. Liberal support for the ASE in the area had been strong during the lock-out and this was now reflected, ironically, in support for Furness. Both the ILP and the SDF vigorously opposed Furness and for their pains had a number of their meetings smashed up by gangs of Liberal and Irish roughs. Commenting upon these events and upon the Engineers'

Lock-Out in general, Rothstein drew attention to the socialists' shortcomings when he analysed the economic factors underpinning class relationships in Britain. In an attempt to explain why it was that socialism had put down strong roots in countries less economically developed than Britain he pointed to the leading role of the continental proletariat in securing civil and personal liberties, as opposed to what he saw as a progressive alliance between middle- and working-class radicals with similar objectives in Britain. In March and April 1898 he published two articles in the SDF's theoretical journal, *Social-Democrat*, asking 'Why is Socialism in England at a Discount?'

> in England the progress which Democracy undoubtedly makes every day is mainly due to the initiative and leadership of the middle classes, so that even such distinctly working class legislation as the Factory Acts, the abolition of the combination laws, and the legislation of the status of the trade unions has been secured by *their* efforts rather than those of the proletariat, it is the latter which in the rest of Europe appears as the champion of the civil and personal rights of the people.[24]

This emphasis on the leading role of the English middle classes led Rothstein to conclude that the working class had merely to develop its own sense of independent political activity to shrug off middle-class patronage and tutelage. For Rothstein, this appeared a rather simple next step owing to a reading of British working-class history that emphasised the essentially passive nature of that class's response to middle-class dominance. To overcome passivity the working class had to become conscious of its own interests and accept the bankruptcy of the British middle classes as a progressive force. The outbreak of the Boer War 18 months later in October 1899 confirmed him in this view leading him to conclude that the progressive side of Liberalism had, by its failure to unequivocally condemn the war, outlived its usefulness. The rift in the Liberal Party over the war, he argued, had become permanent; presenting the socialists with a perfect opportunity for political advance.

However, not all socialists in Britain shared Rothstein's conviction that the war in South Africa had sounded the death knell of the progressive alliance. The Fabians, for example, were as divided over the issue as the Liberals; while Robert Blatchford's *Clarion* movement fully supported the war.[25] The ILP fervently opposed the war, although it 'feared the unpopularity of an anti-war stand amongst sizeable sections of the working class.'[26] British intelligence, too, was not slow to act. William Melville, head of Special Branch, took an active interest in the 'Stop-the-War Committee'[27] and intelligence files were opened on a number of anti-war protestors in 1899.[28]

The 'Stop the War Committee', however, was far from homogenous and Rothstein's arguments in favour of socialist leadership of the anti-war movement were dashed by considerable anti-Semitism from anti-war protestors, including many socialists, who saw the war as essentially a Jewish one.[29] Hyndman, in an outburst of scarcely disguised anti-Semitism, shifted all responsibility for the coming war onto the shoulders of Jewish financiers. In an article in *Justice* on 17 June 1899, he wrote, 'Englishmen are dead against making war with the Transvaal Boers for the sake of such true-born Britons as Beit, Eckstein, Rothschild, Joel, Adler, Goldberg, Israel, Isaac, Solomon, and Co.' In an appeal for anti-war demonstrators to assemble in Trafalgar Square on 9 July the SDF's Executive Committee did so in language which clearly betrayed an anti-Semitic bias:

> There are plenty of common Englishmen left who are not the henchmen of Rhodes and haven't pocketed the money of Beit, or Joel, or Rothschild. To them we Social-Democrats mean to appeal.[30]

The editor of *Justice*, Harry Quelch, spoke in terms of a Jewish conspiracy, maintaining 'that the gold international, the financial ring is dominated by Jews [...] the most virulent jingo organs in this and other countries are in their hands.'[31] Nor did *Justice* hold back from indirect incitement to anti-Jewish violence, using the provocative German term *hetze* (baiting):

> Far be it for us to preach a *'Judenhetze'*, but if such unscrupulous use of the power which their wealth and their control of the press gives them by the wealthy Jew financiers does not promote a reaction against them it will indeed be strange.[32]

Hyndman expressed his fears for the future of the British Empire if the Government permitted itself to be manipulated by Jewish financial intrigue. Linking the decline of the French Second Empire with the self-serving activities of Jewish financiers, Hyndman prophesised a similar fate for the British Empire if Jews were allowed to instigate imperial wars:

> the war in Mexico, like the war in the Transvaal, was undertaken at the instance of Jews and stock-jobbers who had obtained control of the Emperor's entourage, and used their ill-gotten influence to bring about war, in order to give value to the now forgotten 'Jecker Bonds'. The Mexican war of the Second Empire was a Jew's war, and dearly did France pay for the subservience of her rulers to the power of the Semitic money-bags.[33]

Such sentiments as these, coupled with the emotive use of the word *Judenhetze*, raised fears of a national anti-Semitic movement in Britain. A Jewish member of the SDF, whose home had been destroyed by anti-Semitic rioters in Poland, spoke of the growing appeal of Zionism for politically active Jews in London. 'I sometimes wonder if Dr Nordau[34] was not right in saying that "the Jews have no guarantee that they will enjoy peace and equality even in a Socialist regime".'[35] His fears were justified. A widespread campaign against Jewish immigration in the late 1890's prompted the setting up of a Royal Commission on Alien

Immigration, culminating in the 1905 Aliens Act, which reduced 'Aliens' most crudely to European Jews.

In such circumstances the Jewish membership of the SDF became enraged by *Justice*'s anti-Semitic pronouncements on the origins of the Boer War. Rothstein, who had previously complained about 'the unsavoury tendencies of anti-Semitism' within the SDF,[36] spoke for many Jewish socialists – who did not resign their membership – when he spoke of the unlikelihood of an anti-Semitic movement in this country owing to *Justice*'s small circulation:

> Happily for the case, though unhappily for the general cause, JUSTICE is read by a comparatively small section of the community, so that a national anti-Semitic movement is not to be expected.[37]

But of far greater significance was Rothstein's sustained assault on Hyndman's support for imperialism and the British Empire. Taking particular aim at Hyndman's jingoistic pride in the 'honour' of a British Empire threatened by the dishonesty of the 'Jew-millionaire', Rothstein attacked Britain's sense of nationalistic imperialism:

> England is virtuous; the Cabinet is chaste; the capitalists are pure; it is only the Jew-millionaire who pollutes everything and deprives Britannia of her honour.[38]

Hyndman's arguments were not idiosyncratic; he had relied heavily on a series of articles published in the *Manchester Guardian* by J. A. Hobson in the autumn of 1899. Hobson had been sent to South Africa earlier in the year by the paper's editor, C. P. Scott, when war seemed imminent. He used his assessment of the situation in South Africa to develop an overall theory of imperialism, publishing *The War in South Africa* in 1900 and *Imperialism, A Study* in 1902. *The War in South Africa* contained a chapter on 'For Whom are we Fighting?' which concluded that 'it is difficult to state the truth about our doings in South Africa without seeming to appeal to the ignominious passion of the *Judenhetze*; the war, he concluded, 'was being fought in the interests of financiers among whom the foreign Jew must be taken as the leading type.'[39]

At this time the SDF, along with other socialist groups, had not developed a Marxist theory of imperialism and Hobson's theoretical discourse on the subject was widely accepted. Belfort Bax, who had been the first to see in imperialism a major threat to socialism, felt that the search for new markets, whether in the Transvaal or elsewhere, would only serve to prolong capitalism. He maintained that opponents of the Boer War should oppose capitalism *per se*, and not scapegoat one particular group of capitalists, while exonerating others. Together with Rothstein, Bax offered a criticism of the war which did begin to develop a British Marxist or internationalist critique of imperialism. 'I am pro-Boer', proclaimed Bax, because British socialists have the duty to resist 'the violence of Great Britain and international capitalism'.[40] Rothstein saw in anti-war work not only an occasion for broad agitation against war and imperialism; but also an opportunity to promote the continental model of socialism in Britain:

> Now is the psychological moment for which many of us have been on the look-out for the last ten or fifteen years; now is the time to get into line with the continental Socialists whose good fortune it is to have become the sole keepers of and champions of Right a quarter of a century ago. The great obstacle in our way has been forcibly removed by the war; there is not one left to take the wind out of our sails any longer: Liberalism is dead and rotting in its grave.[41]

The following week he was urging British Social-Democracy to cut all ties with Liberal radicalism. Two months later in the June 1900 edition of the *Social-Democrat* he made his point more forcefully, this time chastising the SDF for its sectarian laziness:

we have been more of a sect than a party. We regarded the
world with an eye, not so much of active participators, as of
'intelligent onlookers', and far from thinking to impress
upon it our distinct personality, we contented ourselves with
examining it from our particular standpoint. And that
standpoint was especially adapted to estrange us from life.[42]

Not surprisingly, Rothstein's views provoked the Hyndmanites in
the SDF, who now began to question his ability to understand his
adopted society. Harry Quelch, in the following months' *Social-
Democrat*, attacked Rothstein for his loose understanding of the
Liberal background to the labour movement. Rothstein's
argument, Quelch pointed out, had quite rightly drawn out the
changed political conditions then existing in Britain, but if
socialism was to become more than a continuum of a Liberal
radical tradition it would need to confront the central
economically based problem of Liberalism's relationship with
the trade unions, irrespective of what might be happening
politically. Chastising Rothstein for his purely political thinking,
based on his understanding of working-class history on the
continent, Quelch suggested that 'although expansionism and
imperialism have shattered Liberalism, that does not prove that
Liberalism or what goes by the name, has no longer any hold over
the people'. He continued:

In most Continental countries the trade union movement
having sprung out of the Socialist movement, has a definite
Socialist basis; here, the trade unions, being older than the
present Socialist movement, have been largely hostile;
dominated as in the main they have been, and still in many
cases are, by the economic ideas of the middle class.[43]

Put simply, Rothstein had failed to realise that the British
working class had forged strong economic links with Liberalism
and did not therefore fit continental patterns. To make the
accusation that the SDF was 'more of a sect than a party' meant

that Rothstein was unable to appreciate the difficult conditions under which Marxists in this country laboured:

> it is a change to have Rothstein berating us for being too exclusive and sectarian, seeing how often and for how long we have been attacked for being too opportunist and latitudinarian [. . .] if we had not mingled in the actual life of society, if we had been content to round ourselves up as a doctrinaire sect, the SDF would long ago have ceased to exist.[44]

Following revelations of atrocities committed by the British military in South Africa, the leader of the Opposition and future Liberal Prime Minister, Sir Henry Campbell-Bannerman, attacked the war at a monster meeting of Liberal radicals and socialists held at the Queen's Hall, Peckham, South London on 26 June 1901. At the same time, another future Liberal Prime Minister, Herbert Asquith, confirmed his position as a leading politician by becoming the spokesman for the pro-War Liberal-Imperialists. In practical political terms the anti-war agitation was in danger of succumbing to faction fighting within the Liberal Party. A. J. Benford of Peckham SDF summed up the feeling of those socialists who considered anti-war work a distraction from the main task of spreading Social-Democracy:

> I would suggest that they who call the tune should pay the piper, and that all SDF stalwarts should reserve their energy and enthusiasm for the propagation of Social-Democracy and such work as is called for by their own organization.[45]

These sentiments were shared by Hyndman, who although a speaker at the Queen's Hall meeting, later remarked:

> for my part I think we have devoted quite enough attention to South Africa during the past two years, and I see nothing whatsoever to be gained for Socialism by helping the Liberals, who would not work with us in 1899 when the war could have

been prevented, to gain credit, and probably sooner or later to obtain office, by a belated agitation now.[46]

Hyndman attacked those – Rothstein and Bax in particular – whose anti-war work under the guise of anti-imperialism came dangerously close to pro-Boer[47] propaganda:

> I hold, with our friend Cunninghame Graham,[48] that this is a struggle between two burglars, [...] Some of our eager members of the SDF refuse to look at this side of the question. Feeling strongly for the Boers, they disregard the fact that the independence of the Boers, for which they clamour, necessarily involves the complete submission of the natives. Yet the Zulus would be glad, I take it, if this war between the kites and the crows ended in the disappearance of both.[49]

Hyndman's dominance of the Federation was sufficient to win over the SDF Executive, who passed a resolution in July to the effect that further anti-war agitation was 'a waste of time and money.' There were three dissentient voices, Bax and two Jewish members new to the Executive – Rothstein and G. Saunders Jacobs. On the question of the Zulus, Rothstein expressed amazement that the British could ever be seen as adopting a pro-Zulu position, 'and that to such a degree as to justify the suppression of the national existence of two peoples!'[50] Bax was more scathing:

> Really, when one hears the native trotted out as a stalking-horse for keeping the wicked and ruthless Boer under the tutelage of the 'after all' so decent and beneficent Briton, one's gorge rises to the extent that it is difficult to keep to parliamentary language.[51]

Hyndman, obviously upset by the tone of the debate, called upon Bax to 'withdraw this unworthy letter', which he dismissed as 'a tirade of hysterical misrepresentation'.[52] Rothstein, however, whose position in the SDF had been strengthened as a result of his anti-war work, had the final word:

> Th. Rothstein writes: As comrade Hyndman has thought fit to force the discussion into personal channels, that discussion may now be regarded as closed.[53]

At the Annual Conference of the SDF on 4 and 5 August 1901 Rothstein was re-elected to the National Executive, this time at the head of the poll with 51 votes, one better than Quelch with 50. Hyndman, disappointed both by Rothstein's success[54] and 'by the attitude of the membership which [...] had failed to provide him with an opportunity for fighting the 1900 General Election' withdrew from active politics altogether, remaining inactive until 1903.[55] The party leadership in this period was assumed by Quelch, under whose guidance Rothstein began to develop a more 'orthodox Marxist'[56] understanding of events based on native as opposed to continental and British Liberal radical politics. The external factors making possible Rothstein's theoretical development were two-fold: firstly the House of Lords' decision upholding the Taff Vale Judgement,[57] and, secondly, Quelch's 'class war' policy which led to the SDF withdrawing from the Labour Representation Committee (LRC)[58] in August 1901. Linking both these developments was concern over the 'Impossibilist' revolt in the SDF.

3

Socialist Unity, Revolution 1905, the London Congresses of the RSDLP and the Second International's Condemnation of Militarism

Sometimes they simply sat down with the delegates in a pub and began talking to them. 'I remember on one occasion we ourselves started a conversation with our guardians. We were interested to discover whether they were working for the British or the Russian police. We treated them to a beer and began questioning them about this. The British detectives swore that they were watching both ourselves and the Russian spies, of whom quite a number had travelled in our wake. We knew this, of course, even without their testimony'.

Martyn Liadov, *iz zhizni partii* (*From Party Lives*),
2nd edn Moscow, 1956

Wars between capitalistic States are, as a rule, the consequence of their competition in the world's market, for every State is eager not only to preserve its markets, but also to conquer new ones, principally by the subjugation of foreign nations and the confiscation of their lands.

Report of the Stuttgart Congress of the Second
International: Militarism and International Conflicts, 1907

The 'Impossibilists', followers of Daniel De Leon and the American Socialist Labor Party, were based predominantly in Scotland and Southampton. Initially within the SDF, they had broken away in 1901 following the SDF's support for the German socialist Karl Kautsky's compromise resolution[1] at the 1900 Paris Congress of the Second International. The 'Impossibilists' who later formed the British Socialist Labour Party (SLP)[2] withdrew publicly, though not in practice, from any contact with reformists and reformist institutions. The arguments between the two groups became particularly acute over Taff Vale.[3] Rothstein's position was clear:

> It is surely one of the proverbial ironies of fate that this new current among our Scottish comrades should have made itself prominent just at this moment, when a golden opportunity presents itself of doing something towards the improvement of the abnormal relations between the two movements. I mean the situation created by the decisions of the House of Lords. In any other country where Socialism is really synonymous with the working-class movement of the land, such a mean [. . .] attack on trade unionism would have found the Socialists the first to take up the gauntlet and to initiate a campaign on behalf of the party attacked[4]

In a further article summarising the debate he took a middle course between what he described as 'the Scylla of boneless opportunism and the Charybdis of ossified impossibilism.'[5] Socialists, he argued, must support trade union candidatures on all labour matters; but on political questions they must reserve the right to act according to their own convictions. Rothstein was concerned not to alienate reformists with a policy that dismissed trade union candidatures out of hand; but he tried to win over the Impossibilists by arguing that the external factors which had made possible the political and social alliance between the progressive bourgeoisie and trade unionists in the nineteenth century no longer existed. His attempt to steer a middle course produced the basis of an SDF position on trade union candidatures, but it did not resolve the theoretical and practical impasse that continued to stifle the Federation:

> Socialists MAY run as trade union candidates, and consequently are entitled to our support, if they openly and explicitly, before both the electors and those who bring them forward, reserve to themselves the right to act on all general political questions according to their Socialist convictions. [. . .] In all cases where the trade union candidate does not declare his intention to act on all questions beyond his election programme as a Socialist, Socialists must remain neutral.[6]

During the Impossibilist controversy (1901−3) the SDF was also involved in unity discussions with the ILP. Both the SDF and the ILP had suffered steep falls in membership in the years after 1897 and the right wing of the SDF saw socialist unity as a way of reversing that decline. Rothstein had voted for unity at the 1902 SDF conference, without any great expectations; and when the ILP leadership contemptuously rejected the SDF approach, he sharply attacked the opportunism of Keir Hardie and his associates. While he accused the ILP of 'rank opportunism − opportunism of principle as distinguished from that of tactics' − Rothstein saved his obloquy for the activities of Hardie at a recent Newcastle meeting of the LRC. At this meeting Rothstein stated, Hardie had 'propounded the principle that the movement must be non-political'.[7] He went on to censure Hardie for his activities at the February Guildhall meeting called to set up the National Unemployed Committee, where as chairman he had ignored SDF members wanting to speak. 'Mr. Keir Hardie,' Rothstein concluded, 'is fast becoming a "responsible statesman" who does not wish to give undue offence by obtruding everywhere his socialism.'[8] That this was not a new development led Rothstein to ask why relations between the ILP leadership and its membership had not become strained. Many ILP members had always been attracted by the hope of socialist unity, at the heart of which lay the goal of some sort of link with the SDF. Earlier discussion on fusion in the 1890s had been undermined by the ILP's National Administrative Council (NAC). If, as some ILP members now claimed, they were in all essentials socialists, then it was their duty to resign from the ILP and join the SDF:

> The erratic ways of Mr. Keir Hardie and his satellites do not merely date from yesterday, and if the ILP is really a Socialist party, their ways should have proved by now a sufficiently strong strain upon the loyalty of the members to break it down. If it does not if these gentlemen are allowed to go on as before, then really I, for one, must assume that the party endorses their actions and that, consequently, as I said at the beginning, there are no two Socialist parties in England, which it is in the interests of the cause, desirable to see fused into one, but only one, the SDF, which must and shall remain alone.[9]

There was now an ever-present emphasis in Rothstein's writings on 'orthodox Marxist' principles particularly on the question of socialist unity. It was evidence of a realisation by Rothstein and the SDF National Executive (on which he sat from 1901–1906) that in order to develop a more independent Marxist line, socialism in Britain would not advance if they simply stole Liberal radical clothes; rather they had to stand on an independent understanding of class action. What finally gave a material as opposed to abstract quality to these developments was the outbreak of revolution in Russia in 1905 alongside the spread of Marxism among the East End of London's Russo-Jewish community.

Special Branch fears of political extremism among Britain's Jewish population had increased dramatically in November 1901 when the Whitechapel Branch of the SDF amalgamated with the Karl Marx Reading Association to form the East London (Jewish) Branch of the SDF, led by Rothstein's brother-in-law Boris Kahan. In 1903 a May Day demonstration in London's East End drew 3,000–6,000 people, marching behind four brass bands, 'two provided by various Jewish trade unions, and two by the East

London (Jewish) Branch of the SDF', despite 'a violent downpour of rain.' Between 8,000 Yiddish and 2,000 English leaflets were distributed.[10] Throughout the month numerous protest meetings were held across the country following reports of a massacre of Jews in the Russian town of Kishiniev. On 16 May, *Justice* published an article condemning the pogrom, and three days later Rothstein set up a national committee to organise demonstrations against the Tsarist autocracy for its complicity in the massacre of Russian Jews.

Jewish institutions imported into the UK such as the General Jewish Labour Bund,[11] with its ambitious programme of recruiting all Jewish workers across the Russian empire into a united socialist party, including those in emigration, found significant support in London's East End. Special Branch, set up in 1883 to combat Irish terrorism, extended its activities 'into areas that were assumed originally to be none of its business',[12] when all the main centres of Russian and Jewish refugee activity – their clubs and cafés – were placed under surveillance in 1902.

Between 1900 and 1902 the RSDLP's journal *Iskra*[13] had been printed in Germany and smuggled across the Russian border. Following publication of the RSDLP's political programme in April 1902 the German authorities had seized the printing press, and production of the paper had been moved to England. Lenin along with two other members of the editorial board, Iulio Martov and Vera Zasulich, had moved to London where the newspaper offices of *Justice* and the socialist Twentieth Century Press in Clerkenwell Green were put at their disposal.[14] The newspaper itself was produced in London's East End where there were several small printing shops possessing Russian type. With Lenin, Martov and Zasulich now in London the *Okhrana* converged on the capital and began monitoring anti-regime activity among Britain's Russian political émigré community. In this activity they were often helped by Scotland Yard detectives who were happy to engage in 'moonlighting', taking paid jobs in their spare time for the Okhrana, and reporting back to William Melville, the former head of Special Branch and head of the newly created counter-espionage service MO3.[15] Officially, however, if they wished to pass information to their Russian counterparts the British police were expected to 'do it only through normal diplomatic channels – through the Home Office, who would alert the Foreign Office, who would then pass it on to the Russian ambassador in London'.[16] There were very good reasons for this, if it became widely known that Special Branch was collaborating with the Okhrana then their sources among the Russian and Jewish communities would certainly dry up 'through dread of the vengeance of their comrades'.[17]

Lenin's forays into the East End could often be boisterous. On 29 November 1902, he lectured in Russian on the programme and tactics of the Socialist-Revolutionaries (SRs), the spiritual heirs of the *People's Will*, condemning individual acts of terrorism as futile and provoking a noisy debate with some of their followers. Lenin in London did not shy away from political activity and he met with several labour leaders from across the political spectrum including the dock workers' leader Ben Tillett, Henry Hyndman, as well as James Keir Hardie. The Secretary of the General Federation of Trade Unions, I. H. Mitchell, supported his application for a reader's ticket for the blue-domed reading room of the British Museum where he met Rothstein for the first time. The two men were close in age, Lenin was 32 and Rothstein was 31, in their youth they had both been members of the *People's Will*, and both men fully understood the conspiratorial world of Russian émigré politics. On the 21 March 1903, Lenin addressed the East London (Jewish) Branch of the SDF to commemorate the 32nd anniversary of the Paris Commune, and spoke at a May Day 'Continental Meeting' of socialists held in Alexandra Park, in the North London Borough of Haringey.

Although *Iskra* moved to Geneva later that month Lenin returned to London in the summer of 1903 for the Second Congress of the RSDLP. The Congress – 57 delegates representing 26 labour organizations – had opened in Brussels on 30 July but had been ordered out of the country on the same day. Rothstein made the arrangements for the Congress to move to

London where a number of rooms at different locations were hired to make it difficult for the Okhrana and Special Branch to monitor their activities. The Congress did not spend more than one day in the same place and neither, presumably, did the secret policemen. It was at this Congress that the famous split in the RSDLP between the Bolsheviks and Mensheviks took place.[18]

In the very first number of *Iskra* Lenin had written a short article entitled 'Urgent Tasks of Our Movement' in which he argued that the revolutionary party should consist only of full-time professionals 'who shall devote to the revolution not only their spare evenings, but the whole of their lives'.[19] The Second Congress voted against Lenin in favour of a broader-based political party more in keeping with the 'revisionism' of Bernstein and the tactics of the German SPD. The two factions split, with Lenin winning a small majority on another issue after many of the delegates had left for the continent. His faction then claimed the title Bolsheviki (majority), dubbing his opponents the Mensheviki (minority) and the two titles stuck. From then on the RSDLP was organised effectively as two separate parties, although they continued to be nominally members of one party until 1912.

In April 1905, the RSDLP (Bolsheviks) held their Third Congress in London; while the RSDLP (Mensheviks) held a conference of their own at Geneva. The Russo-Japanese War was raging and Russia was on the brink of revolution. Rolling strikes on an increasingly large-scale had unfolded across Russia in 1904, culminating in a general strike in St Petersburg on 20 January (O.S. 7 January) 1905. Two days later, Sunday 22 January (O.S.9 January), a peaceful demonstration of workers led by an Orthodox priest, Father Gapon, marched on the Winter Palace in St Petersburg to present a petition to the Tsar demanding an eight-hour day and a constitution. As the demonstrators approached the Winter Palace they were met with rifle fire and several hundred protestors were killed; once news of the 'Bloody Sunday' massacre had traveled from St Petersburg into the interior, strikes, mutinies and rural insurrections spread rapidly across Russia. The question of whether the Tsar's government would be overthrown had become a practical issue. Demonstrations of sympathy with the Russian people were held in Vienna, Budapest, Paris and elsewhere.

A general strike in Moscow spread to St Petersburg and other major cities bringing the nation to a standstill – no railways, no post, no telegraph, no newspapers, no public transport and no electricity. On 30 October (O.S. 17 October) 1905 Nicholas II issued his October Manifesto agreeing to the formation of a state Duma with limited powers, to be elected by universal suffrage. The Manifesto proved divisive. While those liberals who feared the revolution spiraling out of control accepted it, the workers and peasants who rapidly set up their own instruments of government in the form of the Soviets did not. Disturbances continued, with strikes and mutinies taking place at Kronstadt and Sevastopol. In December street fighting in Moscow resulted in a heavy loss of life with artillery being used to break up demonstrations and to shell workers' districts. During nine days of disturbances the heirs of the Narodniki, the Socialist Revolutionaries (SRs), assassinated the head of the Moscow Okhrana and bombed their headquarters. On 19 December (O.S. 3 December), with around 1,000 people dead and parts of the city in ruins, the workers surrendered.

The first elections to the state Duma took place in March 1906, with all male citizens over 25 entitled to vote except those enlisted in the military and with criminal records. The Russian Fundamental Law of 23 April (O.S. 10 April) 1906, in effect the Russian Empire's first constitution, however, reinstated most of the old principles of autocratic Tsarism. Nicholas II retained full sovereignty by divine right and retained the authority to initiate, amend or repeal legislation, with or without the endorsement of the Duma. These developments were watched closely in Britain, and in France, where an unprecedentedly large loan of 2,250 million francs (£91 millions) was being negotiated with the Tsarist autocracy.

Those opposed to the loan included the French Socialist Party, the *Societe des amis du people russe et des peoples annexes* (SAPREPA), the Russian Constitutional Democratic Party, and a number of Russian revolutionaries living in Paris. In March 1906 they began to scheme against the loan by convincing the French cabinet and public of its moral and financial unsoundness.[20] The primary organizers of the campaign were S. E. Kalmanovich, 'listed by the secret police as active in the Social (*sic*) Revolutionary Party'; the Russian-born French citizen, Il'ia Rubanovich, for many years the SR's representative on the Bureau of the Second International and the editor of the Paris-based bi-monthly official organ of the SRs, *La Tribune Russe*;[21] the writer Anatole France; and Pierre Quillard, who had access to the Minister of the Interior and future President, Georges Clemenceau. Okhrana archives show that this group organised a hurried meeting on 10 April held at the *Hotel des Societes Savants*, where SAPREPA often met under the observant eye of the Russian secret police.[22] On the same day *The Times* newspaper published an impassioned plea from the Russian writer Maxim Gorky against the French loan. 'He declared that the Duma was only a farce created to deceive Europe to give more money to Russia [and] reminded the Jewish bankers that part of their money would be used to organize pogroms against their Russian brothers.'[23]

Despite these protests a loan agreement was signed between the Russian Government and a consortium of French, British, Austrian, Dutch and Russian banks on 16 April 1906. In Russia the political parties in opposition to the government of Nicholas II resented what they considered a hurried bargain with the autocratic government on the eve of the first meeting of the newly elected national assembly.[24] They branded the French government's decision to lend the money to the Witte-Durnovo[25] government as siding with the forces of reaction against the people. Threats were even made that the Duma would repudiate the debts incurred by the Russian government without its consent. A special Franco-Russian committee was formed in Paris to combat the loan.[26] In France, following the flotation of the 1906 loan on the Paris and London money markets subscribers and participating bankers were subjected to retaliatory threats and intimidation. As a result, the *Zagranichnaia agentura* (Foreign Agency)[27] of the Okhrana now found itself confronting a new and extremely difficult situation.

The creation of the Foreign Agency had marked a sea change in the work of the Russian secret service and had been the first serious recognition of the new direction anti-regime activity was taking. The old Third Section had focused almost exclusively on the activities of the nobility at the court and the officer corps. The creation of the Foreign Agency in 1885, however, had been a tentative acknowledgement, and an early attempt, to comprehend the changing class forces taking place in Russia caused by industrialization.[28] A separate London office of the *Zagranichnaia agentura* had been established in the early 1890s and its members and its activities were well-known to Scotland Yard. The principal tsarist agent in London at this time was a French citizen by the name of Edgar Jean Farce. The Okhrana's strategy of 'émigré-control' was based on 'creating a situation in which he [the émigré] could operate only with great insecurity – a situation corresponding as closely as possible to what he would endure in Russia – to make him feel that his activities were neither approved nor safe.'[29] This strategy had been completely blown apart by the 1905 Revolution and the increasing confidence of the Russian political émigrés and Jewish refugees working inside both the French and British labour movements.

The First Duma would be dissolved after a mere ten weeks and while the Second Duma, convened in February, remained in existence during the RSDLP's London Congress it too would soon be dissolved, on 16 June 1907.[30] The delegates who assembled in London for the Fifth Congress represented both Bolshevik and Menshevik factions, all sections of the RSDLP, including strong Lettish and Polish Social-Democratic Parties, and The Bund.[31] The Congress had been initially scheduled to meet in Copenhagen, but on arrival the Danish police had informed the delegates that the Congress was prohibited, and gave them 12 hours to leave the country or face arrest and deportation to Russia. Apparently, the Tsarist Ambassador to Denmark had informed the

Danish Government that 'holding the Congress in Denmark would be taken as a personal insult to the Russian Empress-Dowager, a sister of the King of Denmark.'[32] When the delegates were refused permission to travel to Sweden, the British Government intervened. The President of the Local Government Board in the Liberal administration of Campbell-Bannerman, the ex-socialist John Burns, granted permission for the Congress to be held in London, as long as it didn't do anything illegal.[33] The Congress met at the Brotherhood Church in Southgate, run by a Socialist (Congregationalist) parson, the Rev. F. R. Swan, an alleged pacifist and a follower of William Morris whose flock included Ramsay MacDonald.[34] Owing to the size of the Congress the meeting could not escape the attention of the British public, and from day one the Brotherhood Church was surrounded by reporters and photographers.

> The place where the Congress is being held is literally besieged by reporters and photographers, who in spite of all requests persist in hovering round the delegates like a swarm of wasps, trying to elicit their names and to get a snapshot of their faces. Only on one occasion was a reporter with a camera [. . .] prevailed upon to give up the plates, having been given to understand that he was simply doing volunteer service for the Russian police. In other cases, similar efforts proved unavailing.[35]

A *Daily Mirror* report for 10 May informed the public that the delegates were being shadowed by 12 detectives, two of them from the Tsarist Embassy.[36] The *Daily News* reported on 14 May that 'a large number of secret police had been sent to England to watch the movements of the Social-Democrats.'[37]

By 23 May the Congress had nearly exhausted its money and an approach was made to Rothstein, who had been one of the organizers of the Congress, for additional funds. In 1906 Rothstein had worked as a sub-editor on Campbell-Bannerman's short-lived radical newspaper *Tribune*. The paper's foreign editor, George Herbert Perris, Secretary of the Cobden Club, a Tolstoyan and an occasional contributor to *Free Russia*, was impressed by his journalistic skills and in 1907 he secured Rothstein employment as a sub-editor on the Liberal *Daily News*.[38] A colleague on the *Daily News*, H. N. Brailsford, introduced him to Joseph Fels, an American of German-Jewish origin, now a wealthy soap manufacturer and a supporter of Henry George's 'single tax' movement. After listening to a debate from the public gallery he agreed to an interest-free loan of £1,700 on the condition that all the delegates agreed to sign up to the bond acknowledging the debt. This was done on the last day of the Congress, apparently not in their own names. The loan was due to be repaid 'on or before the first of January 1908' but by the time of Fels' death in 1914 it had not been paid. However, his widow was repaid in full by the Soviet Trade Delegation to Britain in 1922.

Once the Congress had closed and the delegates had departed for their various destinations co-operation between Special Branch and the Foreign Agency of the Okhrana continued. Following the suppression of the Second Duma on 16 June a protest demonstration was organised in Trafalgar Square for the 14 July. The demonstration was violently broken up by a newly trained section of the police force, giving rise to accusations that Scotland Yard was acting on orders issued by the Foreign Office, who were in the final stages of concluding an anti-German agreement with Russia. The violence followed the arrest of a member of the SDF, Jack Williams, who called upon the demonstrators to 'form up and march from the Square to the Foreign Office. He asked them if they had pluck enough to go there [. . .] he did not wish to surprise the police, and hoped they would go in a perfectly orderly manner.'[39]

Hyndman and Williams led the procession, which was peaceful up until its arrival at Whitehall, where Williams was informed they could not enter Downing Street. Williams then mounted what *Justice* referred to as 'a small parapet of the Foreign Office for the purpose of speaking and putting the resolution' and was promptly arrested and manhandled, provoking the crowd into an assault on the police to secure his release.[40] The fighting continued for some time, with a section of the procession managing to break away and make its way down Whitehall. Williams, meanwhile, jumped onto a passing omnibus and made good his escape.

There were two disconcerting conclusions to these proceedings. The first was the arrival of 'an additional body of police ... [who] had evidently been specially sent for.' The second was the arrest of two foreigners – one a Russian and the other a German – 'both working in the tailoring industry and absolute strangers to each other.'[41] The Liberal publisher, T. Fisher Unwin, provided them with bail.

The arrests led to accusations that the police and the Home Office were acting in complicity with the Russian Government. The police had seized a number of demonstrators at Whitehall, including known leaders in the agitation, yet 'the only persons who were actually arrested and taken to the station were two foreigners'. Both men were subsequently fined on a technical offence. The reason for their arrest, as well as for the police disturbance, appeared clear to *Justice*:

> The object of the Russian autocracy, and of its agents in this country, to whose orders the British government appears to be entirely subservient, would be to make out that the demonstration was not representative of the people of London, but consisted of a dangerous and riotous mob of Russian and other refugees.
>
> It was actually stated in court that the demonstration was made up largely of foreigners; although, as a matter of fact, these, on the urgent representations of the organizing committee, who wished to make it a distinctly English demonstration, were conspicuous by their absence.[42]

Justice also commented upon the appearance of a new body of police at Whitehall, who seemed to be carrying out 'definite orders to stir up a riot.'

There is no doubt that had matters been left in the hands of Inspector Jarvis (who was in charge of the police), the whole affair would have passed off without any disturbance. It was the irruption of a new body of police, who acted as though they had been instructed to create disorder at any cost, which caused all the mischief.[43]

The events at Whitehall formed part of a wider attack upon the Russian political emigre community during the negotiations leading up to the Anglo-Russian Agreement of August 1907. In April, a Glasgow member of the SDF was charged with storing cartridges and explosives, with intent to supply arms to the Russian revolutionaries, in what became known as the 'The Edinburgh 'Cartridge' Mystery. The accused faced two charges, one of possessing '15,000 cartridges under such circumstances as to give rise to a reasonable suspicion that he did not have them for a lawful object, contrary to Section 4 of the Explosive Substance Act, 1883;' and secondly, of keeping in 'an unauthorized place, 15,000 cartridges containing 85lbs of gunpowder or other explosive substance, contrary to Sections 5 and 39 of the Explosives Act.'[44] At this time it was not illegal to import or export arms or ammunition, and the accused, J. F. Reid, was acquitted on the first charge. It was, however, illegal to store arms on unlicensed premises, or to the public danger. Although it had been proved that the cartridges had been 'charged with a nitre compound', and, therefore, 'would only explode when put into a gun and fired off', Reid was found guilty on the second charge. He was fined £8 10s (£8.50). *Justice* felt this to be a severe punishment for what had been a technical offence, and argued that the law had been stretched in order to obtain a conviction. 'There can be no reason whatever for this action unless it be a desire to curry favour with the Russian despotism.'[45]

This court case, given the recent events at Whitehall, the Russophile policy of the British Foreign Secretary Sir Edward Grey and the shadowing of Russian political émigrés by Scotland Yard detectives – led British socialists to conclude that specific instructions had been issued to deal with any protest from Russian émigrés during the negotiations leading to the Anglo-

Russian Convention. The Convention, devised to settle disputes between the two Powers in Asia, had effectively divided the region into two main spheres of influence:

> We are told [wrote *Justice*] just after Parliament has risen, that the Treaty has been signed, and are vouchsafed a little information about the partition of Persia, the independence of Afghanistan, the security of India [. . .] we are informed [. . .] that the relations between the two countries are 'excellent', and that no difficulties will arise either in relation to the Balkans, Asia Minor, or the railway to Baghdad. The two greatest European Powers in Asia have [. . .] come to terms on their respective areas of spoliation.[46]

In the same issue Hyndman, who had been one of the main speakers at the Trafalgar Square demonstration and had led the protestors to the Foreign Office alongside Jack Williams, had a complete change of heart. Abandoning the Russian émigrés, he welcomed the Anglo-Russian Convention, and blasted the Kaiser for the 'reaction' spreading across Europe; while the Tsar was portrayed as both a nonentity and a reasonable fellow:

> the Czar, after all, is not nowadays such a very formidable enemy to progress. The Russian revolution has only just begun. The Romanoff dynasty is manifestly doomed. And Nicholas himself, with all his turpitude, counts personally for so little that the Terrorists don't think him worth assassinating.[47]

Following the Anglo-Russian Convention and the signing of the Anglo-Russian Entente on 31 August 1907 leading to the Triple Entente between Britain, France and Russia, the SDF split over the issue of whether or not the socialist movement should develop an independent foreign policy openly critical of the dominant imperialist and 'jingo' policies of the government of the day. The Second International had debated colonial policy and militarism at its Seventh Congress held in Stuttgart in August 1907, and had adopted a socialist foreign policy that affiliated groups and parties were expected to implement. A resolution, moved by the German Social-Democrat August Bebel, condemning the colonial system for 'increasing the danger of international complications and war, thus making heavier the financial burdens for navy and army', was carried unanimously:

> Wars between capitalistic States are, as a rule, the consequence of their competition in the world's market, for every State is eager not only to preserve its markets, but also to conquer new ones, principally by the subjugation of foreign nations and the confiscation of their lands.[48]

To the left of Bebel stood Lenin and the German SPD firebrand Rosa Luxemburg, who together won the Congress over to the concept of 'revolutionary defeatism'. The duty of socialists facing the threat, or the actual outbreak, of war was to bring the conflict swiftly to an end and engineer the collapse of the capitalist system:

> If a war threatens to break out, it is a duty of the working class in the country affected, [...] to make every effort to prevent the war by all means which seem to them the most appropriate [...] Should war nonetheless break out, it is their duty to intervene in order to bring it promptly to an end, [...] and precipitate the fall of capitalist domination.[49]

In adopting this resolution the Second International had committed itself 'to a great deal more than it was really prepared to do.'[50] Nevertheless, the resolution had been warmly endorsed by the Congress, and had given the impression of unanimity among delegates. Rothstein, who had attended the Congress as a Branch delegate (Central Hackney), remarked favourably upon the changed nature of the Second International in *Justice*:

> Since the extinction of the old International[51] the International Socialist movement has been proceeding in national sections,

bound to each other by sentiments of solidarity and mutual help, but withal separate, independent, and distinct. At Stuttgart, however, [...] we had a real working congress which did presume to prescribe to the national parties represented what they should demand and how they should act in their respective countries. In other words, instead of confining itself to the functions of mere deliberation the Congress has usurped the powers of an International Socialist Parliament, treating the national sections as sort of semi-autonomous branches of an indivisible party.[52]

This loss of national sovereignty was anathema to Hyndman, who rejected outright the authority of the Second International, arguing that Britain was bound by certain Treaty obligations to guarantee the independence of Belgium, Holland and Switzerland. 'The independence of those small States', he maintained, 'can only be preserved, under conditions which may arise almost at any moment, by force of arms.'[53] He spoke out in support of an Anglo-French-Russian alliance, describing German foreign policy as traditionally bellicose, thwarted only by 'an irresistible combination of forces being formed against her.'[54] He published articles in *Justice* and Robert Blatchford's *Clarion* denouncing German ambitions, and accusing the Kaiser of embarking upon a 'Teutonic world mission' with the conquest of Britain as the ultimate goal. He was widely supported within the Social-Democratic Party (SDP),[55] importantly by both the editor of *Justice*, Harry Quelch, and the SDP's party secretary, H. W. Lee. Between them they held the reins of power in the SDP. Nevertheless, a formidable opposition group, predominantly Russian-Jewish in composition, emerged centred upon the Central Hackney Branch of the SDP, which included Rothstein, his sister-in-law Zelda Kahan, his brother-in-law and former secretary of the old East London (Jewish) Branch of the SDF, Boris Kahan, an Englishman, E. C. Fairchild, and a Russo-Polish Jewish tailor, Joe Fineberg from Stepney Branch SDP, all of whom held to an internationalist position. The sixth member of this group, the

English correspondent of the German socialist paper *Vorwaerts*, J. B. Askew, resided in Berlin. During the 1908–9 Bosnia-Herzegovinia annexationist crisis Askew warned that while German socialists were confronting their own government over Bosnia, the chauvinistic pronouncements of Hyndman were making it very difficult for them to continue that opposition.[56] The German Press was constantly alluding to the fact that prominent English socialists were supporting the foreign policy aims of their Government:

> We render the work of Socialism only the more difficult in Germany if *we make it appear that the work of the Socialist movement is only anti-German and not anti-capitalist*. [Askew's emphasis][57]

Throughout the crisis, Anglo-German naval rivalry occupied centre stage in British politics. In 1908 a back-bench rebellion of Liberal radical MPs succeeded in reducing the estimates for naval expenditure by £400,000 and a large-scale propaganda campaign to force a restoration of these cuts was got underway by the Tory press. They found unlikely allies in Hyndman and Quelch, who, alongside Blatchford and other influential figures in the labour movement, repeated Tory claims that Germany was preparing 'to attain supremacy on sea as well as on land.'[58] Rothstein disputed this claim and produced figures to show that Britain had, in fact, exceeded the two-Power standard that determined British naval construction:

From *Brassey's Naval Annual*, published by Rothstein in *Justice*, 10 October 1908

	Battleships	Armoured Cruisers
England	57	34
Germany	22	8
United States	25	13
France	21	19
Japan	11	11[59]

To emphasise this point, Rothstein quoted from *Brassey's Naval Annual*, 'that even if *England were not to construct a single ship* [Rothstein's emphasis] between now and the end of 1911, she would still possess a supremacy over Germany in the proportion of 52 to 30.'[60] In respect of naval construction Britain spent almost twice as much as Germany, obtaining a tonnage far in excess of those obtained by her rival; to ignore these facts played into the hands of the Navy League and their supporters in the Press who were engaged in conducting their 'nefarious agitation against [. . .] Germany.'[61]

Matters came to a head in 1909 when Asquith's attempt to compromise with the Navy League and the Conservative Party with his four-plus-four formula, led to a Tory campaign for the immediate laying down of eight battleships. The jingoistic nature of the campaign, playing on fears of invasion, whipped up a great deal of anti-foreigner feeling and working-class support for an increased naval building programme. The Tory Party's slogan of 'We Want Eight and We Won't Wait' obscured what Rothstein referred to as 'bourgeois party manoeuvres.'[62] In order to contest the Liberal Party's policy of social reform,[63] and drive the Liberal Free Traders into financial bankruptcy, the Tory Party was demanding an increase in armaments. 'It was very shrewdly calculated,' Rothstein pointed out, 'that if most of the money available on the present system of taxation were spent on armaments, nothing would be left for the social reforms to which the Liberal Party stands pledged, and the Tories would then come to power swimmingly with a mandate to 'broaden the basis of taxation.' Naturally the cry raised was, 'The Empire is in danger!' and as Germany was the only country which was building a large fleet, Germany was pointed out as the quarter from which that danger threatened.'[64] Rothstein, by now a prominent critic of the British Government's foreign policy from the standpoint of the left was also working closely with Radicals and progressives who opposed Asquith's policy of Liberal-imperialism, among them the Arabist, ex-diplomat, notorious philanderer and adventurer Wilfrid Scawen Blunt.

4

Imperialism and the Struggle of the Working Class[1]

It would seem [...] in view of the fate of Morocco bartered away to France, of Northern Persia bartered away to Russia, of the Comoro Islands permitted to be annexed last year by France, of the South Orkney Islands grabbed by Britain herself at the same time, and last, but not least, of the intrigues now going on with a view to a protectorate in the Persian Gulf and South Eastern Arabia − it would seem, I say, in face of these facts, that comrade Hyndman might with more consistency have appealed, if not to Germany, at least to the peoples of this country to stop the aggressions of the British Government all over the world.

Theodore Rothstein, *Justice*, 11 February 1911

Blunt, a relative and hero of the future Cambridge spy Anthony Blunt,[2] had seduced his way across Europe during the 1860s, destroying a budding diplomatic career by running off with the most celebrated prostitute in Paris (Catherine Walters, aka 'Skittles') before marrying Byron's granddaughter, 'to whom he was systematically unfaithful.' Anthony Blunt's father, the Reverend A. Stanley Blunt of Holy Trinity Church, Bournemouth, regarded him 'as politically unsound' and his name was never to be mentioned in the Cambridge spy's household.[3]

A member of the landed gentry and the owner of an Arab stallion stud farm at Crabbet Park, Horsham, Scawen Blunt had gained political notoriety in 1889 when he stood for Parliament as an Irish Home Ruler, and had gone to prison for inciting Irish tenants to resist eviction. In 1906, he was the leading figure in the protest movement against Britain's illegal occupation of Ottoman Egypt, publishing a book under the title *Atrocities of Justice under British Rule in Egypt*. The following year he formed the British-Egypt Association in support of the Egyptian nationalist movement of Mustafa Kamil, and campaigned for the withdrawal of British troops. Among its more notable members were Hilaire Belloc, H. N. Brailsford, James Keir Hardie, Mustafa Kamil, the physicist Lord Rutherford, an unnamed member of Sinn Fein working for the British secret service and Theodore Rothstein.[4]

Blunt and Kamil had established a daily newspaper, the *Egyptian Standard*, published in Cairo, London and Paris and in 1907 Rothstein was employed as the paper's London correspondent. A foreign daily newspaper, however, taxed the Association's resources and the *Egyptian Standard* soon became a weekly. On 14 September 1909 Rothstein addressed the 'Second Egyptian National Congress' in Geneva and denounced British finance capital for arresting the social and economic development of the country and derailing Egypt's constitutional movement. At that time there was a sizeable Egyptian community in Geneva, the majority exiled members of the Young Egyptian Party seeking national liberation. On 9 October Rothstein published an article in *Justice* stating that the overwhelming support for the nationalist movement in Egypt had triumphed over the purely constitutional desire for political reform. British opposition to constitutional reform had convinced the majority of Egyptians that reform would never take place without the removal of the British.[5]

A British intelligence report on Rothstein compiled from papers filed between 25 July 1911 to 8 October 1918 remarked on the virility of Rothstein's opposition to the British Empire, as opposed to other imperial systems, and referred to the *Egyptian Standard* as a 'pro-Turk Egyptian paper' that 'took up a very anti-British position'.[6]

The assassination of the Egyptian Prime Minister Boutros Ghali Pasha and the execution of his assassin Ibrahim Wardani in 1910 led Rothstein to place the Egyptian Question within the context of the European system of alliances. Following Wardani's execution a wave of anti-British rioting swept across Egypt, which the British Government struggled to control. Rothstein, whose sources now appeared to include the Ottoman secret service, commented in *Justice* that the British Government could not dispatch troops to Egypt without facing the common censure of the European powers, in particular, Germany and Austria. Britain, he pointed out, had no mandate from Europe condoning her occupation of Egypt. She was allowed to remain there solely at the discretion of the European Powers, as long as she didn't infringe the substantial rights of those Powers by seeking to annex or appropriate any exclusive advantage; nor could she make any alteration in the status quo without the consent of Europe. To send troops to Egypt would raise not only a diplomatic row with Turkey, who in face of the illegal occupation of her autonomous province by foreign troops would have no other choice but to demand the withdrawal of those troops, and the occupation of Egypt by her own. In making such demands, Turkey would be confident of the support of Germany and Austria, and Britain would be left with no alternative but to fight or to surrender. Faced with such an alternative Britain could not afford to risk military repression in Egypt. 'To dispatch troops at this point', Rothstein argued, 'would inevitably clash with the standing and equal rights of Europe, and either on that account or by themselves raise the question of her stay there!' Britain's illegal occupation of Egypt, he concluded, was destabilising international relations and threatening the European 'balance of power'.[7]

That same year Rothstein published *Egypt's Ruin: A Financial and Administrative Record*, exposing the systematic 'spoliation' of Egypt by British financiers and financier-backed government officials, including the previous Consul-General, Lord Cromer. 'I think', Blunt wrote in his diary, 'the book will be worth it politically. It has given me a deal of trouble, besides writing the introduction.'[8] The introduction attacked the British secret service, who Blunt accused of acting on behalf of the Suez Canal Company, and claimed that Egyptians were 'under the control of a new secret police, with espionage, domiciliary visits, arrests, deportations, and imprisonments, just as in the worst of former times, treating all demands that we should fulfil our promised evacuation of their country as "sedition," and threatening, if these lighter methods of coercion fail, to fall back with them on plain martial law.'[9]

Soon afterwards Blunt sent a copy of Rothstein's book to Asquith, 'with a letter requesting him to read it', a foolish attempt to influence British foreign policy that cost Rothstein his application for British citizenship.[10] The book, however, was warmly received by opponents of British imperialism both in Britain and Germany, a condensed version appearing as a supplement to No. 10 of the *Neue Zeit*, 14 July 1911. Rothstein's journalism now gave him considerable opportunity to attack British foreign policy, and to reach out to a wider audience. Between 1910 and 1914, alongside his paid work as a sub-editor for the *Daily News*, he became a *Manchester Guardian* correspondent and worked as the London correspondent for a number of foreign socialist papers. These included *Neue Zeit*, the more extreme left-wing *Leipziger Volkszeitung*, and from 1912 the American *International Socialist Review* and the Bolsheviks' *Pravda*. Articles from Rothstein also appeared in the *New York Call* and the *International Echo*. From 1906–14 he edited the *Socialist Annual*, and until its formal closure on 9 April 1913, he continued to write for the *Egyptian Standard*.[11] His output was indeed impressive.

On 6 July 1910 Hyndman published a letter in the Conservative *Morning Post* in which he repeated his claims that Germany was preparing for war against Great Britain. Attacking the Labour Party's 'turn-the-cheek-to-the-smiter-pacifism', and their refusal to sanction further expenditure on the fleet, Hyndman argued that the Royal Navy was not only vital to Britain's food supply but also guaranteed political liberties, including the Right of Asylum. In response Rothstein's branch of the Social-Democratic Party (SDP),[12] Central Hackney passed a resolution on the 30 July calling on the SDP to dissociate itself from Hyndman's anti-Germany policy and his recent statements made in the capitalist press:

> This meeting of the Central Hackney branch calls upon the Executive Council publicly to dissociate the SDP from the anti-German policy of comrade Hyndman and from his demands for further expenditure on the Navy. It further urges the E. C. to call upon Hyndman to desist from these utterances, both in 'Justice' and particularly the capitalist press, since his views on this subject are contrary to the spirit and policy of the SDP.[13]

A number of letters from other London branches in support of the Central Hackney branch now appeared in *Justice*. On 6 August the North Islington branch announced that the resolution of Central Hackney had also been passed by its own branch and on the 13 August, Enfield, Brixton and Whitechapel registered their approval for the action taken by Central Hackney. Further resolutions dissociating themselves from Hyndman's support for a 'Big Navy' policy were received from Bethnal Green, St George's and Finsbury and Camberwell branches. The following month Hammersmith, Mile End and Walthamstow added their voices to the growing chorus of disapproval of Hyndman's anti-German policy.

Hyndman was stung by the widespread criticism of his leadership of the SDP aroused by the Central Hackney resolution. In the September issue of the *SDP News* the Executive censured the branch for a breach of party convention, and for not informing them of their intention to canvass the London branches. To counteract the loss of support in London the Executive called a conference of London members, 'so that an expression might be given to various points of view.' The matter, however, was not resolved until the SDP party conference of 1911 when Rothstein's sister-in-law, Zelda Kahan, moved a resolution calling for 'the organization, its Executive, organ, and individual members to combat, with their utmost energy, the demands for additional armaments, [...] and to demand from the Government, [...] the abandonment of all Colonial and financial aggression, and the cessation of any provocative or obstructive policy in its relation with the powers.'[14]

Kahan's resolution undoubtedly bore the hallmark of a series of articles from Rothstein entitled 'The German Menace', which had appeared in *Justice* between 28 January and 15 April 1911. Although Rothstein's ostensible purpose had clearly been to discredit Hyndman's July *Morning Post* letter their main objective was the winning of support for the Central Hackney resolution at the forthcoming Easter conference. Rothstein, influenced by recent events in Egypt, was by now totally committed to the destruction of the British Empire and saw the left-wing of the British labour movement as central to any campaign against British imperialism. Britain, he argued, was cynically manipulating fears arising from Germany's challenge to the European balance of power in order to advance her imperial claims in South Persia, the Persian Gulf and south-eastern Arabia:

> It would seem [...] in view of the fate of Morocco bartered away to France, of Northern Persia bartered away to Russia, of the Comoro Islands permitted to be annexed last year by France, of the South Orkney Islands grabbed by Britain herself at the same time, and last, but not least, of the intrigues now going on with a view to a protectorate in the Persian Gulf and South Eastern Arabia – it would seem, I say, in face of these facts, that comrade Hyndman might with more consistency have appealed, if not to Germany, at least to the peoples of this country to stop the aggressions of the British Government all over the world.[15]

The British Empire, he continued, was far from a satiated beast requiring only peace and leisure for digestion. Imperialism was inextricably linked with the capitalist system, and it was no more feasible for the British Empire to stop and rest content with what it had got, than it would be for a capitalist undertaking, having reached a certain degree of prosperity, to cease the expansion of production:

> There is as little finality in Empire building – that is, in grabbing new territories and in subjugating new nationalities and races – as in the capitalist process of production, of which it is itself but a counterpart.[16]

For this reason, Rothstein continued, Britain had a far worse record against the weaker nationalities than any other Power. In order to stave off criticism and manage popular opinion in respect of her imperial policy, the British Government had embarked on her anti-German campaign. In an article on the British response to the Balkan Crisis of 1908–9, published in *Justice* on 20 March 1911, Rothstein berated the British Government for its pro-Russian stance, and for the belligerence underpinning its dealings with Germany. The annexation of Bosnia-Herzegovina by Austria-Hungary, territories formally within the sovereignty of the Ottoman Empire, while technically an aggressive act had not, Rothstein argued, threatened the status quo of Europe; yet the British Foreign Office and Press continued to fuel anti-German prejudices by suggesting that Russia had been forced to step back from supporting Serbia during the crisis for fear of a German declaration of war.[17]

On 8 April Rothstein, somewhat provocatively, went so far as to suggest that Britain was actively seeking an armed conflict with Germany, with the aim of crushing an economic rival. The campaign against Germany waged by the British press, he said, 'had one, and only one purpose – to justify such an increase of armaments as would enable this country one day to attack and to crush her economic rival.'[18] The following week Rothstein accused Britain of pursuing a foreign policy more relevant to the closing of the eighteenth and opening of the nineteenth centuries than to the beginning of the twentieth century. Then, the object of British foreign policy had been to form and to lead a coalition of the willing continental Powers against revolutionary and Napoleonic France. The European situation, however, had since changed dramatically. Napoleon had not only threatened the commercial supremacy of Britain; but also Britain's social and political make-up. Consequently, it had been a relatively simple task to mobilise all the reactionary forces of Europe against revolutionary France. This situation did not apply to present-day Germany who, despite archaic political forms, was still 'the most progressive capitalist country in Europe; and so far from there being any economic and social antagonisms between her and the rest of the Continent, the most intimate financial and commercial co-operation [...] was seen to exist among them. Britain', he continued, 'was in real danger of becoming isolated from the continental Powers, who, in the absence of any political conflict among themselves would come to identify Britain and her policy towards her main economic rival as the biggest threat to world peace.' Rothstein's pro-German and anti-British sentiments were barely disguised:

> It is, therefore, clear that in the absence of all antagonism between Germany and other continental Powers; [...] in fact, of the closest commercial and financial co-operation between the capitalists of the different countries, England's endeavours to stir up a hatred of Germany and a coalition against her is foredoomed to failure [...] And what is still more important is, as I have said, that any further pursuit of this policy on the part of England is bound to result in a coalition against her, since not only the Governments, but even the peoples, are beginning to understand that the menace to the world's peace is England, and that all the heavy naval armaments of recent years have been imposed upon them by the British 'menace'.[19]

Were these opinions, verging on sedition, being monitored by the newly established British secret service? Surely so, on 25 July 1911 there took place one of the most bizarre incidents in the history of British intelligence:

In July 1911 – at the time of the Agadir incident[20] – a letter was picked up in the Strand and taken to the 'Property Found' Office at Scotland Yard. It was markedly opposed to the policy then being adopted by the British Government, which, it alleged, was eager to 'beat off all demands of the German Government for compensation and order it to clear out from Agadir'. The letter further urged that France should not be made the 'dupe of British policy'. The addressee was J. LONGUET, grandson of Carl MARX, and author of a book called 'Egypt's Ruin'.[21] The writer was Theodore ROTHSTEIN, of 28 Gladsmuir Road, Highgate. He was born in 1865[22] in Russia and Scotland Yard's papers shewed that in 1908 he applied for naturalization but was refused on account of his extreme socialistic views.[23]

As a result of this chance discovery in the Strand a security service file[24] was opened on Rothstein and his anti-British, anti-Tsarist and pro-Ottoman activities were henceforth closely monitored. A later document showed that he had established strong ties with the Young Turks through the *Daily News*:

> In 1906–7, as London correspondent of a pro-Turk Egyptian paper, he [Rothstein] took up a very anti-British position. In 1911 [and][25] 1912 he worked for the 'Daily News' which became about [that time][26] very favourable to the Young Turks. Sir E. PEARS (Constantinople correspondent of the same paper) said in 1912 that ROTHSTEIN got on to the paper through I. SACHER a pro-Turk and anti-Russian Jew.[27]

I. Sacher, 'a Viennese Jew relative of the SACHER family of Vienna who are the "JOSEPH LYONS" of that City', was an influential figure in Viennese society and an important contact for Rothstein during the Agadir Crisis of 1911.[28] It was reported that Rothstein had exploited

> his position and information as a journalist to send warning of the strong [*sic*] line to be taken by the British Government and

of the tenor [*sic*] of LLOYD GEORGE's famous speech (which he knew of 'eighteen days [*sic*][29] in advance') to LONGUET[30] and his party, whom he urged to 'persuade [*sic*][31] the French Cabinet to become more conciliatory and not to allow France to be made the dupe of British policy.

He added that he had already sent a similar warning to 'our German comrades', that is, that they should be on their guard and watch their diplomacy and government. He takes up a strongly anti-British standpoint, and remarks how all the British daily papers except the '*Manchester Guardian* have come instantly to heel at the "*mot d'ordre*" of the Government.'[32]

The Agadir Crisis, caused by the dispatch of the German gunboat *SMS Panther* to the port of Agadir in protest against the French occupation of the Moroccan interior in April 1911, led to renewed calls from the Hyndmanite faction within the SDP for an increase in naval expenditure. This was bitterly opposed by Rothstein and the Central Hackney Branch with matters coming to a head at the British Socialist Party's 1912 conference. The previous year delegates to conference had again voted for socialist unity and had joined together with the *Clarion* newspaper and the left wing of the ILP to form the Marxist-oriented British Socialist Party.[33] At the inaugural conference of the BSP, held in Manchester over the weekend of 25–27 May 1912, the split between the Hyndmanites now dubbed the 'social patriots' and the 'internationalists' led by Rothstein and Zelda Kahan increased in acerbity.[34]

The debate on armaments was introduced by Harry Quelch, who urged on delegates the need for a civilian army and a bigger navy. After a noisy debate – in which Quelch was accused of dividing the Party – the motion was approved by 83 votes to 65. In the elections to the nine-man National Executive that followed, however, only three – Harry Quelch, Dan Irving and Victor Fisher – represented the old Hyndmanite wing of the SDP; while the two co-signatories of the ILP's 'Green Manifesto'[35] who opposed any restricting alliance with moderate trade unions, along with E. C. Fairchild and Zelda Kahan, both delegates from the Central Hackney branch, formed an effective opposition. The remaining two members, London dockers' leader Ben Tillett and Conrad Noel, swung between the two factions.[36]

These divisions came to a head in December when a resolution dissociating the Executive Committee from the propaganda for increased naval expenditure was moved by Kahan. It was passed by a majority of one, and caused Fisher to offer his resignation from the Executive Committee citing the absence of Noel and Tillett from the meeting and the Executive's failure to ascertain their votes on such a crucial and potentially divisive question nor had any attempt been made to consult the party membership on such an important issue.[37] In a letter to *Justice* defending her actions, Kahan wrote that to consult absent members from Executive meetings had never been standard practice and it, therefore, hadn't occurred to her to do so. On the question of consulting the membership, however, she was on shakier ground. The Executive, she argued, was there to give 'members a lead on important questions of the day, and Anglo-German relations and the ever-increasing expenditure on armaments was certainly one of the most important of these.'[38] Many branches objected to Kahan's explanation and complained about a lack of democracy in the party and the apparent ease with which the National Executive could overturn Conference decisions.[39] Fisher's attack on Kahan, however, gave evidence of a more worrying trend in the party. The anti-Semitism and xenophobia that had scarred sections of the British left during the Boer War had not entirely disappeared. Fisher's resignation letter, published in *Justice*, expressed fears 'that the general public might equate the BRITISH Socialist Party [Fisher's emphasis] with treason.' The party, he suggested, was following a policy 'largely inspired by comrades alien in blood and race'.[40] The following week a further letter appeared in the correspondence section of *Justice* complaining of 'alien Socialists' receiving 'more than their fair share of the columns of Justice', while it was doubted that 'Miss Kahan had the interests of this country at heart in this German menace business; every action, every word, of hers breathes hatred of Britain and everything that is British – except its hospitality.'[41]

The Hyndmanite 'old guard', past masters at political scheming, now set about reversing the Kahan resolution on armaments at a meeting of the National Executive on 15 February 1913. Only five members were present when the vote was taken (the ex-ILPer Leonard Hall, Tillett and Noel were absent and Fairchild did not turn up until after the vote had been taken). The reappearance of Fisher, who had been personally invited by the Chairman and granted full voting rights on the grounds that his resignation had not yet been considered, won the day for the Hyndmanites. 'Technically correct, I suppose', commented Kahan, 'but it seems to me a somewhat curious proceeding.'[42]

Furious, she resigned from the Executive, and threatened to resign from the BSP altogether if the matter was either shelved or decided in Hyndman's favour at the forthcoming Annual Conference. Accepting that this would 'seriously damage' unity within the BSP, Kahan cited the policy of the Second International on the question of armaments; arguing that those who supported the International would have no alternative but to resign from a party advocating increased expenditure on armaments, or permitting its Chairman and most prominent figure the freedom to do so. For the sake of party unity, however, she gave notice of her willingness 'to drop the whole subject providing Hyndman and those who think with him pledge themselves to do likewise. I think that the majority of those who think with me on the Armaments question will agree with this policy.'[43] The way was open, therefore, for a compromise resolution to be adopted at the Annual Conference in 1913. Introducing the debate, F. L. Kehrhahn (Marxian Club), while condemning Hyndman's views on armaments, remarked that 'first and foremost they must have Socialist Unity [...] He hoped that Hyndman would drop all agitation for an increase of armaments as things were.'[44] Kahan's speech was more conciliatory. She 'spoke with great feeling of what Hyndman had done for the Socialist movement [...] She knew he was no Imperialist and no jingo, but his views on armaments made people here and abroad think that he was, and was putting the BSP entirely outside the International.'[45]

Hyndman, realising the strength of the opposition, was forced to compromise. For the sake of unity he agreed 'to hold his own view, and not to enter upon a discussion of the question or to raise it in any way that might upset the Party.'[46] The following resolution from Hampstead branch was carried with nine dissentients:

That this Conference congratulates our French and German comrades on their vigorous opposition to the increase of armaments in their respective countries, and pledges the British Socialist Party, as an integral part of the International Socialist Party, bound by the resolutions on war of Stuttgart and Basle, 1912, with the object of checking the growth of all forms of militarism.[47]

As a gesture of unity and reconciliation Kahan and Hyndman shook hands, and the issue was effectively 'shelved' for a year. At the elections to the National Executive, however, Kahan was defeated by Quelch and the Hyndmanite, Moore Bell, in a contest for the London seats; while Hall, Smart and Noel did not stand for re-election. The new executive was completely devoid of internationalist representation.[48] Following the death of Quelch on 17 September 1913 the Hyndmanites further strengthened their position by passing responsibility for the editorial policy of *Justice* to the party secretary H. W. Lee and the major shareholders who were largely synonymous with the Hyndmanite 'old guard'. However, Lee's resignation as secretary of the party, a position he had held for over 30 years, 'cost the Hyndman group their direct control of the party machine.'[49] Albert Inkpin, who had been appointed Lee's deputy seven years earlier, succeeded Lee as secretary; as a member of the Central Hackney branch he was a staunch ally of both Rothstein and Kahan. This opposition group grew in number during World War I, providing the leadership for anti-war work on the left of the labour movement and in 1920 would provide most of the membership of the Communist Party of Great Britain, 'the enemy within'.

5

War and MI7(d): Chicherin, the Zimmerwald Manifesto and Trotsky's *Nashe Slovo*

One thing is certain 'the long services to the cause of Russian freedom' have utterly failed to disclose to Mr. Green the meaning of the eternal, fateful question which the Russian – not Jewish-Russian, but 'real Russian' – Radical or Socialist, has to put to himself in every international crisis in which Russia is involved: will not victory so strengthen the Russian political system based on unlimited despotism as to make it for Russia necessary and inevitable to be drenched in blood again in order to secure some form of tolerable political conditions?

E. J. Zundelevich, *Justice*, 5 November 1914

MI7(d) originated in the work of an officer of the old MO6[1] who got his friends and acquaintances of the Press and of the Civil Service to read and translate articles from foreign newspapers and other documents. A news sheet, 'Daily Extracts from the Foreign Press', was produced at irregular intervals and was very soon in great demand from every Government department. In June, 1916, Treasury sanction was obtained for the payment of a small staff. Already in March the summary had changed its title to the 'Daily Review of the Foreign Press'. It was found necessary to publish four weekly supplements dealing with Economics, Allied Press, Neutral Press and Enemy Press and other supplements at irregular intervals,

e.g. Medical and Technical supplements. In this form the review
continued until August, 1919.

TNA Kew WO32/10776, MI7

The creation of the Secret Service Bureau (SSB) in 1909[2] to combat
German espionage in Britain was purely a military and naval affair
and had not been set-up to deal with 'the enemy within'. The
officers selected by the War Office and the Admiralty to run the SSB
were Captain Vernon Kell and Commander Mansfied Cumming
RN.[3] By inheriting William Melville and his assistant Herbert
Dale Long, however, Kell gained access to Special Branch files and
began recruiting informants in the labour movement. According to
Melville's biographer, Andrew Cook, 'Melville had always been
good at snooping on outfits like *The Syndicalist* and following up
suspicions about where their money was coming from, and Kell was
ever-vigilant in case dissidents were being funded abroad.' Cook
makes clear that these fears increased after the creation of the SSB
in 1909:

> The Government was particularly suspicious of pacifist and
> trade-union organizations from about 1910 onwards. Late that
> year a series of strikes, persisting through the summer of 1911,
> led to civil disorder and a few rioters were killed by troops in
> Liverpool and North Wales. Syndicalist unionism should it get
> mass support, would make a dangerous alternative power-base.
> In case of war the dockers, transport workers and miners acting
> in unison could paralyse the country. And such a syndicate of
> unions could ultimately make common cause with the working
> classes abroad. Workers of the world would unite. This would
> undermine nationalism, imperialism and everything the
> Government stood for.[4]

In 1911 the Home Secretary, Winston Churchill, also had to deal
with renewed public concerns about the number of 'aliens' and
dangerous anarchists being allowed into Britain under the political
exemption clause of the 1905 Alien Act.[5] Anti-alien sentiment had

been on the increase following the murder of three City of London Police Officers by Latvian anarchists during a bungled robbery at a jewellers' shop in Houndsditch on 16 December 1910. When Churchill visited Sidney Street, Stepney, the scene of a fierce gun battle between two of the Latvian gang and a combined police and army unit in East London, he was greeted with angry cries of 'Oo let 'em in?'[6] One of his first actions after the siege was to try and persuade Parliament to pass an 'Aliens (Prevention of Crime) Bill' enabling governments to deport any immigrant of less than five years' standing guilty of a criminal act or whose continued stay was 'owing to his consorting with criminals, or for any other reason, likely to be prejudicial to public safety or good order.'[7] The bill, which would have drawn a distinction between British subjects and aliens and given governments the power to deport aliens before they had committed a crime, was rejected by Parliament. However, Churchill's good working relationship with Kell meant that the spirit of the bill did not recede.

Part of Kell's brief in 1909 had been the creation of an Aliens agency, which in March 1910 had resulted in the setting-up of the Aliens Sub-Committee of Imperial Defence under the Chairmanship of Churchill. One of its first acts was to approve 'the preparation by Kell of a secret register of aliens from probable enemy powers (chiefly Germany) based on information supplied by local police forces.'[8] The 1913 Census recorded 'the particulars of all male aliens aged eighteen and above of eight nationalities (in particular Germans and Austrians) living in areas which would be closed to aliens in wartime. Information on aliens taken from the Census was then circulated to chief constables, who were also asked to take note of those on the Register in their areas.'[9] Kell could also draw on the support of the Chief Constables and in December 1913 he wrote to the Home Office expressing his 'gratitude to the Chief Constables and their Superintendents for the excellent work they have done for us during the last three years'. Their work was invaluable and he requested that they keep their local registers 'under constant current revision'.[10] The monitoring of aliens in Britain during the early twentieth century, therefore, had from the very beginning been the joint responsibility of Kell's MO5(g),[11] Special Branch and the ordinary police. The appointment of Basil Thomson as Assistant Commissioner at Scotland Yard in charge of the Criminal Investigation Department (CID) and the 114-man Metropolitan Special Branch in June 1913 saw Thomson working alongside Kell investigating espionage, sabotage and subversion in Britain; both men took a keen interest in the labour movement.

On 5 August, the day after Britain's declaration of war on Germany, the Home Secretary Reginald McKenna[12] announced that 'within the last twenty-four hours no fewer than twenty-one spies, or suspected spies, have been arrested in various places all over the country, chiefly in important military or naval centres, some of them long known to the authorities to be spies'.[13] While the arrests were intended to reassure the British public the sense of relief was not shared by all. The decision to intern enemy aliens as part of the exercise unsettled the Russian émigré and East London Jewish communities, many of whom were recent immigrants fleeing the pogroms of Central and Eastern Europe.[14]

A month into the war the BSP issued a War Manifesto supporting British war aims and accepted the Government's invitation to 'all political parties to join in a united campaign to secure recruits for service in the European war.'[15] As a result Rothstein, who had consistently taken an anti-war stance in the run up to the conflict, resigned his membership of the BSP and issued a statement condemning the BSP's support for the war. His position as the leading spokesperson for the anti-war movement in the BSP now passed to his few close associates from the BSP's Central Hackney branch – Zelda Kahan, E. C. Fairchild and the brothers H. W. and Albert Inkpin. His decision to resign from the BSP, however, was also influenced by a 'tip off' that he was being considered for internment as an 'enemy alien', and he hoped that his resignation from the BSP would stay the authority's hand.[16] According to Andrew Rothstein, although his father resigned from the BSP he continued his anti-war work by bringing together 'the most determined of the BSP's members together on a platform of struggle against the war'.[17] Throughout the war the security service, MO5(g), regarded him as a German agent of influence:

> According to a report from Paris ROTHSTEIN was in close touch with Germans, and with one LIAKHOVETSKY [Ivan MiKhailovitch Maisky],[18] who is connected with German social democrats. This clique, of considerable influence in literary circles, exaggerates Allied reverses, and spreads false rumours about the Entente, alleging, for instance, that France is on the verge of bankruptcy. ROTHSTEIN is kept informed of what is going on in Germany through his friends.[19]

From the beginning of the war MO5(g) had been intercepting the BSP's correspondence and regarded the Jewish members of the Party as unpatriotic.[20] Following the resignation of the social-patriot, George Moore Bell from the BSP's Executive Committee to enlist in the Army in October 1914 and his replacement by Joe Fineberg, a Russian-Polish Jew,[21] MO5(g) expanded its 'enemy alien' investigations to include 'friendly aliens' and Jews from Russia who opposed the war. Fineberg's election to the Executive sparked an acrimonious debate in *Justice* on the question of 'Foreigners and the War', which centred upon the refusal of East London Jewry to support the Triple Entente.[22]

The debate was started unwittingly by Plekhanov, who had published a letter in *Justice* supporting Russia's involvement in the war on the side of the democracies. A German victory, he warned, would mean that Russia could only survive as an 'economic vassal' of Germany. Russia would be subject to such 'onerous conditions' as to 'render her further economic evolution terribly difficult.' Russia would then find it almost impossible to overthrow Tsardom as 'economic evolution', capitalism and class conflict would be denied the revolutionary forces in Russia.'[23]

The following week J. F. Green, a former Secretary of the Society of Friends of Russian Freedom, wrote in support of Plekhanov welcoming his views as those 'of the real Russians i.e. those of Slav race [. . .] fighting side by side with Britain and France.' It was only the Jews and Russo-Jews in emigration, he argued, who owed their liberty to Britain's commitment to uphold the Right of Asylum, who were pro-German. It was not for these men, to denounce 'the Government for going to war with Germany; their proper role was to remain silent: If they cannot conscientiously support the country which protects them, they might at least preserve a discreet silence.'[24] Not surprisingly Green's letter provoked a response from BSP members irrespective of their views on the war. E. J. Zundelevich, expressed his doubts that such a letter could have been 'written by a Socialist to the Editor of the organ of the British Socialist Party'.

> One thing is certain 'the long services to the cause of Russian freedom' have utterly failed to disclose to Mr. Green the meaning of the eternal, fateful question which the Russian − not Jewish-Russian, but 'real Russian' − Radical or Socialist, has to put to himself in every international crisis in which Russia is involved: will not victory so strengthen the Russian political system based on unlimited despotism as to make it for Russia necessary and inevitable to be drenched in blood again in order to secure some form of tolerable political conditions?'[25]

J. B. Askew and H. Lubert stressed that it would be foolish to expect from people 'who have for decades been inhumanely oppressed by such a country as Russia to have that hatred for Germany which we Englishmen might have.'[26] 'Le Vin' pointed out that the attitude of Russian-Jewish political émigrés towards Russia and the war was shared by the ILP and the *Labour Leader*, and a good many Liberals and Radicals besides:

> The *Labour Leader*, and all who share their views on the war, the Russo-Jewish refugees included, have made out a strong case. Their case must be met with argument and criticism [. . .] it is hardly decent to turn around and instead of argument fling at them a 'shut-up, you foreigner', as Comrade Green does.[27]

'A Russian Socialist' reminded *Justice* that a total of 15 London branches of the BSP had issued a statement condemning the war. 'May not a Russian-Jewish Socialist agree with that resolution without being ungrateful and indecent?' he asked.[28]

Green was defended by Victor Fisher who claimed that the war had ushered in the 'eternal idea of nationality' based upon an 'age old idealism' that evoked a wider spirit of 'racial life.' It was the Jews alone who lacked 'any strong attachment to European nationality'. The Jews had played a prominent role in the development of Socialist thought in the last decades of the nineteenth century, he continued, but to the detriment of nationalism within the International Socialist movement. To move forward the Socialist International has to root itself in Nationality. 'Democracy must develop along the lines of national genius – not according to a vague and nebulous cosmopolitanism. The rights of the nation shall be affirmed as sacred as the rights of the individual. And in the democratization of the fecund idea of national rights we shall find the mightiest lever for the Social-Democratic transformation.'[29] 'Poor Jew!' replied Fineberg the following week, 'Even in Socialist discussions he must fulfill his historical role of scapegoat for the mistakes of others.'[30]

Opposition to both the war and Russian despotism by Russian-Jews encouraged anti-Semitism in the BSP and elsewhere; it soon led to accusations that the Russian Jews were 'pro-German'. At the District Conferences of the BSP held in March 1915 Hyndman, Fisher and the 'old guard' were bitterly attacked for their continuing support of the war. According to Andrew Rothstein his father had drawn up a resolution condemning the Executive for associating the BSP with the Government's recruiting campaign, which was passed unanimously. Enraged, Hyndman began denouncing his opponents in the French press. The Independent Labour Party, however, bore the initial brunt of his anger. In March 1915 two letters appeared in *L'Homme Enchaine*, the journal of the French Radical Party, in which Hyndman accused the ILP of receiving funds from Germany, prompting Karl Marx's grandson, the French Socialist Deputy

Jean Longuet, to point out that 'the ILP was more Quaker or Tolstoyan, than Germanophil.'[31] Unmoved, Hyndman began denouncing his opponents to the authorities for internment under the Defence of the Realm Act (DORA), among them the pro-German Russian Jew Theodore Rothstein.

DORA had been drafted by the Home Office in consultation with Kell and Holt-Wilson (Kell's deputy during the war) and had passed into law on 8 August 1914; it immediately gave the government powers close to martial law. On 1 October 1914 Kell divided MO5(g) into three branches,[32] one of which was given responsibility for the 'Co-ordination of general policy of Government Departments in dealing with aliens.'[33] Kell's main concern here was largely with 'enemy aliens'; however, the Jews, whether German or Russian, were increasingly painted in the British press as both 'foreigners' and pro-German. In these circumstances, Rothstein took steps to safeguard his place in British society by securing newspaper work reading the German and Austrian Press and 'advising the News Department of the F.O. on matters connected with German socialism and the International.'[34] Rex Leeper, then in charge of the Foreign Office's Russian Department, spoke of first making Rothstein's 'acquaintance in 1915 when he was reading Russian and German papers in the small office that had been set up by Mr. Muir and was at that time under the Home Office.'[35]

In May 1915 Rothstein was transferred to MO7 at the War Office and officially began working for British intelligence. MO7 Press Control had been set up in 1914 with the help of MO6[36] as a sub-section of Kell's MO5 and was initially known as MO5(h). The duties of MO5(h) were to draft and furnish to the Press suitable communiques on military events to be communicated to the Press through the Admiralty, War Office and the Press Committee,[37] and consisted of the Secretary of the Admiralty as Chairman,[38] the Director of Naval Intelligence,[39] the Assistant Secretary of the War Office[40] and MO5's Vernon Kell, with the Secretary of the Newspaper Proprietors Association and representatives of the Press of all parts of the United Kingdom as members. This organisation was very quickly expanded and became the War Office branch of the Press Bureau[41] to oversee all military communication with the Press.[42]

The military personnel of the Press Bureau were under the control of the War Office, and following the establishment of the Directorate of Special Intelligence in April 1915, the Bureau was placed under direct military control. Colonel Coleridge, the nominal head of the section, assumed the title of Military Assistant Director of the Press Bureau and MO7 was divided into four sub-sections: MO7(a) in the War Office; MO7(b) in the War Office, with three Press Officers; MO7(c) at the Press Bureau, with Military Assistant Censors; and MO7(d) at the Press Bureau, with Press Cable Censors.[43]

Following the formation of the Directorate of Military Intelligence in January 1916, which saw MO5 assume the title MI5, MO7 became MI7 and MO7(d) became MI7(d), with Colonel W. E. Davies from the W.O. taking over as head of the organisation:

> M.I.7(d) originated in the work of an officer of the old M.0.6 who got his friends and acquaintances of the Press and of the Civil Service to read and translate articles from foreign newspapers and other documents. A news sheet, 'Daily Extracts from the Foreign Press,' was produced at irregular intervals and was very soon in great demand from every Government department. In June, 1916, Treasury sanction was obtained for the payment of a small staff. Already in March the summary had changed its title to the 'Daily Review of the Foreign Press.' It was found necessary to publish four weekly supplements dealing with Economics, Allied Press, Neutral Press and Enemy Press and other supplements at irregular intervals, *e.g.* Medical and Technical supplements. In this form the review continued until August, 1919.[44]

The offices of both MI5 and MI7 were situated in Watergate House, on the Embankment, and the DRFP was produced there.[45]

Kell's office was also at Watergate House. Rothstein's employment by MI7(d), where he occupied an important position in Press Control, not surprisingly raised some eyebrows. He was apparently recruited 'in some panic' when the authorities applied to the *Manchester Guardian* for any translators they could recommend and C. P. Scott, editor of the *Manchester Guardian*, for whom Rothstein 'had been doing just such translation work in the form of articles on foreign affairs, asked him to take on this work.'[46] According to Andrew Rothstein, this gave his father 'a far wider access to foreign press opinions and events abroad than he had ever had before. I don't personally doubt that this helped him in his anti-war campaign'.[47]

Rothstein's employment in MI7(d) generated a considerable degree of alarm, initially in the Special Intelligence Bureau (SIB) (Eastern Mediterranean), which had long suspected Rothstein of having links with Ottoman intelligence. On 11 June 1916 the Assistant Director of SIB (Eastern Mediterranean) wrote to MI5 informing them that Rothstein had been working for the Ottoman secret service since 1908 through his association with Scawen Blunt's British-Egypt Association. One of the London-based editors of the British-Egypt Association's newspaper, the *Egyptian Standard*, was described in this document as 'a Sinn Feiner, but long a good Loyalist'[48] who had successfully infiltrated Scawen Blunt's circle for SIB (Eastern Mediterranean) and had reported back that 'TH. ROTHSTEIN was a very violent man and almost an Anarchist and that he was of German Jewish origin. [. . .] We send you a copy of a note regarding Theodore ROTHSTEIN for your information and such action as may appear necessary'.[49] At this time Rothstein was still in regular contact with Scawen Blunt, who sent him a welcome brace of pheasants in 1916 as a New Year's gift.[50]

Sir Edward Pears, the Constantinople correspondent of the *Daily News*, also informed SIB (Eastern Mediterranean) that Rothstein was working for 'a pro-Turk faction at the *Daily News* (Foreign Department)' concluding that Rothstein in 1914 was probably working for the Ottoman secret service in London:

The writer receives hints at Constantinople in 1914 that a Russian Jewish journalist working for English newspapers was in receipt of Turkish secret service money. This might be ROTHSTEIN.[51]

As a result MI5 opened an investigation into Rothstein's activities. An examination of his bank account on 2 September 1916 revealed that it contained a 'little less than £20'. It was noted that Rothstein had not been in contact with the Egyptian national liberation movement since 1912 and it was decided to ignore the warnings coming from SIB (Eastern Mediterranean), particularly as both the War Office and the Foreign Office spoke highly of his abilities. He was kept on at MI7(d), where he was paid £5 per week for his reports culled from the foreign socialist press. Nevertheless, a Home Office Warrant (HOW) was placed on his correspondence between 13 September 1916 and 23 February 1917,[52] and throughout this period he remained in close contact with Scawen Blunt. On 2 December 1916 he wrote to him predicting revolution in Russia and expressing his conviction that events were bearing out his views on the possible course of the war. If intercepted by MI5, this letter could easily have been misconstrued by Kell as pro-German:

Germany is as formidable as ever, while the position of France and Russia is certainly weakening. The former may collapse at any moment while the latter is so unreliable that a betrayal on her part of the cause of the Allies will not come as a surprise even to the F.O. Moreover, the internal conditions in Russia are such as to head straight for a revolution. In these circumstances a negotiated peace would be the best way out of the growing difficulties, but the men to make it are unfortunately lacking. Our statesmen are mortally afraid of Northcliffe,[53] and as Northcliffe is in favour of fighting to a finish, hundreds of thousands will yet perish [. . .] before the senseless massacre comes to an end.[54]

He also complained to Scawen Blunt of fatigue, 'stress of circumstances has compelled me to take up some work in the day also, [presumably at Watergate House] so that I am leaving home at 10 in the morning and return only after twelve at night.'[55] He continued to work evenings, from 7.30 p.m. to midnight at the offices of the *Daily News* in Bouverie Street (Saturdays excluded), where he selected and translated articles from foreign newspapers for insertion in the following day's edition. He was probably one of the best-informed sub-editors on Fleet Street and shared his knowledge of the international situation not only with MI7(d) but also with a select group of fellow socialists, both Russian and British.

The nature of this work, however, estranged Rothstein from a number of international socialists and Russian political émigrés, among them the future Soviet Commissar for Foreign Affairs Georgii Chicherin, who came to regard him with hostility and suspicion at a time of renewed class tension in Britain.[56] Chicherin, who had arrived in Britain from Belgium shortly after the outbreak of war, had spent six years in Paris and six years in Berlin. In Paris he had been closely associated with the views of A. N. Potresov and the faction grouped around the journal *Zarya* (*Dawn*). Their doctrine opposed both Plekhanov's 'social patriotism' and Lenin's 'revolutionary defeatism', which had called on socialists to work for the defeat of their respective countries in the war as a prelude to world revolution. Potresov argued instead for what he termed a 'defencist' policy of not obstructing national defence while continuing the political struggle against Tsarism. On his arrival in England Chicherin joined with those Russian political émigrés who argued that Socialists should support the nations most likely to advance socialism and democracy in Russia. He, therefore, supported the British and French Governments against the 'feudal monarchist' remnants of Germany and Austria-Hungary; while, in line with Potresov, he continued to advocate that Russian Socialists work for the final overthrow of Tsardom. His support for the Entente, however, collapsed in early 1915, and towards the end of the year he began writing articles for Trotsky's internationalist

Paris-based newspaper, *Nashe Slovo* (*Our Word*) renouncing *oboronchestvo* ('defencism') and advocating internationalism.[57]

Nashe Slovo, edited initially by Menshevik-Internationalists and Trotsky, and later by Trotsky alone, supported Trotsky's contention that the Internationalists should split at once with all non-internationalists.[58] In order to create the conditions for such a split in the British labour movement Chicherin set up the Russian Political Prisoners and Exiles Relief Committee (RPPERC). Ostensibly to collect relief funds for Russian political prisoners and exiles, its main purpose was to broaden this body into an *ad hoc* International supporting the views of *Nashe Slovo*.[59] Having arrived in Britain with little or no experience of the British labour movement, however, he became very much a one-man organisation working outside the Russian political émigré community in London. His internationalist views found him in opposition to the BSP, who were loyal to the Second International, including those émigrés opposed to the dominance of Hyndman. Significant ill feeling developed between Chicherin and other émigrés resident in London, who through the Herzen Circle, an inter-party political club for Russian political émigrés, already operated a broad-based fund for the relief of Russian prisoners and exiles in conjunction with the 'Vera Figner Fund' in Paris and the Krakov organisation in Zurich. Writing to *Justice* on 12 August 1915, the Committee of the Russian Political Prisoners' and Exiles' Fund (RPPEF), consisting of Fanny Stepniak (hon. treasurer), Theodore Rothstein, V. Mitrov, S. Perstovskii and E. Zundelevich (hon. sec.), issued an appeal for funds, in a manner which censured Chicherin for his sectarian approach to Russian émigré politics. However, despite the fact that Chicherin was a member of the Herzen Circle, he persisted in setting up a rival fund-raising organization to the RPPEF with an altogether different political objective. On 15 July 1915 the *Labour Leader* issued an appeal on behalf of a new Russian émigré organisation, the RPPERC, under Chicherin's signature. Chicherin was, ironically, helped in this endeavor by the activities of Hyndman and his outrageous claim made in Georges Clemenceau's *L' Homme*

Enchaine that the ILP was in receipt of German funds. Mistrusting the BSP Chicherin looked for support from the ILP and the trade union movement, effectively cutting himself off from the émigrés in the BSP. Furthermore, disagreements with prominent members of the Herzen Circle whom he accused of taking a 'social-patriotic' stance, most notably (and mistakenly) Rothstein and Maxim Litvinov, the latter having arrived in England in 1908, led him to censure both men along with the Herzen Circle, for failing to unequivocally condemn Russia's involvement in the war.

Litvinov, a leading Bolshevik figure in London in 1915 and the Bolsheviks' representative on the International Socialist Bureau, was not a 'social-patriot', and Chicherin's description of him as such showed that his knowledge and experience of the Russian Social-Democratic Labour Party in London was limited. His understanding of the British labour movement, compared to Litvinov's, was also decidedly poor. Litvinov, a member of the Kentish Town branch of the BSP was also Jewish and consequently had considerable influence in East London branches. A *Litvak* (Lithuanian-Jew) like Rothstein, his first language was Yiddish. Born Meer Genokh Moisseevitch Wallach on 17 July 1876 (O.S. 5 July) in Bialystok, he had changed his name to Maxim Litvinov soon after joining the RSDLP. In 1903 he sided with Lenin and the Bolsheviks, and had his first taste of London émigré life in 1907 when he attended the 5th Party Congress of the RSDLP, apparently renting a house with Joseph Stalin.[60] The two men also purportedly shared a bank-robbing, arms-smuggling past, and on 18 January 1908 Litvinov, back in Paris, was said to have been arrested by French police working closely with the Foreign Agency of the Russian Okhrana. The circumstances of his arrest were reported in the conservative journal *Figaro*. The individual concerned was arrested at the Gare du Nord with 12 500-rouble banknotes in his possession bearing numbers from the 1907 Tiflis bank robbery.[61] In custody the prisoner told his captors that he had been in France when the Tiflis robbery had taken place and had been given the notes by the Russian revolutionary treasury. He had not asked their origin, and his travelling companion, Mlle. Yanpolska, knew nothing about the affair. Requests from the Russian authorities for his extradition were turned down by the French Minister of Justice, Aristide Briand, and along with his travelling companion he was deported to Britain in January 1908.

There is some doubt, however, that this particular émigré was, in fact, Litvinov. An intelligence report on the 1910 Houndsditch Murders and the Siege of Sydney Street written in 1930 claims that the person arrested by the French police was Abraham Borisuk, who was using the alias of Wallach.[62] Nevertheless, Litvinov is known to have arrived in Britain at the beginning of 1908 with an introduction from the writer Maxim Gorky to the Director of the London Library, Charles Hagberg Wright, who found him employment as a clerk in the foreign department of the publishing firm, Williams and Norgate. Litvinov worked there until 1918 apart from a short stint with the publisher John Murray. By all accounts he was an impeccably dressed, respectable businessman, who went by the name of Maxim Harrison. During the early years of the war he taught Russian in Berlitz schools in both London and neutral Rotterdam where he met with German revolutionary socialists who, for obvious reasons, were not allowed to enter Britain.

Chicherin, however, stuck to his task and within a short space of time the RPPERC had proved to be the more successful of the two Russian charitable bodies. Working closely with the ILP's MP for Blackburn, Philip Snowden, the philosopher Bertrand Russell and the suffragette and ILPer Mrs Bridges Adams, Chicherin built up extensive links with trade unionists in Britain. He wrote articles outlining the work of the RPPERC for several trade union journals – the *Railway Review, Cotton Factory Times* and *Yorkshire Factory Times* and promoted the Committee at workplace meetings, on trade councils, at the TUC Congress in Bristol, and in both the *Labour Leader* and *Justice*. Writing in *Nashe Slovo* under the pseudonym Ornatsky he described the Committee's work as evidence of a new internationalist spirit amongst British workers. In particular, he wrote of the 'good contacts' being forged in the engineering and munitions industries, most notably in

Woolwich, Newcastle, Lancashire and Clydeside. His reading of the strikes against the Munitions Act[63] in Scotland organised by the Clyde Workers' Committee, a rank-and-file shop stewards' movement, however, was wildly optimistic, and led to a dispute with Rothstein in the pages of *Nashe Slovo* which would later impact negatively on early Anglo-Soviet relations when Rothstein sought to play down the revolutionary potential of the British working-class movement; while Chicherin was, initially, over-sanguine in his appraisal of the revolutionary potency of the British working class.

The dispute between the two men began in September 1915 when the Russian-language journal *Kommunist*, intended by Lenin to be a monthly review of labour movements in the belligerent nations, published a lengthy article from Rothstein on the British labour movement, which argued that recent strike activity on the Clyde had been neither revolutionary nor international in character. The rank-and-file movement, which had opposed both the Government and the trade union leadership over industrial compulsion, had not achieved 'that level of independence' necessary to bypass the union hierarchy in negotiations with employers. The reluctant acceptance of the Munitions Act,[64] and the suppression of the strike movement by arbitration, had demonstrated this fact. The strike movement, he argued, had involved the craft unions only and internationalism in Britain was 'still a matter for the future.'[65] At the time of writing International socialism looked all but dead.

Recent attempts to revitalise the pre-war Second International and the 1907 Stuttgart resolution calling on Socialists to turn the war into a European-wide social revolution had come to nothing.[66] The French Socialists had refused to take part in any meeting at which Germans were present while German troops remained on French soil, rendering the International obsolete for the duration of the war. An Allied Socialist Conference had been held in London in February 1915 calling for a negotiated peace based on no annexations but the conference had simply supported the allied cause; the French and Belgian delegates going so far as to place the sole guilt for the war on German shoulders. Seven months later, however, a small group of international socialists opposed to the war met in the small village of Zimmerwald high up in the Swiss Alps, about ten kilometers from Berne. Thirty-eight delegates from 11 countries, including Germany and France (British delegates had been refused passports), came together to denounce the war as the outcome of imperialist and capitalist rivalry, urging the conclusion of an immediate peace based on no annexations or indemnities. Apart from Trotsky in France, Lenin and other Bolsheviks living in exile in Switzerland, the remaining 33 delegates represented countries that were either neutral or allied to Germany. Lenin's attempt to win them over to revolutionary defeatism – that socialists should turn the imperialist war into a civil war – failed completely. Instead, the Zimmerwald Manifesto, drawn up by Trotsky, called upon the proletariat to establish a just peace without annexations or war indemnities:

> Working men and women! Mothers and fathers! Widows and orphans! Wounded and crippled! To all who are suffering from the war or in consequence of the war, we cry out, over the frontiers, over the smoking battlefields, over the devastated cities and hamlets: 'WORKERS OF THE WORLD UNITE!'[67]

But it was by no means clear what the Zimmerwald Manifesto could achieve in the *Entente* countries when the internationalists themselves were so divided. In September 1915, the Scottish District Council of the BSP began publishing *Vanguard* as a rival newspaper to the BSP's London-based paper *Justice*, which was still in the hands of the Hyndmanites. The *Vanguard*, edited by John Maclean, came out in support of the Zimmerwald Manifesto and the tactics being pushed by *Nashe Slovo* to split the socialist parties between the internationalists and the social-patriots. The *Vanguard*'s London agent was a Russian-Jewish political émigré by the name of Peter Petrov who had arrived at the Port of Leith in 1907. He had remained in Scotland for two months, lodging with

John Maclean in Glasgow, before moving to London where he had joined the Kentish Town Branch of the SDP.

In December 1915 Petrov published an article in *Vanguard* calling on the opposition in the BSP to 'sit down fast on one of the two stools between which they are wavering.' It was impossible, he argued, for the Executive 'to support the manifesto of the Zimmerwald Conference and at the same time Vandervelde,[68] Hyndman and company.'[69] The BSP's Scottish branches, he triumphantly announced, endorsed the tactics being put forward by *Nashe Slovo* and the Zimmerwaldians. We must immediately split the Party between internationalists and social-patriots.

Petrov's intervention led to an acrimonious debate on the situation in Britain in the columns of *Nashe Slovo* between Petrov, supported by Chicherin, and Rothstein, who argued that party unity should not be sacrificed too glibly. Concern for the 'integrity' of the socialist parties, Rothstein warned, had 'paralysed' the internationalist opposition in Britain, who were determined to prevent any split that might destroy their respective parties. There was a substantial minority in the BSP who supported the war, and to orchestrate an immediate split would be counter-productive. That minority not only controlled *Justice* but was led by Hyndman and the BSP's most popular leaders. There was no guarantee that this minority would not take a considerable part of the membership with them; whereas, a more cautious approach was beginning to pay dividends. At the recent Divisional Conferences the Internationalists had won control of the National Executive, and had secured a majority on the Inter-Party Committee on International Affairs. This dominance had allowed them to nominate a delegate to Zimmerwald, and to effectively marginalise the minority by forcing them to organise their pressure group, the Socialist Committee for National Defence, outside the mainstream of the Party. These successes, Rothstein argued, had been achieved 'without damaging Party unity [...] mining operations, *guerre d'usure*, had proved successful; should they now be abandoned [...] for a full-scale assault?'[70] To do so would be to go against the prevailing current of British left-wing politics. Similar tactics, he argued, prevailed in the ILP, where although disagreements were not so marked, the question of continued affiliation to the Labour Party threatened to divide the membership.[71] If the ILP spoke out strongly against the war a rupture with the Labour Party would inevitably follow, and this, in turn, would lead to a split within the ILP, and a weakening of its overall position. The British, Rothstein observed, were nothing if not pragmatic: 'between inactivity and the issuing of an "excessively sharp statement" they know a number of alternatives remain, not least the skillful manipulation of politics, to the very point where a split becomes inevitable.'[72]

Rothstein was counselling caution while Chicherin and Petrov, believing the situation on the Clyde to be revolutionary, called upon the BSP in England to follow the example of the Scots. Since the appearance of Rothstein's article in *Kommunist* and the issuing of the Zimmerwald Manifesto Basil Thomson's Special Branch and MI5, no doubt liaising with the Foreign Agency of the Okhrana, had taken steps to neutralise the more extreme elements among the Russian political emigration. One of the principal tasks of Krassilnikov, the head of the Okhrana's Foreign Agency between 1909 and 1917, had been 'to maintain liaison with foreign police, evaluate information from both surveillance agents and internal collaborators, and to pass that information in summary form to St. Petersburg.'[73] The activities of Russians in Britain were of great interest to the Okhrana. In October 1915, Chicherin had reported on the setting-up of a Local Committee of the RPPERC at the Woolwich Arsenal (where there were 14 Russian Inspectors) in conjunction with the local trades' council. 'An important step', he argued, in giving to the Committee 'the character of a mass movement', and promoting 'international workers' solidarity.'[74]

6

War, the Clyde Workers' Committee and Peter Petrov

To bring an alien into a district such as the Clyde for the purpose of stirring up opposition to the Munitions Act is simply to play into the hands of the authorities, and to render his position a serious one. We say unhesitatingly that, in times like the present, opposition to the acts of the Government must come from the people of the nation concerned, and not from those of other nationalities, if it is to be effective and above suspicion.

Editorial, Peter Petroff, *Justice*, 13 January 1916

The success of Chicherin's propaganda in key war industries was noted by the British authorities. On 22 October members of the Liverpool RPPERC were summoned to the Central Detective office, where they were 'told [. . .] that the work of the committee and especially the leaflets they had circulated, were exercising a harmful influence upon the British workers', and that they were 'prohibited from having any employment in Liverpool with British workers, unless they signed a statement, pledging themselves never to take part in any Union or Committee that is against the war, against the allied Governments, or against their internal administration, and promised to be in future heart and soul for Great Britain, France and Russia.'[1] Kell and the Home Office were not openly involved, 'Snowden asked questions in the House but the Home Secretary only replied that the Liverpool police had dealt with the matter independently of the Home Office.'[2] That same month the future Soviet Ambassador to Great Britain, Ivan Maisky, had been due to speak in Southampton for the RPPERC when he received a telegram warning him not to travel as detectives were waiting to arrest him on his arrival.[3] Shortly after this four police raids took place on the offices of the Russian Seamen's Union under a search warrant from the military authorities. On 20 December 1915 raids were launched on the private residencies of the Union's secretary Anitchkine and Chicherin. These raids took place against a backdrop of increasing labour unrest, which appeared to threaten the wartime industrial truce agreed with the TUC.

Two days later Petrov was arrested in Glasgow and charged with breaches of the Defence of the Realm Act. The following day an article appeared in *Justice* asking 'Who and What is Peter Petroff?' which many thought only encouraged the authorities on the Clyde to investigate Petrov's activities further:

> Many of us have known of Peter Petroff for some years, though we have known little about him save that he has usually acted as a disintegrating nuisance. That he places a high value on his knowledge of and services to the Socialist movement we readily admit. He has now been for some weeks on the Clyde. What he is doing there, and what may be his object, is best known to himself. It is for the representatives of the Glasgow workers to determine what is his status on the Clyde Workers Committee,[4] and to make whatever inquiries about him they may deem necessary.[5]

Petrov's position on the Clyde Workers' Committee (CWC) was by no means accepted by all trade unionists on the Clyde; his denunciation by *Justice*, however, was a deliberate provocation given his status as an 'alien'. Petrov, a Russian-born Jew with a German-Jewish wife,[6] would have been liable to internment under DORA regulations. He had been given honorary status on the CWC on 27 October 1915 following the arrest of John

Maclean for 'uttering statements calculated to prejudice recruiting'.[7] Expecting a heavy sentence, Maclean had arranged for Petrov to travel to Glasgow to continue the BSP's anti-war campaign, and to prevent the CWC from taking control of the *Vanguard*. Maclean and his deputy James MacDougall, a bank clerk, had already been made honorary members of the CWC, and Maclean thought he could secure Petrov's position in Glasgow by making him a fraternal delegate to the Committee. Petrov, however, had very little knowledge of the labour movement on the Clyde and quickly antagonised the leaders of the CWC.

Established in February 1915 to protest against profiteering among companies producing war materials the CWC was neither revolutionary nor opposed to the war itself. It had its origins in an unofficial strike organised by the Labour Witholding Committee, an organization of the rank-and-file, for a wage increase of 2d an hour.[8] After 17 days the strike had collapsed and the Labour Witholding Committee had been disbanded; an increase of 1d an hour was later imposed by the Government. There followed an uneasy industrial truce, which collapsed in July when a shop steward at Parkhead Forge, Mitchell, was sentenced to three months' imprisonment for 'slacking and causing others to slack' under the Munitions of War Act. The Government, faced with the prospect of widespread industrial action, ordered Mitchell's release; but the damage had already been done. Several members of the old Labour Witholding Committee now joined with a number of shop stewards to form the CWC: 'for the purpose of concentrating the whole forces of the Clyde area against the Munitions Act.'[9] The authors of this plan, however, were anxious not to profess any revolutionary or anti-war pretensions; while Maclean and his supporters in the Glasgow BSP, including Petrov, sought to take control of the CWC and broaden its industrial struggle into one against the war itself.[10]

The dispute between the two groups came to a head on the eve of Lloyd George's tempestuous Christmas Day meeting with the Clyde workers, when as Minister of Munitions he attempted to convince them of the need for the 'dilution of labour'.[11] At a meeting to discuss plans to counter 'dilution', two of the CWC's most prominent figures, William Gallacher[12] and John Muir,[13] were involved in a fierce argument with Petrov over the Committee's failure to condemn the war resulting in Petrov's expulsion from the CWC. Two days before the Lloyd George Christmas Day address to munition workers in Glasgow *Justice* published their 'red alert' to the authorities: 'Who and What is Peter Petroff?' The previous day Petrov had been charged in Fife for contravening the Aliens Restriction Act and fined £3; on his return to Glasgow he was re-arrested and charged with the same offence. On 3 January 1916 he was sentenced to two months' imprisonment without the option of a fine. He protested against the sentence, and was released on bail after lodging an appeal with the High Court.

The Petrov case unnerved socialists in both London and Glasgow as well as in the Russian political émigré community, and shifted the main thrust of MI5's wartime strategy from that of counter-espionage to counter-subversion. Protests began to appear in the socialist press condemning *Justice* for its defamatory article of 23 December, many Socialists, given the recent debate in *Justice* on the activities of foreign elements inside the BSP, objected both to the timing and to the content of the paragraph on Petrov. Chicherin, now claiming to be the Secretary of the Social-Democratic Labour Party of Russia (Central Bureau of the Groups Abroad), wrote to *Justice* condemning the attack on Petrov and expressing the Central Bureau's 'expectation that the Executive of [. . .] the BSP, will not allow under its name the appearance of such publications,' that threaten the security of Russian political refugees in Britain.[14] The Kentish Town Branch passed a resolution calling 'upon the Party Executive to take action to protect comrades of the Party against an organ which is supposed to be the official organ of the Party.'[15] The paper's response was to blame those who had brought Petrov into the Clyde area:

> To bring an alien into a district such as the Clyde for the
> purpose of stirring up opposition to the Munitions Act is

simply to play into the hands of the authorities, and to render his position a serious one. We say unhesitatingly that, in times like the present, opposition to the acts of the Government must come from the people of the nation concerned, and not from those of other nationalities, if it is to be effective and above suspicion.[16]

A similar view was put forward by James Morton, a member of the Maclean-dominated Pollokshaws branch of the BSP, who blamed Maclean's 'one-man movement' on the Clyde for Petrov's arrest:

Maclean tells us that the GDC [Glasgow District Council] invited Petroff to Glasgow. But the GDC did not send Petroff to Bowhill in Fife. Maclean tells us that he sent him to this prohibited area. It is here the mischief was done. [...] Comments have been strong among Socialists at what is now called the one-man movement. [...] For the sake of the Cause it would be best that the Glasgow District Council should take the reins in hand, and not allow any one man to have the power of making such a blunder as the Petroff blunder. I am sorry for comrade Petroff, because it has unsettled him so that he will be suspicious that every agency is directed against aliens.[17]

Morton's fears were soon realised; the Petrov case not only highlighted divisions between the social patriots and the internationalists but also created friction within the émigré community. On 16 January Petrov wrote to Chicherin accusing the London-based opposition to the BSP's Hyndman-dominated Executive Committee of being untrustworthy and manipulated by Rothstein, who he claimed had always been a supporter of Hyndman against the Marxists:

By the way, Rothstein was never connected with the movement. He was only connected with the dirty clique [...] Rothstein always supported the Hyndman clique against the Marxist trend in Great Britain.[18]

This makes curious reading. It suggests that Rothstein's War Office work within British intelligence had become more widely known among socialists than he suspected. Andrew Rothstein told the present author that Petrov had visited his father 'more than once, before and during the war, [. . .] at the latter's home (often I was present).'[19] What exactly Petrov understood about Rothstein's activities before and after August 1914, however, is not clear; given that Maclean and his supporters suspected the authorities were working closely with Hyndman the level of mistrust between socialists was unsettling others beside Petrov. The rift in the BSP was actively encouraged by MI5 who at the beginning of the war had recruited two members of the BSP to inform on the activities of the internationalists in the Party, the longstanding social patriot Victor Fisher and A. S. Headingley,[20] who in 1870 had volunteered as a stretcher bearer during the Paris Commune.

Once Petrov had linked Rothstein with the Hyndmanite clique, the 'dirty clique' as he called it, Rothstein too came under suspicion. Writing in *Nashe Slovo*, Chicherin unleashed a furious attack upon Rothstein for supporting the BSP leadership, and for failing to urge his English comrades to emulate all that their Scottish comrades had achieved; recent events in Scotland, he argued, had been revolutionary in character. They had only been halted by a lack of courage from the BSP's leadership.

Rothstein's reply demonstrated a degree of understanding of British society and history that Chicherin, a much more recent arrival in Britain, simply didn't have; the same criticism could be made of Petrov. The differences existing between the established émigré community in respect of political affairs in Britain and those who had arrived at the beginning of the war were quite pronounced. Chicherin, Rothstein claimed, simply didn't understand how radical politics in Britain had come to rely heavily on London whose role had been quite unlike that of any other European capital city. In the past London's support had been essential for securing victory for radical causes, but it had neither initiated nor led a popular movement. In the current situation

Glasgow was not 'in the rapids of revolution', as Chicherin suggested, waiting only for London to act; the workers' opposition in Scotland, and elsewhere, was a result of 'indignation against the principle of compulsion', it has yet to speak out against the war. Moreover, Chicherin, a relative newcomer to Britain, had failed to appreciate the attachment of BSP members to their newspaper *Justice*, built up over a period of 30 years. Chicherin's exhortation to the BSP 'to appeal to the masses, as in Scotland', is therefore misplaced: 'London is not Scotland, and Scotland herself is not as Comrade Ornatsky [Chicherin] imagines'.[21]

Many workers in Scotland, however, felt that with the arrest of Petrov the Government was testing the mettle of Scottish public opinion on the eve of conscription. The near-riotous reception afforded to Lloyd George during his stay on the Clyde had led to the suppression of four labour newspapers.[22] On 2 February 1916, the police raided the Socialist Labour Party's Glasgow head-quarters:

> They smashed the printing machinery and confiscated the forthcoming issue of the Clyde Workers' Committee paper, *The Worker*. Next day two CWC officials, Gallacher and Muir, were arrested along with Walter Bell, the SLP's business manager. They were charged under DORA with attempting 'to cause mutiny, sedition or disaffection among the civilian population and to impede, delay or restrict the production of war material by producing, printing and circulating amongst workers in and around Glasgow *The Worker*.'[23]

Depicted as dangerous enemy agents, the three men were initially refused bail. But this aroused a massive response: 10,000 'workers decided to have a holiday in honour of the occasion.'[24] After a day's stoppage, the court relented and the three were released on bail. Christopher Addison, Parliamentary Under-Secretary to the Minister of Munitions, now began to talk of 'a systematic and sinister plan' to sabotage 'production of the most important munitions of war in the Clyde district':

His suspicions were fueled by ill-founded reports of German machinations from a small Clydeside intelligence service secretly organized by Sir Lynden Macassey KC, chairman of the Clyde Dilution Commissioners (who dealt with the 'dilution' of skilled by unskilled labour). [...] Macassey's reports prompted the Ministry of Munitions to found an intelligence service of its own (later known as PMS2).[25]

That Macassey's agents believed that Gallacher, Muir and Bell were in receipt of German funds fed fears that German business interests and 'aliens' were fomenting labour unrest on the Clyde. Addison, who was soon to take over from Lloyd George as Minister of Munitions, recorded in his diary:

He [Macassey] has traced direct payment from Germany to three workers and also discovered that [...] the man who is financing the Clyde workers [...] has a daughter, married in Germany, a son married to a German and his chief business is in Germany. He is evidently on the track of a very successful revelation.[26]

To Macassey's 'extreme annoyance' his intelligence agency was wound up and taken over by MI5 with Kell providing the Ministry of Munitions 'with a "nucleus" of MI5 officers under Colonel Frank Labouchere to monitor aliens and labour unrest.'[27] According to Joseph King, the veteran Liberal Radical MP for North Somerset, £620,000 was spent on the use of *agent provocateurs* and police spies in 1916 in Glasgow alone:

The city, to all intents and purposes, had been placed under martial law and 'Russian methods' were being employed; public and private halls were all closed to Socialist organizations by Government order, and anyone attempting to hold meetings in the open air threatened with prosecution under DORA.[28]

He also questioned the 'employment of immoral, disreputable and ungentlemanly' tactics by police agents highlighting the case of

Carl Graves, a convicted criminal described by police as a most dangerous man, who was recruited by Robert Munro, Secretary of State for Scotland, to spy on militants in Glasgow. 'I have personal knowledge', claimed the Liberal MP for North West Lanarkshire, W. M. R. Pringle, 'of cases where important leaders in the trade union movement in this country have been approached for the purpose of spying upon their fellows and making secret reports in regard to their actions to the Government.'[29] The Petrov affair, having first caused divisions within the labour movement on the Clyde, had also created tensions between the Ministry of Munitions and MI5. Chicherin now stoked the flames of émigré discord.

On 11 February Petrov's arrest and internment under Section 14B of DORA was reported in *Nashe Slovo*; two days later an article appeared in the paper from Chicherin censuring Rothstein and Litvinov for their work with the Russian Political Prisoners' Fund and for their activities in the Herzen Circle. Chicherin now claimed that the Fund was taking a 'defencist' position and that statements issued by the Fund, under the signatures of Rothstein and Litvinov, were conciliatory towards the Tsarist regime. At best Chicherin was ill-informed; but his article was picked up by Lenin who recorded his full agreement with Chicherin, 'that it was time for a split in the BSP too.' In his article intended for publication in the Bolshevik journal, *Sotzial-Demokrat*, Lenin wrote that he 'disagreed with Theodore Rothstein for adopting a "Kautskian position" i.e. no split.'[30]

Following the closure of *Vanguard* and Maclean's arrest in Scotland the internationalists in the BSP were denied any public outlet for their views. As a result the centre of the opposition now shifted to London.[31] On 24 February the opposition launched a new weekly newspaper, *The Call* and began a campaign to take over the party orchestrated in the houses of Rothstein and the Inkpins. The first issue of *The Call*, however, exposed the enormous gap separating the London opposition to Hyndman from the supporters of *Vanguard* on the controversial issue of whether or not to become signatories to the Zimmerwald Manifesto or to

remake the Second International and the ISB in the internationalists' image. The case of Petrov continued to ruffle feathers.
The BSP's National Organisation Committee, by now dominated
by London-based internationalists, published a condemnation of
Justice's note concerning Petrov in *Nashe Slovo*.[32] Despite Chicherin
questioning the sincerity of this act, owing to the fact that it was
printed in *Nashe Slovo* and not in an English newspaper, in its first
edition *The Call* did issue a statement 'dissociating the Party' from
the recent attack made on Petrov in *Justice*. On the eve of the party
conference *Justice* not wishing to be seen as out of touch with the
views of the party at large, published an Executive Committee
resolution protesting 'against the unjustifiable internment of Peter
Petroff', and the arrest of Petrov's German-born wife Irma, as an
enemy alien.[33] However, while the case of the Petrovs continued to
give rise to much ill feeling within the BSP, the hostility generated
by the clash between supporters of the Zimmerwald Manifesto and
the national sections of the ISB proved more divisive. In a recent
poll of the party a large majority had endorsed the action of the
Executive in approving the Zimmerwald Conference, and its
appointment of a corresponding secretary to the Berne
International Committee.[34] The Hyndmanite Central London
Branch of the BSP now called upon the forthcoming BSP
Conference to repudiate that decision, and dissociate itself
completely from the Zimmerwald programme. The reasons given
were the British and French Governments' objections to a
Conference that would prove 'likely to forward the interests of
Germany'; that the French Socialist Party had disapproved of
Zimmerwald by 9,947 votes against 545, and that similar
reservations had been expressed by the Belgian 'and other Socialist
comrades'; participation could only be interpreted as an act of
disloyalty to the ISB.[35] In reply the internationalists pointed to the
ISB's failure to carry out the decisions of the International Socialist
Congresses, which had clearly defined its duties in the event of war.

The battle lines were drawn up and both sides confidently
expected a split. The wider question concerned the fate of the
party's newspaper. The social-patriots did not expect to win the

vote censuring Zimmerwald, and were quite prepared to leave the party in order to retain control of *Justice*. As the date of the conference drew closer, Rothstein, writing as John Bryan, argued in *The Call* that in order to be effective the BSP would have to sever its ties with the International Socialist Bureau, and 'form a new ISB.'[36]

The pseudonym John Bryan was necessary. On the same day *The Call* reported on the increasing number of attacks on foreign members of the BSP in the jingo press written by MI5's two agents inside the BSP Victor Fisher and A. S. Headingley. The latter writing under the pseudonym Adolphe Smith[37] (the codename he used when communicating with British intelligence) accused the internationalists of 'acting under instructions from Berlin.'[38] On 20 March 1916 Headingley met with Major H. B. Matthews of MI5 at the National Liberal Club and 'stated that he rather suspects THEODORE ROTHSTEIN of receiving German funds and of being a German agent. ROTHSTEIN, he said, is connected with the "Daily News" and apparently has means from some source. He keeps in the background, but "hovers around, watching his opportunity, sizing up the various members of the Socialist and Labour parties, with a view to influencing them to agitate, by payment of money". Mr. SMITH [Headingley] described him as a dangerous Socialist who required watching.'[39] Headingley also seems to have been aware of Rothstein's employment by MI7.[40]

The BSP's Annual Conference held in Manchester over the Easter weekend (23–24 April 1916) was an acrimonious affair. Twenty-two Hyndmanites, representing 18 of the 91 branches, walked out of the Conference to form the National Socialist Advisory Committee with headquarters in the premises of the Twentieth Century Press at Clerkenwell Green.[41] In the branch ballot for the election of a new Executive, which had taken place in the weeks before the Conference, the victory of the internationalists was complete. Among those elected were John Maclean – who in the week before the Conference had been sentenced to three years imprisonment for sedition – E. C. Fairchild (editor of *The Call*),

Joe Fineberg and Albert Inkpin. A Kentish Town branch resolution endorsed the action of those members of the executive who had voted for a delegate to the Zimmerwald Conference, and condemned the Government for its refusal to grant passports. It welcomed the 'magnificent manifesto' issued by the Conference, and instructed the Executive Committee to support the Berne Commission in its endeavor to bring about a renewal of international relations between socialists of all the belligerent countries; it was carried by 77 votes to 6. A Central London resolution seeking to dissociate the BSP from the Zimmerwald Conference and the Berne Commission was defeated by 77 votes to 7.

There remained the problem of *Justice*. A Pollokshaws resolution to establish a new party organ was withdrawn in favour of a Central Hackney resolution instructing the Executive Committee to acquire effective control over the policy of *Justice*, and was carried by 73 votes to 4. The Central Hackney branch, whose members had been instrumental in setting up *The Call*, still saw *Justice* as the party's rightful newspaper. The issue was not settled until the 24 May when Fairchild, the BSP's sole representative on the Board of the Twentieth Century Press (1912) Ltd., was forced to stand down. *The Call* then became the official organ of the BSP to be issued weekly. In October Fisher denounced the BSP's general secretary, Albert Inkpin to MI5 as 'violently pro-German':

MI5 had been intercepting BSP correspondence for the past two years, reporting in October 1916 that the Party and its general secretary, Albert Edward Inkpin, were 'violently pro-German'.[42] Victor Ferguson, who led MI5 investigations of anti-war movements, noted the following information on Inkpin given him by a former leading member of the BSP, Victor Fisher, who had turned against Inkpin because of his opposition to the war: '?German blood. Has a brother (Christian name unknown) and both are violently pro-German. Funds from German sources may possibly filter through him. Very clever. His influence succeeded in carrying over [BSP] Executive to pro-Germanism'[43]

Following the introduction of conscription, first for unmarried men in February 1916, then for married men two months later, the activities of the security services against socialists and pacifists were stepped up considerably; the lead role in investigating the anti-conscription movement being taken by Major Victor Ferguson.[44] At the same time MI5 ratcheted up its investigations of 'friendly aliens'. On 10 April 1916 a personal file was opened on Joe Fineberg and he was subsequently interviewed by two CID detectives at his home in Hackney where he confessed to being an ardent socialist and a member of the BSP since 1906.

Following the introduction of conscription a campaign was launched to apply the Military Services Act to 'friendly aliens' aimed specifically at the immigrant Jewish population. Jews were accused of taking advantage of absent British shopkeepers and workers to promote their own interests. Calls were issued for a clause to be inserted in the Act empowering the military authorities to either deport Jews to their country of origin for military service or to conscript them into the British Army. As the majority of these Jews were either Russian political émigrés or refugees from the Pale of Settlement escaping religious persecution, there was no guarantee that they would not be prosecuted or ill-treated on their return to Russia. This Press campaign, orchestrated by the *Daily Express* and the London *Evening News*, was creating a situation of near-pogrom mentality in the East End of London. The *Bethnal Green News* of 20 May published an interview with a 'Vice-Consul of a Friendly Power in London', in which it was reported that the Consuls of such 'Friendly Powers' were 'urging the Governments to compulsion of aliens.'[45] Other sections of the Press welcomed this intervention from outside Powers and saw in the Military Services Act an opportunity to launch a wider attack on the Right of Asylum.

In response a campaign was launched amongst Jews to defend the Right of Asylum in Britain. This campaign, under the auspices of the Foreign Jews Protection Committee against Deportation to Russia and Compulsion (FJPC), was restricted to the threat facing Russian Jews. Not all political émigrés, however, were Jewish; and a further organisation, the Committee of Russian Socialist Groups in London (CORSGL), was formed by Chicherin and other Russian socialists with the specific purpose of launching a campaign amongst trade unionists and other working-class organisations to maintain the Right of Asylum, and to oppose any attempts at compulsion of Russians to enlist in the British Army under threat of deportation.

The growing antagonism between the Government and the East End of London forced the Home Secretary, Herbert Samuel, to adopt what the CORSGL referred to as 'a slight change of method' in his plans to conscript immigrant Jews. It was announced in the House of Commons on 22 August that 'an active recruiting campaign' would be carried out amongst the Jewish population with a view to securing the 'voluntary enlistment in the British Army of Russian subjects living in this country who are eligible for military service.' It was agreed 'that until the results of the campaign are seen, the question whether those who do not enlist should be repatriated, shall remain in abeyance.'[46] Voluntary recruitment was to last until 30 September, when the question of repatriation would be reconsidered. No measure with compulsory repatriation as its aim was to be adopted until the House had reassembled in October.

By the time Parliament did reconvene, however, attitudes towards the war had undergone a considerable change. According to Rothstein (again writing as John Bryan) popular psychology was 'in a stage of transition'. Old certainties underpinning the moral justification for Britain's participation in the war were gradually being undermined. The belief that Belgium 'could be had back at any time for mere asking', 'the coercion of Greece and other neutral countries', 'the introduction of compulsory service' all served to undo confidence in the further prosecution of the war. While initial fears surrounding Germany's occupation of the Belgian coast had provided some justification for initial popular support for the war; the rejection of Germany's offer of a withdrawal from Belgium in return for 'free and unfettered connection with Constantinople and Baghdad' had, Rothstein felt, exposed the real nature of Britain's war aims. With Belgian neutrality no longer occupying the place in popular psychology it once did, 'a new ideology' had to be carved out by the British Government to further their imperialist aims. The desire to 'cut Germany's south-eastern connection' gave added impetus to calls for a United Southern Slav State from the Serbian Society to block Germany's path to Constantinople. In this way the new state of Yugoslavia would play a similar role in British conceptions of the European balance of power as that formerly played by Belgium.[47]

Such a policy would undoubtedly imply an attack on Turkish interests in Europe. Arguments, therefore, began to appear in the Press calling for a widening of the front against Turkey. The creation of a Jewish Legion specifically to defend Egypt and assist in the conquest of Palestine was increasingly seen as a viable alternative to the deportation of Russian Jews or their conscription into individual units of the British Army. Lord Milner, a key figure in the Serbian Society, travelled to Petrograd in order to reach an agreement with the Russian Government on the question of conscription and deportation of Russians of military age. Russian interests in the Balkans, and her desire to incorporate the Dardanelles and Constantinople into a greater Russian Empire, played a crucial part in these negotiations. Offering Russian subjects resident in Britain the alternative of service in the British Army or deportation to Russia, where they faced conscription into the Russian Army or prosecution, formed a part of these negotiations. A new offensive was being planned against Britain's Russian political émigré community.

In 1915 MI5 had been sufficiently alarmed by the activities of the Russian political émigré community in London to begin an investigation into the activities of the *Communistischer Arbeiter-Bildungs-Verein* (Communist Working Men's Club and Institute) at 107 Charlotte Street. Kell reported to the Home Office that the Russians in the Communist Club were 'a desperate and very dangerous crowd'.[48] Some of its members, he believed, had been closely connected with the murders of three policemen, and the wounding of two others, during a botched raid on a Houndsditch jeweller in 1910. The chief suspect was the Latvian Yakov Peters, future deputy head of the Bolshevik Party's security service the Cheka, variously described as an anarchist, communist and Tolstoyan. Peters, who had been on friendly terms with Rothstein, was subsequently arrested but was acquitted at his trial in 1911 'after being ably defended by, ironically, William Melville's barrister son James [later a Labour solicitor general].[49] In November 1916, as a result of Major Ferguson's investigations, 'the Communist Club was [again] raided and twenty-two of its members of various nationalities recommended for internment. The Home Secretary agreed to the internment of seventeen.'[50] This would be MI5's last approved act against the Russian political émigré community working within the British labour movement for the duration of the war. In December 1916, the Minister of Munitions, dissatisfied with PMS2's investigation into labour unrest on the Clyde, asked Basil Thomson 'to undertake the whole of the intelligence service on labour matters for the whole country'. Thomson accepted and 'in a clear snub to Kell', 12 sergeants from the CID were drafted into the Ministry of Munitions to run the new intelligence system.[51] Thomson's appointment had coincided with Kell's investigation into the activities of the Communist Club and was due partly to Kell's absurd 'conclusion that the Communist Club had 'fomented' the strike wave at Clydeside munitions factories in the early spring of 1916.'[52] With Kell seeing opposition to 'dilution' in terms of conspiracy Thomson's ascendancy was all but assured. At this time MI5 were relying on the dubious information furnished by an informant in the Communist Club, Alex Gordon, real name F. Vivian. His covert activities at the Communist Club and at the International Workers of The World (IWW) hall in Whitechapel, had led to raids on their premises.[53]

Undeterred, in January 1917 Kell warned the Home Office that the Communist Club's purpose was 'the hampering by all possible means (e.g. by anti-recruiting propaganda, fomentation of strikes etc) of the Execution of the War in the present crisis'.[54] Chicherin's activities on behalf of the RPPERC were singled out for particular censure:

> Perhaps the greatest immediate danger arises from the instigation of enmity to the British Government on the part of the thousands of immigrants and refugees from Russia (and their offspring) now in this country. [...] That the active enmity thus engendered may be cunningly manipulated at some opportune time by Germany very considerably adds to the danger of the moment.[55]

Despite Kell's pleas for Chicherin's internment on the grounds that he 'has openly expressed anti-British sentiments, and has freely associated on intimate terms with Germans and pro-Germans', the H.O. refused to act.[56] Thomson regarded such reports as alarmist and questioned their source. The hidden hand of the Okhrana did not appear to be far away. A Foreign Office memo dated 6 February on the 'Committee of Delegates of the Russian Socialist Groups' contained wild reports from the Russian Government that plans were being hatched for the assassination of the British Home Secretary, Herbert Samuel, and other acts of terrorism emanating from London's East End listing five persons it regarded as most dangerous, among them Chicherin. The Committee, it was alleged was working closely with influential members of the BSP, 'whose pacifist tendencies are well known.'[57]

Among those who Rothstein passed Russian revolutionary literature to, culled from the 'Daily Review of the Foreign Press', was the Latvian-born socialist Alexander Sirnis.[58] Sirnis, a disciple of Leo Tolstoy had joined the BSP in 1906 and had met Rothstein through Tolstoy's literary executor, Count Vladimir Chertkov, while both men were working on translations of Tolstoy's works at Tuckton House, Bournemouth. Chertkov had set up a Tolstoyan community in the village of Tuckton on the outskirts of Bournemouth in the wake of the Doukhobor affair where he housed the Russian writer's manuscripts in a closely guarded safe and arranged for their translation into English and French.[59] A printing works housed in a disused water works in nearby Christchurch boasted Russian type, Russian compositors, printing machines, machinists, guillotines for cutting and all the other necessary plant of a small printing and paper-binding factory. Sirnis kept a diary for much of this period and was visited by 'Rothstein and Mrs. Rothstein' on 10 August 1916. They had called upon Sirnis with MI7 material on Lenin and the Bolsheviks taken from the European socialist press. Four days after this visit Sirnis noted in his diary 'Lenin's art. To Paul' (Lenin's article to William Paul, editor of *The Socialist*).[60]

Rothstein at this time remained in close contact with his old mentor in the anti-imperialist movement, Scawen Blunt. At the beginning of 1917 he wrote to Scawen Blunt thanking him once again for the seasonal brace of pheasants and outlining his horoscope for 1917. His pro-Turkish and pro-German sympathies were by now well-established and he remained committed to the Egyptian nationalist movement; his hatred of British imperialism in the 'Mahommedan world' by now barely, if at all, disguised:

in the autumn, if not earlier, we shall have peace. [. . .] All the changes will take place in the East, and to the good. Bulgaria will be the predominant power in the Balkans, and Turkey will have saved her independence, and will enter upon a new and better stage of her development. By means of the Danube, which will become the new economic axis in Europe, and the Baghdad railway she will be brought into close contact with modern life, and the Russian danger will forever disappear. I think the entire Mahommedan world will be the gainer through the war (even Tripoli, I think, will be given back to Turkey), and India will not rest until she obtains at least Home Rule. The alliance between the Hindus and Moslems in India is now complete, and this spells the death-knell of British domination and exploitation. The position of Egypt, too, will gradually change with the change of the balance of power in the Mediterranean. The Germanic bloc with Greece as its advanced post protruding in the very centre of the Mediterranean and the emergence of Russia's warships in the same sea (Germany will give her a free outlet through the Dardanelles) will impair England's position in Egypt, and the railway connection between Egypt and Syria, which Germany is going to construct, will do away with Egypt's isolation, the chief strength of the British rule.[61]

With continued unrest in India and Egypt, Rothstein continued, Britain would be irrevocably damaged and Europe would be in decline: 'our liberties will everywhere be crippled and social conflicts will become the order of the day. I think Russia will open the ball by a grand revolution, Austria may follow suit, and everywhere the political and social fabric will be shaken severely. But America and Japan will prosper, and South America will make great strides. Such is my horoscope for the new year.'[62] Two months later, on Friday, 16 March 1917, Sirnis wrote in his diary: 'Russian Revolution could not believe my eyes when I opened the Daily Chronicle'.[63]

7

Revolution

The Bolsheviks, like the French revolutionaries, realise that the Governments of Europe are unfriendly; but they separate the peoples from the Governments. They realise that the Imperialist-capitalists of all nations are their enemies, and that the workers of all nations are their friends. The *Manchester Guardian* suggests, and some British Socialists who should know better suggest, that if the Allied Governments had shown more sympathy for Russian aims and treated Russia more generously, this Bolshevik view would not have been held. To argue thus is completely to ignore the outstanding fact that the Russian Revolution is a Socialist revolution, and that its aims and ideals are incompatible with those of capitalism.

Sylvia Pankhurst, *Workers Dreadnought*, 17 November 1917

On Thursday, 7 March (O.S. 22 February), workers at Putilov, Petrograd's largest industrial plant, went on strike. The following day, a series of meetings and rallies were held for International Women's Day, which gradually turned into economic and political gatherings. By Sunday, 10 March (O.S. 25 February) Petrograd was gripped by a general strike. On Monday, 11 March (O.S. 26 February) troops began to mutiny and join the strikers. The Tsar abdicated on 15 March (O.S. 2 March) nominating his brother Grand Duke Michael Alexandrovich as his successor. The Grand Duke declined the Crown the following day and a republic was declared.

While many émigrés wished to return to Russia to assist the revolution, it was by no means clear what the war aims of the new Government were or whether they were essentially different from those of the Tsar. The British Government permitted only those émigrés who supported Russia's continued involvement in the war to return to Russia. Initially, most sections of British society welcomed the February Revolution, and it was felt that the question of the compulsion of aliens would no longer prove such a contentious issue. However, the revolution gave rise to different responses. Public opinion was initially favourable but socialists, labour organisations and the Government all appeared equally bemused by the aims of the revolution. The British Ambassador to Russia, Sir George Buchanan, in a dispatch from Petrograd, wrote of the necessity of the British Press to report the revolution as the work of the entire Russian nation.[1] *The Times* and other organs of the commercial Press complied and put forward the view that the revolution had been carried out by the 'united forces of the Duma and the Army,' in order to strengthen Russia's war effort.[2] The Foreign Office commenting on Buchanan's dispatch: 'As a matter of fact this is the line which our Press has taken. Nothing could have been better than the attitude of our Press. No action required.'[3]

That both the F.O. and *The Times* equated the Duma with 'the entire Russian nation' was evident from the nature of their response to Buchanan's dispatch; while the attempt to place the revolution firmly within the Duma's history as an expression of Russian patriotism was viewed by many on the left as 'both significant and sinister.'[4] *The Call*, in its report on the revolution dismissed the claim that 'the Liberals and the Radicals of the Duma' had been the main driving force of revolution as a falsehood:

> The real truth of the matter is that the revolution was begun and carried out with the utmost success by the masses of the people themselves against the previous exhortations of the Duma, who had feared nothing so much as a revolution, that it was the masses who, ever since Thursday, had been fraternizing with, and gaining over to their side the troops, and that it was

not until Monday that the Liberals and the Radicals of the Duma appeared on the scene.[5]

On the question of war aims *The Call* was adamant that the 'revolutionary people of Russia were not out for the conquest of Constantinople, nor even for the re-conquest of Poland. Their watchword is "Reform and Peace" – of course, peace, not by surrender, but by negotiation and on the principle of no-annexations, but still peace in preference to the continuation of the war for Imperialist objects.'[6]

The situation in Russia remained uncertain, and while *The Call* welcomed the revolution as the 'first tremendous breach in the walls of the enemy' the triumph of the revolution was by no means assured. The *Labour Leader* published articles by J. Bruce Glasier and Philip Snowden suggesting that sinister plots were underway 'to capture the Revolution from the democracy in the interests not of the Russian commonwealth, but in the interests of a powerful political faction.'[7]

Nevertheless, the British labour movement's support for the Duma was regarded as critical if the revolution was to survive. When General Poole, Military Attaché to Russia, interviewed Alexander Kerensky[8] on the day of the Tsar's abdication he expressed his dismay at the total stoppage of all munition output in Petrograd. In reply, Kerensky drew attention to the important role to be played by British labour in ensuring that the revolution went the way the Entente and all sections of the Russian Government desired:

all the new Government realized situation but that in his view present was an unsuitable time to attempt to coerce the people as they are now within a measurable distance of Anarchy and he feared that any drastic steps might only precipitate matters [. . .] He hopes that by gentle persuasion and in time that Government may get situation in hand but that at present they are powerless. He thinks strong representations of English labour party would have good effect here. Poole says there is no doubt that he realizes situation and is afraid of what may result.[9]

Kerensky's fears were repeated by Buchanan who suggested in a F.O. memo that 'labour leaders in England [...] send a telegram to Messrs. Kerensky and Chkeidze[10] [...] expressing their confidence that they and their colleagues will know how to strengthen the hands of free peoples fighting against the despotism of Germany whose victory can only bring disaster to all classes of the Allies.'[11] The F.O. then drafted an 'Appeal to the Russian People' that was signed by leading figures of the Parliamentary Labour Party and the TUC, stating that they 'confidently look forward to the assistance of Russian labour in achieving the object (victory over Germany) to which we have devoted ourselves.'[12] The despatch of this telegram on 16 March provoked protests across Britain and resolutions from the ILP, BSP and other socialist and labour groupings dissociating the British working class from the actions of those 'termed the "leaders of the British labour movement", who are fast winning for themselves the bad eminence of being the most obtuse and self-centred politicians in our country.'[13] The decision that followed to send a Labour Party deputation to Russia caused a similar sense of outrage, and led to demands that a second deputation from the ILP National Council, ILP Members of Parliament, the BSP and some of the larger trade unions be sent to Russia. Philip Snowden asked the Prime Minister in the House whether the Labour Party deputation had been undertaken at the request of the Government, and if so 'what credentials these men have to represent the English labour movement?' The Chancellor of the Exchequer, Andrew Bonar Law, left the House in no doubt as to the true nature of their visit.

> These gentlemen are going with the one object of encouraging, so far as they can, the present Russian Government in the prosecution of the war.[14]

The ILP and the BSP took immediate steps to distance themselves from the Labour Party's support for the Government's position on the Russian Revolution.

Following news of the revolution the Russian émigré position as regards deportation to Russia underwent a dramatic change, and a number of émigrés returned to Russia, despite the Government's attempts to prevent those who were anti-war from returning. The future Minister of Agriculture in the Provisional Government, M. V. Chernov, returned to Russia on 4 April carrying with him a personal message from the ILP and the BSP to the Committee of the Council of the Soviet of Workers' Deputies. This message stated that the Labour Party Delegates in no way represented British labour and that they had been sent to Russia by the British Government who paid their expenses and used them to help their imperialistic designs and the continuance of the war. The full message was published in *Pravda* and helped ensure that the delegation's visit to Russia did not serve the purpose Kerensky and Buchanan had intended.[15] Further difficulties were caused by the publication of a letter from Chicherin in the soldiers' newspaper *Soldat-Grazhdanin (Soldier-Citizen)* carrying news of the ILP's Conference resolution dissociating the ILP from the Labour Party deputation, and warning Russian socialists that the delegates were 'agents of the British Government.'[16] Both the ILP and BSP based their understanding of events unfolding in Russia on the views of the majority of the Petrograd Soviet who were calling for a negotiated end to the war.

British Marxists had been talking enthusiastically about the coming social revolution ever since the foundation of the SDF in 1884. On 22 March 1917, the week the news of the February Revolution was received, *The Call* gave its front page over to a banner headline, 'Long Live the Revolution.' The BSP organised an immediate mass meeting called 'To Celebrate the Russian Revolution'. Seven thousand attended the meeting in London's East End addressed by, among others, the Jewish Marxist Joe Fineberg. *The Call* exulted: 'It may well be that we are only in the initial stages of the revolution, [. . .] The first tremendous breach in the walls of the enemy has been made; the hour is close at hand when we too, in this country, will plant the Red Flag on the grave of Reaction and shout Long Live the Revolution! Long Live the International!'[17]

In Russia, Lenin's return on 3 April (O.S. 22 March), in a sealed train put at his disposal by the German government, shifted the balance of power away from the Duma towards the Soviets. The following day Lenin presented his *April Theses* to comrades in the Tauride Palace calling for 'the party to build up majorities in the soviets and other mass organizations and then to expedite the transfer of power to them. Implicitly he was urging the overthrow of the Provisional Government and the inception of a socialist order.'[18] Lenin was confident that socialist revolution in Russia would soon engulf a war-weary Europe and called upon the internationalists to prepare for revolutionary war. Following publication of the *April Theses* on 16 April 1917 (O.S. 3 April) calling for the overthrow of the Provisional Government and Russia's immediate withdrawal from the 'imperialist war' the British Government found it difficult to respond. They knew precious little about Lenin.

In such circumstances, MI7(d) regarded Rothstein's knowledge of Russian socialism as a prized intelligence asset. MI5, however, who had been monitoring Rothstein ever since the Agadir Crisis of 1911, counselled caution. On the 8 May they received intelligence from the historian Dr R. W. Seton Watson, then working in the Propaganda Office of the F.O., 'that an extreme Russian socialist called Theodore Rothstein at present employed on economic reports on conditions in Germany (Based on German Press) in G. H. Mair's[19] [*sic*] office, is a completely unreliable person who should on no account be employed in any office where he could have access to confidential documents or even get any insight into the general trend of events.'[20] Seton Watson's source was the veteran socialist leader Hyndman who had recently told him that Rothstein was 'hand in glove with Lenin, the most absolute of Russian pacifist-socialists.'[21] 'The worst of it is', the MI5 officer responsible for monitoring Rothstein complained, 'this man [Rothstein] is almost certain to be transferred to the Propaganda Office, F.O. now in course of construction under

John Buchan.[22] Seton Watson is himself employed there. He wishes his name kept out of any enquiry for this reason. But in view of what Hyndman both told and wrote to him, he could not help reporting it.'[23]

MI5 now approached Lieutenant-Colonel Wake of MI7 and questioned the wisdom of Rothstein's continued employment. Wake defended Rothstein, stating that he was 'a very valuable man' and that he would be 'very averse' to part with him but would 'do so without demur' if it was considered absolutely necessary. He spoke of his concern 'that if he [Rothstein] was dismissed from MI7 he would be immediately snapped up by Count Gleichen, ex-head of Section E (Austrian and Turkish) of the Intelligence Department at the FO and a leading figure in Lloyd George's Special Intelligence Bureau.'[24] 'Count Gleichen', he observed, 'had already borrowed Rothstein's services on one occasion and envies MI7 the possession of them.'[25] Wake then told his interviewer, Major Ferguson, that Rothstein was 'in close touch with Russian Socialists in London, and an opportunity of acquiring knowledge of them and at the same time seeing Rothstein could be obtained by despatching a Minute to MI7(d): "Have you anyone on your staff who could furnish any information regarding Russian Socialism here and abroad?"'[26] Major Ferguson acted promptly:

> The only thing I can suggest for the moment with reference to Lt. Col. Wake's minute is that one of you get into touch with Rothstein (you can no doubt find a good excuse for this) and see what you make of him. But do not bring him here[27] nor let him know where you are employed (except at the W.O.).[28]

The interview with Rothstein was conducted by an MI5 officer called Anson on 6 June. Anson reported back that he 'took a dislike to the little man who from a short interview, I shd. say does not love [our] country overmuch. He's [sleazy] and oily, and no [doubt] useful at his present work and as [he] is thought a good deal of in MI7d. He's not [a] man *I'd* care to trust: such at least was [the] impression he made on me. The report on [Russian] Socialism which he wrote is distinctly [interesting]. I left it with Col. Wake, who is [going] to get another employee to criticise it – [?] a Russian, or rather Russian Pole.'[29] Kell minuted on the 9 June 'I will raise no objection to his remaining on at his present job; but should be glad to be informed if and when he changes.'[30]

MI7(d) continued to defend Rothstein informing Kell that he 'was extremely useful in preparing the "Daily Review of the Foreign Press"', both because of his languages and of his knowledge of Russian socialist parties. They added that he had no access to confidential documents, beyond the 'Review' itself. It was therefore 'decided (9.6.17) that ROTHSTEIN might be allowed to continue his work at MI7(d). MI5 was to be informed if any change was proposed.'[31] The matter, however, did not rest there. On 15 June the Liberal MP Donald Maclean, father of the future Cambridge spy Donald Maclean, wrote to Kell expressing his concern at Rothstein's employment by the F.O. as a translator and offering to speak personally to Robert Cecil about the case. 'I am informed by a high official of the London Labour Movement [probably Hyndman], whom I know well and have every confidence in, that this man was well known to them as a strong pro-German, and it gives them much uneasiness that he is in the Foreign Office.'[32] Kell thanked Maclean for his letter and reassured him that Rothstein was 'not now employed by the Foreign Office in any capacity, but his good knowledge of languages and other attainments are being made use of by the War Office in a capacity which he could not possibly do any harm, even if he were so disposed.'[33]

Rothstein's ability to remain impartial when it came to the summaries he was preparing for the DRFP was boosted by his son Andrew's call-up by the British Army, which convinced him that he should remain in Britain despite a dream to return to 'Russia to fight her battles'. On 26 June he wrote to his old friend and mentor in the anti-imperialist cause, Scawen Blunt, recording the divided loyalties that he felt towards both Britain and Russia now that his son had been conscripted:

Dear Mr. Blunt,

You may think, judging from my silence, that I have, perhaps, gone back to Russia! No such luck. Most of my friends have gone, and soon I shall be left alone. But I have struck my roots too deeply here, and it will take sometime before I can release myself. I think it will not be before the end of the war. My eldest son is now being called up by the army authorities, and this alone will keep me and my family here. You can realise with what feelings I am looking forward to this event. He has been passed for garrison duty abroad; but for one thing, there is now no reliance to be placed on the official classification, and if the authorities chose they can "advance" him for general service and send him to the trenches. For another, even if he is allowed to remain in his class, he may [be] sent to Mesopotamia or to some other such pleasant place. Anyhow this is a new trouble and a new disagreeable [sic] feature of the present war. [. . .] My dream is now to go to Russia to fight her battles, but, as I have said above, this at present is impossible.[34]

The developing crisis in Russia ensured his continuing employment by MI7(d). 'I get most of the new Russian papers, and exciting reading they are. My God, what an amount of writing and [. . .] talking they do now in Russia! It is as if they wanted to compensate themselves for the long centuries of silence.'[35]

In midsummer the head of the Provisional Government, Prince Lvov, and his War Minister, Alexander Kerensky, believing that a military victory would undermine the power of the Bolsheviks in the Soviets, launched an offensive on the Eastern front's southern sector. The Bolsheviks countered by calling an armed demonstration in the capital, Petrograd, on 16 July (O.S. 3 July). Between 16 and 17 July a series of spontaneous demonstrations by soldiers and workers against the Provisional Government ended in widespread rioting. On the afternoon of 17 July the Bolshevik Military Organization, without initial authorisation from the Central Committee, led a peaceful demonstration of 500,000 workers, soldiers, and sailors under the slogan 'All Power to the Soviets'. It was met with violent repression not seen since the bloody massacres of 1905; more than 700 people were killed or wounded by troops loyal to the regime. The offices and printing plant of *Pravda* and the headquarters of the Bolshevik Central Committee were destroyed, and on 19 July (O.S. 6 July) the Provisional Government issued an order for the arrest of Lenin who went into hiding before making his way across the Finnish border. The July Days forced the resignation of Prince Lvov. Kerensky, with Menshevik and SR backing, became Prime Minister on 24 July (O.S. 11 July). 'There was', as one historian noted, 'a growing atmosphere of counter-revolution. Newspapers called for the Bolsheviks to be hanged and the Soviet to be closed down.'[36]

Kerensky now faced a multitude of problems, not least the need to re-impose the government's authority over the towns and the front. He appointed General Lavr Kornilov, an advocate of stern measures against unruly Soviets, as Supreme Commander of the Russian armed forces and summoned him to Petrograd to stiffen the resistance of troops loyal to the government. Fearful of Kornilov's ambitions, however, Kerensky changed his mind and countermanded his order. On 27 (O.S. 14 August) Kornilov 'pressed onwards to Petrograd in open mutiny' leaving Kerensky with little alternative but to turn to the Petrograd Soviet for help. Bolshevik, Menshevik and SR emissaries were despatched to the troops who were persuaded to halt their own trains and place Kornilov under house arrest. Kornilov's mutiny now ended in 'fiasco.'[37]

In an article written for *Plebs Magazine* Rothstein, writing as John Bryan, spoke of the growing strength of the 'Jacobins (Bolsheviks)' and predicted that 'if the Provisional Government failed to deal with the worsening economic, political and military situation then it would pave the way for the Jacobins to assume power.'[38] In Rothstein's view the comparison with the Jacobins was an indication that the 'struggle of classes', in a Marxian sense, had become 'the main factor in the Russian situation' and that the class struggle alone would determine the 'logical' outcome of the revolution. The revolution if it was to survive had to 'proceed to the next ascending phase of development.'[39] On the eve of the October Revolution Rothstein was undoubtedly using his position in MI7(d) to promote the Bolshevik's programme in Britain's left-wing press at a time when very few people in Britain, or for that matter in Russia, knew what the Bolsheviks intended to do.

Seizure of land owned by the gentry now took place at an alarming rate. Simultaneously the slogan of 'workers' control' gained in appeal to the working class; elective committees of workers claimed the right to monitor and regulate managerial decisions on finance, production and employment; managers and foremen were removed and the committees completely took over the enterprises; 'workers' control' involved a massive interference with capitalist practices. In July it was in force in 378 enterprises, by October it had spread to 573 and involved two-fifths of the industrial working class.[40] Central power was rapidly disintegrating; the disbanding of the Tsarist police force limited Kerensky's scope for repression; soldiers' and sailors' committees scrutinised and challenged the orders of their officers; the hierarchy of military command simply collapsed, all but disappearing after the Kornilov mutiny in August. 'By September Lenin was urging his party to seize power immediately. [...] Disguised as a footplateman, [he] hastened back to Petrograd. On 10 October he cajoled his Central Committee colleagues into ratifying the policy of a rapid seizure of power.'[41] On 25 October the Military-Revolutionary Committee of the Petrograd Soviet and the Red Guards under Trotsky's guidance overthrew Kerensky's Provisional Government. At the Second All-Russia Congress of Soviets of Workers' and Soldiers' Deputies, due to be held later that day, the Bolsheviks, who represented only 300 out of the 670 delegates were forced to compromise with the Mensheviks and SRs. Fearing that a socialist coalition government was about to be foisted upon him Lenin simply took power before the Congress opened:

The Bolsheviks, operating through the Military-Revolutionary Committee of the City Soviet, seized power in a series of decisive actions. The post and telegraph offices of the railway stations were taken and the army garrisons were put under rebel control. By the end of the day the Winter Palace had fallen to the insurgents. On Lenin's proposal, the Second Congress of Soviets of Workers' and Soldiers' Deputies ratified the transfer of authority to the soviets. A government led by him was quickly formed. He called for an immediate end to the Great War and for working people across Europe to establish their own socialist administrations. Fundamental reforms were promulgated in Russia. Land was to be transferred to the peasants; workers' control was to be imposed in the factories; the right of national self-determination, including secession, was to be accorded to the non-Russian peoples. Opponents of the seizure of power were threatened with ruthless retaliation.[42]

Disgusted, the Mensheviks and SRs 'denounced what they described as a Bolshevik party *coup d'etat*' and stormed out of the Congress, the minority Left Socialist Revolutionaries alone remained, leaving the Bolsheviks in complete control. They proclaimed themselves the new government, which they called the Council of People's Commissars (or *Sovnarkom*, its Russian acronym). Lenin justified the 'victorious uprising' by reference to 'the will of the huge majority of workers, soldiers and peasants' and set out his plans for the future. These included the bringing of 'an immediate democratic peace to all the peoples'; the convocation of a Constituent Assembly, workers' control over industrial establishments; 'democratization of the army'; and the transfer of gentry, crown and church lands to the peasant committees. There was opposition; railwaymen and postal workers called a strike but this soon petered out; the Bolsheviks, jubilant, expected revolutions abroad; the Red Revolution in Russia was to be the clarion call. Trotsky, as People's Commissar for Foreign Affairs, issued a decree calling on governments and to 'all the warring peoples' to bring about a 'just, democratic peace'.[43]

But who was this Lenin? Very little had been written about him, or by him, in Britain apart from two articles translated by Alexander Sirnis who had recently resigned from the BSP to join the SLP. These had been published in the June and September editions of the SLP's paper, *The Socialist.* There was little else in print. The initial response of the BSP towards the October Revolution, despite their Marxism, displayed little real under-standing of the fierce class struggles that had wracked Russia between the Kornilov Affair and the Bolshevik seizure of power. *The Call* merely assumed that Lenin's second revolution had been made to defend the democratic ideals of the first and in pursuit of a democratic peace. Responsibility for the salvation of the Revolution, therefore, rested with the *Entente* Powers:

> The programme of the new revolutionary Government brings the immediate objects of the Revolution back to what it was at the commencement: immediate democratic peace, the granting of land to the peasants, and the convocation of the Constituent Assembly. Russia must have peace now, there is no question about that [. . .] Russia once again holds out the offer of a general democratic peace, which, if the peoples of Europe desired it, can be secured now. Revolutionary Russia does not desire a separate peace. The Soviet prevented Miliukoff from doing the same. It is the reactionary Minister of War, Vertchovsky, who proposes a separate peace to Kerensky. But if Russia is compelled through sheer exhaustion to make a separate peace the responsibility will rest on the Governments and people of the Entente. Their treatment of the revolution has been shameful.[44]

The BSP had simply come out in support of the views of the *Manchester Guardian* – that the failure of the Entente Governments to respond positively to the Provisional Govern-ment's peace overtures had created the conditions for the October Revolution. It now remained for the Entente to salvage the situation by seizing the opportunity for peace offered by the October Revolution.

A democratic peace, however, was not the mainstay of the revolution as the firebrand daughter of the suffragette leader Christabel Pankhurst and leader of the Workers' Socialist Federation (WSF), Sylvia Pankhurst, was the first to point out in an article welcoming Lenin's revolution in the *Workers' Dreadnought*. The October Revolution, she argued, was a Socialist Revolution, and that its aims and ideals not only differed from those of capitalism; but were sincerely held by the Bolsheviks who could not simply change course once peace had been declared:

> The Bolsheviks, like the French revolutionaries, realise that the Governments of Europe are unfriendly; but they separate the peoples from the Governments. They realise that the Imperialist-capitalists of all nations are their enemies, and that the workers of all nations are their friends. The *Manchester Guardian* suggests, and some British Socialists who should know better suggest, that if the Allied Governments had shown more sympathy for Russian aims and treated Russia more generously, this Bolshevik view would not have been held. To argue thus is completely to ignore the outstanding fact that the Russian Revolution is a Socialist revolution, and that its aims and ideals are incompatible with those of capitalism.[45]

Pankhurst's bold assertion that the Russian Revolution had changed the fundamental relationship between States was missed by the other major socialist parties, the BSP, SLP and the ILP. Philip Snowden commenting on the Bolshevik Revolution in the *Labour Leader* questioned the practicality of peace negotiations without formal recognition of the Revolution by the Entente and Central Powers. Germany's refusal to enter into 'communications with a Government which is not supported by a Constituent Assembly' convinced Snowden that the 'dominant party in Russia' must hold elections as soon as possible.[46] Unlike Pankhurst, Snowden did not discuss the socialist objectives of the Bolshevik Revolution; his concern was to point out the dangers inherent in not having a legitimate government in Russia with whom the

Entente and Central Powers could negotiate. He did not see any future ideological incompatibility between the foreign policy of the Bolsheviks and other Powers.

Trotsky's peace decree, sent to all the belligerent Powers, was therefore seen by many to be the prime mover of the October Revolution, and the negative response of the belligerent Powers only served to make the point that the revolution's survival was dependent on an *Entente*, and to some extent German, brokered peace. Even the militant SLP, unswerving in its support for industrial unionism, could see little further than Russia extricating herself from the war in the absence of a 'thoroughly organised industrial movement.'[47] In December 1917 the SLP asked Sirnis to submit a short biography of Lenin for a special Russian supplement to *The Socialist* to be published in January; his revolution was not expected to survive:

> Can you get a photo of Lenin, and supply a short outline of his life and activity together with a reference to his theoretical writings? If he manages to hold out successfully, we may need to translate his other works.[48]

British socialists were so far removed from fulfilling Lenin's desire for world revolution that the SLP, probably the most militant of the socialist groups, almost three months into the Russian Revolution, laboured 'under the impression' that Lenin had 'written something on theoretical Marxism on either economics or history.' In January 1918 they pushed Sirnis once more for a translation of one of his pamphlets:

> We think you would be the better judge of what would be most topical from Lenin's writings to be presented to British readers. Something about 32 pages, as per any of our pamphlets, would be sufficient as a preliminary feeler regarding Lenin's popularity in this country. I was under the impression that he had written something on theoretical Marxism on either economics or history.[49]

Sirnis sent them a translation of Lenin's *Collapse of The Second International*, which castigated the old International for its readiness to admit other than avowedly socialist bodies. When the war came, Lenin argued, the Second International had proved too broad-based to organise any effective opposition against it. Any future International would need to be based on revolutionary principles and exclude all but 'left-wing' parties. The etching of Lenin on the second page of the pamphlet was the first picture of to be published in Britain of the revolutionary leader. By now, however, the British government was monitoring the SLP's correspondence, and quickly moved to shut down the SLP's printing presses.

The National Labour Press in Glasgow, which was part-owned by the SLP, and the SLP's own Socialist Labour Press, which had printed Lenin's pamphlet, received a 'special letter' from the Home Office telling them that 'if they did any matter in connection with blocks and Russian revolution their Press would be dismantled and closed down.'[50] Sirnis was warned by the SLP to be extra cautious: 'You put your address on the order to the Photo Company and our "friends" got it. Had the blocks not been delivered up there is no doubt they would have been on your track.'[51] The SLP now began experiencing difficulties obtaining paper, and it was feared that *The Socialist* would be closed down at any moment. Sirnis offered to buy paper from a supplier in Southampton to keep the paper alive. He also made arrangements for an alternative printing press to be set up should the authorities dismantle the existing one, using equipment from the old Tuckton House printing works at Christchurch.

> Your offer re machine will most likely turn out very timely and I would like further particulars of it. It is most likely that the Press will be closed if we get out many more issues like the last, for although it is legally all right, it is not wise for an unscrupulous government to tolerate such for long. If we can rely on using the one you name it would be a help. If you can get the bursted portion mended I will be glad to cover cost even

if we cannot use it. I presume it is in Bournemouth? If not you need not send details through the post. If you can give me a more detailed description of plant I will be very glad.[52]

The British government's response to the October Revolution was uncompromising. It rejected Trotsky's call for a general negotiated democratic peace on the grounds that the Bolshevik Government was not a legitimate body with whom it could negotiate. A significant minority, largely confined to the FO, however, took an opposing view. In September 1917, with the revolutionary crisis in Russia approaching its peak, the British Vice-Consul in Moscow, Robert Bruce Lockhart, returned to London. Seven months previously Lockhart had met with British members of the military inter-Allied delegation to Russia, among them Lord Milner, who had questioned him on the likelihood of revolution in Russia. On his arrival in London, Lockhart was approached by a number of politicians anxious for news from Russia, including Lord Milner. Lockhart's views were radically different from those prevailing in London and at a December meeting with Milner he expressed the view that the Bolshevik regime was not on the point of collapse. 'It was madness', he told him, 'not to establish some contact with the men who at that moment were controlling Russia's destinies.'[53]

Lockhart's arguments made a favourable impression on Milner and he arranged a meeting between Lockhart and Lloyd George, where 'the necessity of getting into touch with Lenin and Trotsky' was agreed upon.[54] Diplomatic relations between Britain and Russia post-October had effectively ceased.[55] Trotsky had appointed Litvinov Soviet *charge d'affaires* in Britain on 30 December 1917 and Britain's Ambassador, Sir George Buchanan, had left Moscow for London on 3 January 1918. As a gesture of good will, Chicherin, who had been arrested on 25 August for associating with Germans and pro-Germans at the Communist Club, was released from Brixton gaol and deported to Russia along with the Petrovs.[56] On 4 January 1918, it was decided to send Lockhart to Russia as head of a special mission to establish unofficial relations with the Bolsheviks. It was hoped that the Bolsheviks would grant Lockhart the necessary diplomatic privileges without being recognised by the British Government. An introduction to Lenin and Trotsky and the setting-up of a *modus vivendi* with Litvinov, who was to be granted similar privileges in Britain, was to be arranged through Rex Leeper, who Lockhart later recalled 'was on friendly terms with Rothstein [...] then an official translator in our own War Office.'[57] Lockhart kept a full record of his meetings with Rothstein:

> I had a long talk with Rothstein, the substance of which I carefully noted in my diary. Rothstein, who had lived for years in England, was an intellectual armchair revolutionary. He said Trotsky's ambition was not a separate peace but a general peace. He pointed out that if he were Lloyd George he would accept Trotsky's offer of a conference unconditionally. England would be the chief beneficiary. The Russian stipulations about self-determination would fall through with an ineffective protest from Trotsky, and England and Germany could arrange the colonial questions between them. Germany would agree to almost all other terms – that is, no annexations and no contributions. She might even be prepared to compromise on the Alsace-Lorraine question. In any case, it was absurd for England to prolong the war for the sake of Alsace-Lorraine. There was nothing easier to destroy than sentimental causes which were not rooted in a people itself, and we should have to consider very seriously whether we should get a better peace nine months hence.[58]

A few days later Britain all but recognised the Bolsheviks when unofficial diplomatic relations between the British and Russian governments were concluded at a Joe Lyons coffee shop[59] in the Strand, by Charing Cross station:

> It was an amazing meal. Outside, the January sky was like lead, and the room, poorly lit at the best of times, was grey

and sombre. Leeper and I were just thirty. Litvinoff was eleven years our senior. Rothstein was a year or two older than Litvinoff. Both men were Jews. Both had suffered persecution and imprisonment for their political convictions. Yet Litvinov, whose real name was Wallach, was married to an Englishwoman. Rothstein had a son – a British subject – in the British Army.[60]

After a nervous beginning it was Rothstein, whose diplomatic skills had been honed in the seemingly intractable internecine squabbles of British Marxists, who ensured that the 'negotiations went smoothly':

> The success of that luncheon was made by Rothstein, who supplied to the conversation the necessary mixture of banter and seriousness which afterwards I was to find so useful in my negotiations with the Bolsheviks in Russia. Small, bearded with dark lively eyes, he was a kind of intellectual cricket, whose dialectical jumps were as bewildering to us as they were amusing to himself.[61]

There was, however, to be no official recognition; officially the Russian Embassy of the Tsarist regime located at Chesham House still existed; unofficially, both Litvinov and Lockhart would be granted certain diplomatic privileges and the right to a diplomatic courier and cyphers. Litvinov's letter of recommendation to Trotsky was written out there and then 'on the rough linen of a standard Lyons' table – an event that would dramatically change the course of Anglo-Soviet relations:

> Citizen Trotsky,
>
> The bearer of this, Mr Lockhart, is going to Russia with an official mission with the exact character of which I am not acquainted. I know him personally as a thoroughly honest man who understands our position and sympathises with us. I should consider his sojourn in Russia useful from the point of view of our interests.

My position here remains indefinite. I learnt of my appointment only from the newspapers. I hope a courier is bringing me the necessary documents without which the difficulties of my position are greatly increased. The Embassy, Consulate and Russian Government Committee have not yet surrendered. Their relations to me will be determined by the relations of the British Government.

[. . .] I shall write more fully by the first courier. I have not received an answer from you to my telegram of January 4th, new style, No. 1. I request you very much to confirm the receipt of all telegrams and to number your telegrams.

The ciphers will, I trust, be delivered to me by the courier. Greetings to Lenin and all friends. I press your hand warmly.

Yours (signed) M Litvinoff

Rothstein begs me to greet you.
London, January 11th (new style), 1918.[62]

The meal concluded on an ominous, if humorous, note: 'As we were ordering a sweet, Litvinoff noticed on the menu the magic words: "pouding diplomate." The idea appealed to him. The new diplomatist would eat the diplomatic pudding. The Lyons "Nippy" took his order and returned a minute later to say there was no more. Litvinoff shrugged his shoulders and smiled blandly. "Not recognised even by Lyons," he said.'[63]

8

The 'Dual Policy'

The Russian Soviet Government [...] declares its readiness, if necessary, to include in the general agreement with the Entente Powers a pledge of non-interference in their internal affairs.

The policy which allowed of these compromises represented a repetition of Lenin's tactics during the Brest Litovsk period. Russia needed peace and the Bolsheviks had decided to buy it at a great price in the confidence that the sacrifice was temporary.

Louis Fisher, *The Soviets in World Affairs*, p. 116

The meeting between Leeper, Litvinov, Lockhart and Rothstein at Joe Lyons coffee shop in the Strand was a dramatic moment in the history of early Anglo-Soviet diplomatic relations, and an indication that some common ground remained. Leeper was genuinely fond of Litvinov, having introduced him to his future wife Ivy Low at a literary *soiree* in Bloomsbury. The granddaughter of Austrian Jews who had converted to Anglicanism, Ivy Low Litvinov introduced her *Litvak* husband to a number of influential figures in British society.[1] Her father worked closely with H. G. Wells on the *Educational Times* while her uncle, Sir Sidney Low, enjoyed the friendship of the future foreign secretary, George Curzon, as well as Lord Milner. Both Curzon and Milner advocated military intervention in Russia and the overthrow of the Bolsheviks. Her Aunt Edith's first husband was Leslie Haden-Guest,[2] whom she divorced in 1909; her second husband was the Fabian and Zionist Dr David Eder.[3]

Initially, Lockhart had wanted to take Leeper with him to Moscow as his assistant but settled instead for an MI6 agent, Captain Hicks.[4] It was felt that Leeper, who had been a witness at the Litvinov's' wedding in 1916, would be more useful at home liaising with Litvinov whose office at 82 Victoria Street was situated above the rooms used by Leeper and some of his colleagues in the Foreign Office Political Intelligence Department. Early contact between the British and Russian governments, therefore, owed much to the unofficial Leeper-Litvinov link.[5]

Litvinov's first act as unofficial Soviet 'Ambassador' had been to issue an appeal addressed 'To the Workers of Great Britain' calling on them to force their Government to comply with Russia's request for an immediate armistice and to participate in the negotiations for a general peace.[6] On 17 January, six days after his meeting with Leeper and Lockhart in the Strand, the Executive Committee of the BSP issued a Manifesto calling on the Labour Party to support Litvinov's appeal at its forthcoming Labour Party Conference to be held in Nottingham that month, and to take the initiative in 'restoring peace':

> Let the forthcoming Labour Party Conference at Nottingham give the answer to Russia's urgent and imperative appeal.
> [...] Say to the Government: 'If you will not comply with Russia's request for an immediate armistice and negotiations for a general peace. Labour will thrust you aside and take up itself the task of restoring peace to a sorrow-stricken world.'[7]

The Home Office, however, was less accommodating than the Foreign Office when it came to dealing with Litvinov. On the eve of the Conference police raided the BSP's London premises and confiscated copies of its Manifesto and Litvinov's appeal to British workers thus preventing their distribution to delegates at Nottingham. Nevertheless, his speech to the Conference, which stopped just short of calling for an armed revolution in Britain, was warmly received by many in the audience prompting the F.O.

to despatch a note to Trotsky protesting against Litvinov's 'impossible behaviour'.[8] Litvinov's speech, however, had been more emotional than pragmatic and did not reflect Lenin's increasing pessimism about the prospects for world revolution, and the need to accept German peace terms in the absence of a negotiated 'general peace.'

In November 1917, an Armistice had been agreed between Germany and the Bolsheviks at Brest-Litovsk, the town nearest the trenches of the Eastern Front's northern sector. The following month the German negotiators 'delivered an ultimatum to the effect that *Sovnarkom* should allow national self-determination to the borderlands and cease to claim sovereignty over them.'[9] Lenin was asked to cede half of imperial Russia's European territory, including the Ukraine and the Baltic States, and a quarter of Russia's entire population, 'most of Russia's coal mines, half of its other industry and more than a third of its most fertile agricultural land.'[10] In January 1918 the Central Powers made it clear that, unless a separate peace was quickly signed on the Eastern front, Russia would be overrun. Following the elections to the Constituent Assembly earlier that month, the Bolsheviks had obtained less than a quarter of the votes, making Lenin's grip on power uncertain. Needing to buy time for his revolution he had one single aim – to survive in power. On 8 January he put forward his proposals for a separate peace to the Third Congress of Soviets of Workers', Soldiers' and Cossacks' Deputies. Despite arguing that peace would enable the Bolsheviks to 'strangle' the Russian bourgeoisie and prepare better for an eventual revolutionary war in Europe the majority of delegates, 65 in total, voted against; while only 15 supported him.[11]

Nevertheless, Russia was not in a position to continue the war with Germany; nor could the Bolsheviks garner enough support to launch a revolutionary war. A Russian army no longer existed; the party was divided on the question of war and peace, and the opposition ready to exploit any military failure. Lenin had little choice; he rejected calls for a revolutionary war and immediate world revolution and sued for a separate peace.

On 18 February the German Army advanced from Riga and overran Dvinsk, 600 kilometres from Petrograd. 'That evening [...] a shaken Central Committee adopted Lenin's policy of bowing to the German terms.'[12] In an article prompted by accusations from the newly formed United Labour Party of Russian Social-Democrats, in effect the Menshevik opposition, circulated through the Second International's International Socialist Bureau, Litvinov defended the Bolsheviks against charges of having broken with the policy of International struggle for a democratic peace.[13] It became a matter of some urgency to discover Britain's position on the separate peace and the renewed German offensive. Rothstein and Leeper were to be consulted. In February Litvinov received a telegram from Russia saying that the Petrograd Telegraph Agency had cabled Rothstein requesting him to contribute by cabling daily.[14] At this point Rothstein was invited to join the Labour Party's Advisory Committee on Foreign Affairs (Westminster Branch). Leeper, who was then working on the Reconstruction of Eastern Europe under top civil servant Sir William Tyrell, along with historian Lewis Namier at the Foreign Office, was also on the Committee. The arrival of Kamenev on 23 February and the confiscation of £5,000 intended for the purposes of Litvinov's Embassy and the arbitrary deportation of one of Litvinov's secretaries, Stefen Wolf, without charge or trial, was an indication of shifting attitudes towards the Bolshevik Government. The conclusion of a separate peace with Germany at Brest-Litovsk on 3 March 1918 strengthened those in Government calling for allied military intervention in Russia. A schism began to appear in the official labour movement, with Henderson and a majority of the Parliamentary Labour Party and the Parliamentary Committee of the TUC moving away from reluctant support for Litvinov and the October Revolution, towards a more pro-Government stance of open opposition. Given such support for the Government the BSP's continued affiliation to the Labour Party came up for renewed discussion on the eve of the BSP's Annual Easter Conference. Joe Fineberg, who was to advise Lenin on this issue during the negotiations leading to the formation of the Communist Party of Great Britain (CPGB), opened the debate with three articles in favour of continued affiliation to the Labour Party in *The Call* between 7 and 21 March. Only two articles appeared opposed to Fineberg's views, from Albert Ward and M. Jacobs. The issue was debated at the BSP's Annual Conference where a North West Ham branch resolution in favour of disaffiliation was defeated by 102 votes to 17.

Steps were also taken to consolidate moves towards Socialist Unity among the various socialist and syndicalist groups; while Rothstein, publishing his first article for nearly five months in *The Call* under the pseudonym WAMM, strongly criticised the ineffectual response of both the German Majority and 'Independent' Socialists to the 'peace of force concluded at Brest-Litovsk,' and the renewed German offensive against Russia. Of far greater significance, however, was a later Rothstein article, also under the signature of WAMM, calling for a break with the Second International and the creation of a new International of Revolutionary Socialists.[15] Published on the eve of moves to reconstruct the Second International, Rothstein's article raised a number of difficult questions. In all likelihood, he wrote, there will be two Internationals, one revolutionary and the other reformist, splitting the Labour Party and the Trade Unions from the Marxian Socialists. In such circumstances, the BSP would find it difficult to justify continued affiliation with the Labour Party. On the eve of the second 1918 Labour Conference to be held in June, as a gesture towards Socialist Unity, Sylvia Pankhurst of the WSF was added to the BSP's delegation to the Labour Party Conference. The other members of the delegation were H. Alexander, E. C. Fairchild, Boris Kahan, Dora B. Montefiore and J. T. Walton Newbold.

The Conference was remarkable for two events: the resolution moved on behalf of the BSP by Pankhurst calling on Labour Ministers of the Cabinet to withdraw from the Government and the speech from Kerensky calling for military intervention in Russia. Kerensky's speech, and the manoeuvrings behind the scenes to bring Kerensky to the platform, was an indication of the extent to which the Labour Party had moved since the

Brest-Litovsk Treaty, in favour of the Government's policy of intervention. The refusal to allow Litvinov to speak gave evidence that Henderson did not want to flout the F.O. by allowing him to oppose the policy that Kerensky had just outlined.

At the beginning of July 1918 4,000 British, French, American, Canadian, Italian and Serbian soldiers occupied the port city of Murmansk. On 4 July, writing in *The Call*, Litvinov indignantly asked 'Whom Does Kerensky Represent?' and called upon British labour to support 'the great Russian Proletarian Revolution':

> Do not allow yourself to be misled by the presumption that Kerensky pleaded for one Labour Party in Russia against another. The overthrow of the Bolsheviks *cannot* mean that any other Socialist or even Democratic party will take over the power. The Soviet Government, if overthrown at the present juncture, can only be superseded by the most brutal and barbaric military dictatorship, resting on foreign bayonets, with the inevitable subsequent restoration of Tsarism. Is British labour going to be a party to these dark schemes? Is the British proletariat prepared to take upon itself the responsibility before history for the crushing of the great Russian Proletarian Revolution?[16]

Litvinov's semi-official diplomatic activities were now superseded by a campaign against military intervention in Russia. Launching a propaganda offensive that the British authorities found difficult to contain, Litvinov and his supporters made use of the socialist press and the *Manchester Guardian* to publicise Bolshevik aims.

Rothstein's continued employment by MI7(d), where he had access to foreign socialist newspapers, was again causing some disquiet. Rothstein and Sirnis, at this time, were pioneering the publication of Trotsky's works in Britain. On 17 June MI5's Captain Bray revisited the case; describing Rothstein as 'a nasty little Russian-Jew with extreme socialist sentiments' and remarking on Rothstein's close connections with Litvinov he concluded that

Rothstein's 'employment by any Government Department seemed most undesirable.'[17] That same month extracts from Trotsky's *War and Revolution*[18] were published in *The Socialist* prompting a second police raid on the Glasgow headquarters of the Socialist Labour Press under Defence of the Realm Regulation 27c:

> On Saturday July 6th without any previous warning, a body of Police, accompanied by an engineer, entered our printing establishment [...] and dismantled the machinery, and removed the vital parts, together with stocks of paper and printing materials to the Police Office. On being asked by our representatives for their authority for such action they replied that it was done on the order of the Crown, no other reason being given.[19]

In a letter to Sirnis appealing for paper, W. R. Stoker summed up just how effective the authorities had been in muzzling the socialist press in Scotland:

> This will play havoc with us, for I believe it will take several hundreds of pounds to replace what was stolen. Where the money is to come from goodness knows. I expect this will prevent the publication of the works in hand, for I think it will take us all our time to keep the Socialist going if we can find someone to print.[20]

The London-based *Call* was more fortunate. A collection of Lenin's articles, written in the summer of 1917, recently translated in Petrograd had been passed to the BSP for publication. They were published as a pamphlet in July 1918 under the title *Lessons of the Russian Revolution*, priced very cheaply at threepence. At the end of the month MI5 intercepted two letters from Albert Rothstein in Leeds to his brother Theodore Rothstein, written in Russian, calling for Litvinov to issue 'an official circular' discussing in 'detail the preliminary steps necessary to induce local labour organisations in England 'to react in connection with the intervention by the Allies in the internal affairs of Russia'.[21] The second letter dated 30 July impressed 'on his brother that the information on the circular must be absolutely reliable, as the people he is in touch with are "all capable people, not empty talkers, holding important positions".'[22] Both letters were retained by MI5, who decided to deport the Rothstein brothers as soon as possible. MI7, however, although they 'expressed themselves ready to dispense with Theodore's services at once', suggested that, 'until his passage could be arranged, it might be best to keep him at MI7, where he could be watched and where the harm he could do in a few more days would not make much difference, rather than turn him away and thus leave him loose in the country, with a grievance to incite him to do fresh damage.'[23] Nevertheless, on 14 August Scotland Yard was asked to arrange as soon as possible Theodore and Albert Rothstein's repatriation to Russia.[24] The head of Special Branch, Basil Thomson, however, appeared to share MI7's reticence and the case appears to have been shelved until October. Meanwhile, Rothstein continued to pass items of interest from the foreign Press to Litvinov and Sirnis.

In August the *Manchester Guardian*[25] published a heavily censored article on the Bolshevik Constitution with the caveat that lack of space prevented them from printing the whole Constitution. Stoker wrote to Sirnis asking him to translate the complete Constitution if a copy could be located:

> Now this document will rank as important or even more important than the Communist Manifesto. I have today sent an article to A[26] and asked him to obtain full text from Litvinoff. If he should do so, could you translate quickly for the Press. Perhaps you yourself are in possession of the Constitution. [...] It would be a masterstroke as well as good propaganda if we could get it out quickly.[27]

On 14 August Sirnis's name was added to a list of Bolsheviks, which included the Rothstein brothers, to be deported to Russia.

His address was given as Tuckton House, Bournemouth, where it was stated 'a good deal of Bolshevik literature is printed'. The man himself is undoubtedly a Pacifist, but as he is a naturalised British subject he may be difficult to deal with.'[28] On the 17 November 1918 Rothstein sent the manuscript of Trotsky's *History of the Russian Revolution* to the publisher George Allen & Unwin, Limited.

Further evidence of Rothstein's propaganda work was disclosed in an intercepted letter to Theodore Rothstein from a 'Mrs. E. Bouvier, of, 32 Mount Pleasant Road, Lewisham, S.E. [London] – who writes very poor Russian'.[29] This letter, dated 13 September, referred 'to some translation work (presumably propaganda)' that Mrs. Bouvier was doing for Rothstein and requested a meeting with him to discuss 'a mysterious something which Rothstein wants [. . .] at Bigwood Road.' As Bigwood Road was Litvinov's residence, MI5 believed it 'possible that what is referred to may be the circular asked for by Albert in his letter of 29.7.1918.'[30] This was unlikely as Albert Rothstein's letter of 29 July remained in MI5's hands. However, Rothstein had a connection in Paris, 'V', who he sent money and propaganda material to and it seems likely that Mrs Bouverie was connected with this group. A registered letter intercepted by MI5, signed 'V' dated Paris 28 September 1918, requested 'copies of the Secret Agreements, any new pamphlets by LENIN, or certain other papers" 'and 'an advance of £250 for expenses already undertaken towards a forthcoming publication for which a certain "PAPASHA" [Litvinov] has subscribed'. The letter was 'not allowed to go on'; instead, on 1 October the letter was sent to B.C.I. [*sic*],[31] 'with the suggestion that they might pass it to the French *Sûreté* in the hope that the author could be traced.'[32]

MI5 was now very eager to deport Rothstein. On 8 October Kell wrote to Scotland Yard 'pointing out that the departure of the next party for repatriation to Russia was not likely to be at any near date, and suggesting, in view of the strong evidence of their mischievous activities, the brothers ROTHSTEIN should be dealt with without further delay.'[33] On 12 October Kell wrote a further letter to Thomson on the repatriation of Bolsheviks to Russia that barely disguised what had become a common belief in MI5: that all Russian Jews were Bolsheviks:

> With regard to the further deportation of Bolsheviks here are some names which I have collected. As you probably know, however, apart from the usual difficulty of obtaining first class evidence there is the extreme desire of Russian Jews (the majority of whom I firmly contend are potential Bolsheviks) to claim [...] they may be Social Revolutionaries but anti-Bolsheviks. It is difficult to draw the line, and my own opinion is that the more Russian Revolutionary Jewish Refugees are deported the better. They are only a source of danger to this country and merely await opportunity to make mischief.
>
> I consider that the following anyhow can be fairly described as Bolsheviks or Bolshevik sympathisers although there must be hundreds of the latter.
>
> (I have already written to you about the Brothers ROTHSTEIN).[34]

By now, however, the Foreign Office had renewed its interest in Theodore Rothstein and was staunchly opposing his deportation. The arrest of Bruce Lockhart in Moscow on 1 September following an assassination attempt on Lenin at the Mikhelson Factory in Moscow had been followed swiftly by the arrest of Litvinov and his incarceration in Brixton gaol; Rothstein remained the F.O.'s only means of communication with the Bolsheviks. On the day that Lenin was shot the Cheka, convinced that British agents in Russia were behind the attempt on Lenin's life, stormed the British Embassy in Petrograd.[35] The British clerks resisted and one of the Commissars was killed by the naval attaché, Captain Cromie, before he too was 'shot down at the top of the staircase.'[36] At 3.30 a.m. Lockhart had been awakened by a rough voice ordering him to get up at once:

> As I opened my eyes, I looked up into the steely barrel of a revolver. Some ten armed men were in my room. One man, who

was in charge, I knew. [. . .] I asked him what this outrage meant. 'No questions,' he answered gruffly. 'Get dressed at once. You are to go to Loubianka No. 11.' [Loubianka No. 11 was the headquarters of the Moscow Cheka.][37]

Lockhart, whose experiences of the war and of the Russian revolution had left him with a very poor opinion of secret service work,[38] now learnt that he was at the head of an Allied plot to overthrow the Bolsheviks:

On the Tuesday [3 September] we[39] read the full tale of our iniquities in the Bolshevik Press, which excelled itself in a fantastic account of a so-called Lockhart Plot. We were accused of having conspired to murder Lenin and Trotsky, to set up a military dictatorship in Moscow, and by blowing up all the railway bridges to reduce the populations of Moscow and St Petersburg to starvation. The whole plot had been revealed by the loyalty of the Lettish garrison, whom the Allies had sought to suborn by lavish gifts of money. The whole story, which read like a fairy-tale, was rounded off with a fantastic account of my arrest. I had been surprised, it was stated, at a conspirator's meeting. I had been taken to the Cheka and, as soon as my identity was established, I had been immediately released. An equally fantastic story described the events in St. Petersburg. Cromie's murder was depicted as a measure of self-defence by the Bolshevik agents, who had been forced to return fire. Huge headlines denounced the Allied representatives as 'Anglo-French Bandits', and in their comments the leader-writers shrieked for the application of a wholesale terror and of the severest measures against the conspirators.[40]

Lockhart's imprisonment lasted for exactly one month; he was exchanged for Litvinov in early October. Despite calls from MI5's Colonel Bray for Rothstein to 'be deported with the Litvinoff crowd' he remained in London where he took over Litvinov's 'unofficial' responsibilities and continued working for MI7(d). His role would be markedly different from that of his predecessor. Whereas Litvinov had acted in a quasi-official diplomatic capacity, Rothstein was tasked with building a communist movement in Britain capable of challenging British imperialism while normalising relations between Soviet Russia and its capitalist counterpart.[41] Rothstein's close ties with the British labour movement, his ability to court Liberal radical opinion alongside his links with both the W.O. and F.O., meant that he was very well-placed to play both sides of what the historian E. H. Carr referred to as Lenin's 'dual policy', a simple 'choice between principle and expediency,' which rested on the premise that Soviet national interests were compatible with the interests of world revolution.[42] Rothstein now found himself operating as an important 'back channel' for the Foreign Office in its dealings with the Bolsheviks.

These events, taking place against a backdrop of fierce debate in the columns of *The Call* on 'The Reconstruction of the International', paved the way for Communist Unity. E. C. Fairchild, opening the debate in July as editor, warned of the possibility of two Internationals if the left adopted a rigid approach towards membership. His emphasis on the International's reconstruction rested upon an analysis which saw the responsibility for the breakdown of the old International not in terms of the policies pursued by its leaders, but in the loose structure of the International itself, whose resolutions had not been binding on affiliated bodies. Fairchild's overall concern, therefore, was for a reformed International, broad based in membership, with a more 'authoritative' structure.[43]

Of the five articles that followed, only two, by G. Davey and the International Secretary of the ISB Camille Huysmans, agreed with the line taken by Fairchild.[44] Rothstein, writing as WAMM, suggested that the failure of the Second International was due more to its readiness to admit other than avowedly Socialist parties to the International; thereby weakening the integrity of the International as a repository for Socialist ideals and practice. When the war came the International had proved too broad-based to organise any effective protest against it. Any future International, therefore, would need to be based on revolutionary principles and to exclude all but the parties of the '"left wing" if Labourism' and 'Centrism' were to be prevented from again undermining the revolutionary movement.[45]

Rothstein's views were echoed by John Maclean's leading lieutenant on the Clyde, James D. MacDougall, who argued that the 'main weakness of the International Socialist movement during the period 1880–1914 was the enormous importance attached to Parliamentary action.'[46] At the time, he continued, the needs of the International were subordinated to the needs of the German SPD whose eagerness to avoid Government persecution and build up their electoral strength, had 'snuffed out' the French socialist Gustave Herve's call for a general strike against war at the Stuttgart Congress of 1907. The strength of the German party had come to dominate the International Congresses and their success had led the other parties in Europe to model themselves upon 'the "great" German organisation'; the British Labour Party was no exception. MacDougall's view of the future international was of a revolutionary body developing different forms of political action alongside industrial organisation.[47]

Dora B. Montefiore, who had spoken out against military intervention in Russia at the recent Labour Party Conference, also disagreed with Fairchild's editorial articles. She felt that all those responsible for allowing Kerensky to address the Labour Party Conference should be automatically barred from membership. Her position that only revolutionaries should be considered was based on the belief that the new International could function 'as a weapon of offence'. Interestingly, she also saw the 'supreme test' for admittance into the 'Red International' as 'the manner in which the workers in various lands are either supporting or helping to destroy the Soviet administration in Russia.'[48] Montefiore's views were consistent with Lenin's management, through Rothstein, of the negotiations for a Communist Party in Britain reflecting not only the long-term ideological goal of world communism; but also the survival of the revolution and the Soviet state. Lenin's insistence on the formation of a Communist Party in Britain was bound up with the need to conclude a much-needed trade agreement with Great Britain, in reality *de facto* recognition of the Soviet government, by exerting domestic pressure on the British government through the labour movement.

However, the dualistic nature of Soviet foreign policy – attempting to hasten the downfall of capitalist governments while at the same time attempting to negotiate with them – elicited a more cautious approach from the British labour movement towards the Soviet experiment than Montefiore anticipated. Rothstein would play a canny game. Between 1917 and 1920 he kept Lenin informed of political developments in Britain, while assessing the potential threat of militant, if not revolutionary, activity by the British labour movement. To do this, he was entrusted with Soviet funds in order to publish pro-Soviet material, and to oversee the negotiations leading to the formation of a British communist party affiliated to the Communist International. MI5 had an inkling of Rothstein's activities but owing to the overlapping nature of Kell's MI5 and Thomson's Special Branch, and the renewed interest of the F.O. in Rothstein, they were unsure how to respond. At one point Rothstein was said to be languishing on a ship in the Pool just below London Bridge awaiting deportation. According to Leonard Woolf he succeeded 'in getting a letter to Lloyd George smuggled out, and orders were immediately given to the police to release the Russian "ambassador"'.[49] Woolf who had worked closely with Rothstein and Leeper on the Labour Party's Advisory Committee on International Questions,[50] was privy to much of Rothstein's clandestine activities and wrote in his memoirs that Rothstein had managed to gain access to Lloyd George and was conducting off-the-record talks with him on Lenin's behalf. In October Thomson and Kell made one last attempt to have him deported.

On 23 October 1918 Thomson telephoned MI5 and requested that they ask MI7 'to hand Theodore ROTHSTEIN his dismissal to-day, in order that he should be arrested to-morrow and shipped to Russia'. MI7's Colonel Fisher, however, informed MI5 that 'he could not dismiss ROTHSTEIN as he had no grounds to do so, his work being entirely satisfactory.' He did not, however, have any 'objection to ROTHSTEIN being arrested or taken away from MI7 by the Scotland Yard authorities for shipment to Russia. [. . .] It was therefore arranged with Sir Basil THOMSON that ROTHSTEIN should be arrested before going to the office on 24 October and that he should merely be told he was to be deported as an undesirable Bolshevik.'[51] On that day, however, Rothstein was said to be laid up with a heavy bout of flu, it was the middle of the Spanish influenza epidemic, and his deportation was postponed. On 4 November MI5 asked MI7 to let them know when Rothstein had 'resumed his activities' so that a deportation notice could be enforced. At this point Thomson, who had been approached by C. P. Scott on behalf of Lloyd George, interviewed Rothstein and had a complete change of heart. In a letter to E. H. Carr, then a junior F.O. official working in the Northern Section of the Department, he was adamant that no 'further action' should be 'taken against him', stressing the point that he 'will continue to be employed by the War Office.' 'I think', he concluded, 'that the decision to allow him to continue his work at the War Office is a wise one'.[52]

Leeper who wrote a detailed report on Rothstein's activities warned that 'if now sent back forcibly to Russia' Rothstein would damage the interests of the British government:

> Owing to his very real ability, doctrinaire though he is, and his intimate knowledge of this country, extending over many years, he would be a dangerous opponent to us and of great assistance to the Soviet Government. On this ground I think his deportation inadvisable.[53]

Leeper, who had known Rothstein since 1915, claimed to be ignorant of his covert activities and asked to be allowed to approach him privately. That way he could warn him that any further activity on behalf of the Soviet Government would end in his expulsion. As a result Rothstein remained employed in the War Office until 16 August 1919,[54] where he continued to cultivate unofficial contacts with junior F.O. officials, most notably Leeper. Following Litvinov's departure, E.H. Carr, Leeper, and even Thomson had all argued against Rothstein's immediate deportation; with the Under-Secretary of State for Foreign Affairs, Lord Robert Cecil the only dissentient Foreign Office voice.[55]

Theodore Rothstein's brother Albert, however, was less fortunate; or more fortunate, depending on your point of view. He was removed from Leeds to Aberdeen for deportation on the 24/25 October 1918. However, because a 'last-minute' decision had been taken not to deport Theodore it was explained to him 'that this was all a misunderstanding' and he was put up overnight in Aberdeen's 'best hotel' at Government expense and returned to Leeds the following day in a First Class carriage. Once back in Leeds he wrote to Theodore describing his experience as 'exactly like a nightmare' and letting him know that he was putting all his spare cash into War Bonds. [...] one must', he explained, 'help one's country in these times'. He also went to a solicitor. The Government agreed to pay him £35 in compensation and his solicitor £10 along with 'an official letter expressing regret at the mistake which had been made.'[56]

On 11 November 1918 the Armistice was declared ending the war. In Germany the Kaiser abdicated and a Republic was declared. Soviets on the Russian model were set up across Germany. In Britain calls were made for the withdrawal of Allied forces from Russia at the 'earliest possible moment'. The Labour Party's December 1918 general election manifesto also called for the 'immediate withdrawal of all Allied forces from Russia'.[57] Labour's request for a statement of Allied war aims regarding Russia, however, was ignored. 'Up to May 1919', the executive complained, 'it had not been possible [...] to secure any official indication of the objects sought to be achieved by the Allies in their Russian policy.'[58] Opposition to what was known as the War of Intervention now passed to the industrial wing of the labour movement. The Birmingham Trades Council took the first step shortly after the general election, adopting a resolution calling for a conference to consider action to 'compel the Government to withdraw all troops from Russia'.[59] Other local labour bodies followed suit. At its national conference on 26 March 1919 the Miners' Federation of Great Britain unanimously adopted an executive resolution calling on the government to immediately 'withdraw all British troops from Russia, and to take the necessary steps to induce the Allied Powers to do likewise'.[60]

On 18 January 1919, an *ad hoc* body, the London Workers' Committee, organised a conference with the purpose of uniting under one umbrella all the organisations willing to bring 'about a cessation of the Allied powers' violation of Russia.'[61] Five hundred delegates representing nearly 350 organisations discussed calling a general strike unless the government withdrew troops from Russia, and adopted the name 'Hands Off Russia'. The debate was remarkable not merely for the expression of unanimity regarding non-intervention in Russia, but also for the varying responses of delegates to the implications of a strike for political ends. T. J. Smith, a delegate from the National Union of Railwaymen, and Arthur MacManus (SLP) moved a resolution that a general strike would, with 'more scientific organisation of the workers [...] aim at the overthrow of the capitalist State,' thereby compelling 'the abandonment on the part of the Allies to maintain capitalism in Russia, the true purpose of intervention.'[62] Not since the days of Chartism had the British working class shown the confidence to call a strike for political ends; uniting both the industrial and political wings of the labour movement in defence of the Russian revolution. In the spring of 1919, Basil Thomson reported to the Cabinet that 'every section of the workers appeared to be against conscription and intervention in Russia.'[63]

Following the inaugural conference of the Communist International (the Comintern) on 3 March 1919 'Hands Off Russia' took on a new significance, incorporating the defence of Soviet Russia with the organised political and industrial strength of the British labour movement. The first historian to make a detailed study of British communism, Henry Pelling, remarked in

1958 'that there can be few topics more worthy of exploration than the problem of how it came to pass, that a band of British citizens could sacrifice themselves so completely over a period of almost forty years to the service of a dictatorship in another country'.[64] The explanation can largely be found in Lenin's 'dual policy' and the attempts by British labour to marry industrial with political action. 'Hands Off Russia' was a double-edged sword as Carr and Lloyd George appreciated. E. H. Carr, 'had no sympathy' for intervention in Russia, and 'warmly' approved 'Lloyd George's resistance to War Minister Churchill's[65] schemes for finishing off the Bolsheviks'.[66] Lloyd George was quite prepared to lecture Churchill: 'An expensive war of aggression against Russia is a way to strengthen Bolshevism in Russia & create it at home. We cannot afford the burden'.[67]

On the eve of the BSP's Annual Conference in April Rothstein, writing under the pseudonym John Bryan in *The Call*, called for affiliation to the Comintern on the grounds that the BSP was a revolutionary party opposed to Parliamentary forms of warfare. Rothstein was convinced that the British working class, despite being 'traditionally wedded to Parliamentary methods,' confronted 'the same social factors – modern industry, capitalism, proletariat; and, now, the world-war' that had led to revolution in Russia, Germany and Hungary. In these circumstances, he believed, a similar revolutionary crisis was developing in Britain, and events would eventually mirror those that had taken place in the aforementioned countries. In such a situation the British working class would 'forget their Parliamentary "traditions", and confront both Parliament and the Government with some such tangible expression of their will as a Labour Convention, a congress of delegates from the rank and file, call it a Soviet' rivalling Parliamentary Government.[68] Undoubtedly optimistic; but in 1919 the British Government, too, feared general unrest if not revolution. In April Basil Thomson was asked to upgrade the fortnightly Reports on Revolutionary Organisations in the United Kingdom, and to submit weekly reports in their place.[69] These reports circulated by the Home Secretary and issued by the newly formed

Directorate of Intelligence, led by Thomson, pointed to a damaging split unfolding within Britain's postwar intelligence services. In January 1919 a Secret Service Committee had been set up under Lord Curzon to review the performance of the intelligence agencies and to co-ordinate their work.[70] Curzon, a strong admirer of Thomson, who he described as 'an invaluable sleuth hound', oversaw the creation of a 'Civil Secret Service'.[71] In its first report issued in February 1919 they had 'recommended Thomson's appointment as head of a new Directorate of Intelligence under the Home Office', effectively side-lining Kell.[72] 'His new office, which he assumed on May Day 1919, formally confirmed him as the chief watchdog of subversion and left him in control of the Special Branch.'[73]

The setting up of the Comintern ended all attempts by the British government to establish a *modus vivendi* with Soviet Russia and all-out aid, short of direct military action and a formal declaration of war, was extended to the counter-revolutionary 'Whites'.[74] On 2 May 82 Russians were deported to Odessa, all of whom were known to have Bolshevik sympathies. The following day the *Manchester Guardian* asked Rothstein to give them 'something about the present Deportation of Russians, and how Scotland Yard are acting. What result are the Authorities after and how they are doing it? What are the abuses of the method?'[75] Slightly ironic as, unbeknown to Rothstein, Kell had included him on the next deportation list; Thomson, who was 'letting Rothstein run', and was closely monitoring his activities and noting his associates, simply removed it.[76]

According to Thomson's weekly report to the Home Secretary the deportations were having 'a marked effect upon the Russian Jews in the East End of London, and the fear of Deportation seems to have put an end to revolutionary propaganda among them.'[77] This was hardly surprising as the 'Whites' campaign in South Russia had given rise to an unprecedented wave of pogroms in which more than 100,000 Jews lost their lives. Nationalist forces effectively made war on the Jews for their alleged collaboration with the Bolsheviks.[78] As a consequence, Jewish anti-government activity was stepped up in the East End of London and on 12 June

Thomson informed the Home Secretary that a conference had been held at the Old King's Hall on the sixth to protest against the pogroms in Poland. 'Judaism,' he wrote, 'from the Chief Rabbi's Court to the anarchists, was well represented. The Jewish community has been profoundly moved by the pogroms and it was decided that on a date to be fixed this month there should be a general strike of every Jewish worker in shops, kinemas and theatres and that black flags and badges should be displayed. A permanent committee has been elected to make arrangements.'[79] Thomson was then working closely with the Jewish editor of the *Daily Express* and controlled a number of Yiddish-speaking agents among the 'foreign' Jews of the East End. He was well-informed.

The atmosphere in the East End at this time was tense and on 26 June Thomson reported that the veteran syndicalist, Tom Mann, had 'been rather active among the dock labourers' and that a room at 147 East India Dock Road had been 'taken for pickets of the Communist Party, who are stopping men and munitions from going to Russia.'[80] In the same report he remarked that Sylvia Pankhurst 'has stated to friends that she has access to late Russian journals, obtained for her by someone [at] the War Office on loan for a few hours. This is being investigated.'[81] That this 'someone' was Rothstein was known to Thomson. The following week he revealed that leading Bolsheviks in England, France and America were in touch with one another and were receiving directions from Moscow. His sources told him, however, that the 'principal Bolshevik agent in this country [Rothstein] [. . .] confesses that he has had no communication with Moscow for four months.' Paying 'tribute to the effectiveness of the control at the ports' in disrupting this traffic, Thomson informed the Home Secretary that it 'has been thought better not to interfere with the Bolshevik agent in London for the moment. He is not aware that his identity is known, and it is desirable to obtain evidence against other persons before any action is taken.'[82]

The previous month a Soviet courier travelling between Britain and America, Jacob Nosivitsky, a Russian-American Jew, had been arrested on arrival at Liverpool. He was taken to Scotland

Yard where he was apparently 'turned' by Thomson, and given the task of uncovering the chief soviet agent residing in Britain. Nosovitsky wasted no time in identifying Rothstein:

> Nosovitsky claims that, after a visit to Pankhurst and a hurried trip to Paris to meet Boris Souvarine,[83] he succeeded in getting an introduction to Theodore Rothstein, whom he later identified to Scotland Yard as the sought-after Russian representative. On his subsequent voyages Nosivitsky carried messages to and fro between Rothstein and Martens the Soviet representative in the United States. All these communications were opened at Scotland Yard and transcribed before delivery.[84]

Rothstein's role as a Bolshevik agent was set out in some detail by Thomson in his weekly reports to the Cabinet on Revolutionary Organisations in the United Kingdom. As early as January 1920 Thomson was warning that:

> Special attention is called to the secret negotiations now proceeding on the Continent between adherents of the Third Moscow International. British subjects are taking part in it and there is an intention to transform the British Socialist Party into the 'Communist Party'. The money has been furnished by Theodore Rothstein, a Russian Jew journalist formerly employed in the War Office, he is believed to have received it by courier from Moscow. Quotations are given from a letter written by Lenin to a British Communist, in which he declares that the cause of Communism will be best used by using the parliamentary machine.
>
> The flow of Bolshevik propaganda, which is very ably written, will inevitably be greatly increased when trade is opened with Russia, and there is no way of stemming the flow without legislation.'[85]

Certainly, those responsible for disseminating Bolshevik propaganda were resourceful, and could call on sympathisers across the full spectrum of the labour movement. Leonard Woolf a British-born Jew and a member of both the Labour Party and the Fabian Society had first met Rothstein when the two men worked together, along with Rex Leeper, on the Labour Party's Advisory Committee on International and Colonial Questions. In 1919 he became the editor of the *International Review* and Rothstein asked him to publish the full texts of a number of Lenin's post-April 1917 speeches. This he agreed to do, expecting to receive the documents in the normal way through the post. Rothstein corrected him:

> The question was how the typescript of the translation of Lenin's speeches should be physically handed over by Rothstein, his agent, to me, the editor. Having had no experience of revolutionaries, secret agents, or spies, I naturally thought that it would be sent to me in the ordinary way through the post. Rothstein was horrified at such a crude and naïve idea. [...]
>
> On Wednesday afternoon I was to walk down the Strand towards Fleet Street, timing it so that I should pass under the clock at the Law Courts precisely at 2.30. I must walk on the inside of the pavement and precisely at 2.30 I would meet Rothstein under the clock walking from Fleet Street to Trafalgar Square on the outside of the pavement. He would be carrying in his right hand an envelope containing Lenin's speeches, and, as we passed, without speaking or looking at each other, he would transfer the envelope from his right hand to mine.[86]

This early example of how to execute the 'brush pass' was a good illustration of the lengths 'the real underground revolutionary' was prepared to go to overcome Thomson's desire to control the reading matter of the working class. Despite Rothstein's elaborate precautions he was observed by one of Thomson's agents handing over an envelope containing Lenin's speeches to Woolf at precisely 2.30 under the clock outside the Law Courts on the Strand. A few days later the police raided the printers of the *International Review*, seized the documents, the type that had already been set and forbade publication of the material. Rothstein was not arrested.

As well as managing propaganda Rothstein was working frantically behind the scenes to unite Britain's fractious Marxist groups into one communist party affiliated to the Comintern. He was probably the right candidate for the job. He had a long history of involvement with both the socialist movement in Britain and the Radical rump of the Liberal Party stretching back to his turn-of-the-century opposition to the Boer War. His activities on behalf of the Bolsheviks in Britain had an equally long history, and he both understood and contributed to Lenin's 'dual policy' that now dominated Bolshevik thinking. By intervening in the negotiations for Socialist Unity as a British-trained Marxist, the spokesperson of the Bolsheviks in Britain and the bearer of 'Moscow Gold', he was irreplaceable; managing artificially created splits among the Marxist groups and keeping these ill-funded parties and groups alive as he oversaw the creation of the Communist Party of Great Britain (CPGB). Basil Thomson by keeping Rothstein under surveillance, as opposed to ordering his immediate arrest, was able to gain an insight not only into the complexities of British Marxism and those who professed the new 'faith'; but also into Moscow's involvement in pointing out the path British Marxism should follow. Thomson later wrote in his memoirs that Rothstein was 'the intermediary for subsidies to the revolutionary organizations and his secret activities were far reaching.'[87]

A number of left-wing groups received funding from Moscow through Rothstein: a faction within the SLP calling itself the Communist Unity Group, the Hands Off Russia Movement, the ILP Left-Wing, the BSP, the People's Russian Information Bureau, the South Wales Socialist Society, and the Workers Socialist Federation (WSF). Of the three political parties that received 'subsidies' the industrial unionist SLP regarded the Bolsheviks as the 'Russian wing of the SLP' and, along with the WSF, opposed affiliation to the Labour Party; while the BSP, which had the largest number of Russian political emigres and 'foreign' Jews in its ranks, was essentially reformist and remained affiliated to the Labour

Party. In October 1919 the BSP branches voted overwhelmingly in favour of affiliation to both the Labour Party and the Communist International. Rothstein's arguments, having combined two presumably irreconcilable sets of belief in a *union sacree* – Sovietism and Parliamentarianism – had brought the majority of the BSP into support for the Comintern line:

> This line does not by any means imply that we must abandon parliamentary warfare, just as it does not mean that we must leave our trade unions. Any opportunity or place for our propaganda is good for us, whether it be an election platform, or the floor of the House of Commons, or the meeting of our trade union branch. What we must bear in mind, and what we must propagate, is that the Revolution will not come about through the instrumentality of Parliament or the trade unions, but by the direct action, political and economic of the rank and file through their politico-economical organisations of the Soviet type.[88]

Rothstein found it more difficult to bring about a change in the SLP and the WSF. All the revolutionary socialist parties, including the BSP, were agreed on the establishment of a Communist Party on the principles of the Dictatorship of the Proletariat, the Soviet System and the Communist International. The SLP and WSF, however, were opposed to unity with the BSP on the grounds that their anti-parliamentary views would be swamped by the parliamentary ambitions of the BSP in an unholy alliance with the Parliamentary Labour Party. They were certainly swimming against the tide of communist opinion. On 6 January 1920 Britain ended her 'economic blockade' of Soviet Russia and warmed to the idea of trade negotiations; a major victory for 'expediency' over 'principle'. By strengthening the positions of the parliamentarians in the revolutionary movement and of those politicians in the government seeking a normalisation of relations, the promise of a trade agreement with Russia, ushered in by the ending of economic sanctions, put the negotiations for a Communist Party in Britain on a very different footing.

9

The CPGB and 'Hands Off Russia'; 'Zionism versus Bolshevism'; Enter Zinoviev

Listen, Brother Pollitt. I can see through your game. This strike is to help Russia, not Poplar.

Harry Pollitt, *Serving My Time*, p. 97

it may well be that this same astonishing race [the Jews] may at the present time be in the actual process of producing another system of morals and philosophy, as malevolent as Christianity was benevolent, which, if not arrested, would shatter irretrievably all that Christianity has rendered possible. It would almost seem as if the gospel of Christ were destined to originate among the same people; and that this mystic and mysterious race had been chosen for the supreme manifestations, both of the divine and the diabolical

Winston Churchill, 'Zionism versus Bolshevism. A Struggle For The Soul Of The Jewish People,' *Illustrated Sunday Herald*, 8 June 1920

We have to state again that the most vital part of the struggle must be outside of Parliament – on the street. It is clear that the most effective weapons of the workers against capitalism are the strike, the revolt, armed insurrection. Comrades have to keep in mind the following: organisation of the Party, instalment of Party groups in the trade unions, leadership of the

masses, revolutionary agitation among the masses, etc.
Parliamentary activities and participation in elections must
be used only as a secondary measure – no more.

Zinoviev, quoted in *The Call*, 22 April 1920

The revolutionary crisis that had overtaken Russia and Central
Europe in 1917 appeared to be on the wane in 1920. 'Citizen
History' was at last beginning to impose itself upon the principal
actors of the period. 'Re-reading the parliamentary debates on the
war of intervention against revolutionary France in the 1790s'
British Prime Minister Lloyd George concluded that the French
war of intervention had done 'more harm than good'. It had simply
acted as 'the catalyst that brought Napoleon Bonaparte to power',
and had led to 'the great war that lasted until 1815 and the
introduction of income tax into Britain.'[1] Overruling Churchill and
other diehards in the governing coalition he agreed to pull British
troops out of Russia by the end of the year; while Lenin, for his part,
drifted away from world revolution towards parliamentarianism
and acceptance of a non-revolutionary British road to socialism. In
effect, the 'dual policy' was in the making.

Towards the end of 1919 and January 1920 Lenin began
collecting material on Britain for his pamphlet *Left-Wing
Communism: An Infantile Disorder* from three main sources: Joe
Fineberg, who had returned to Russia in June 1918 and was
advising Lenin on the question of Communist Party affiliation to
the Labour Party;[2] George Lansbury during the latter's visit to
Moscow in January 1920; and his agent inside MI7(d), Theodore
Rothstein. Of the three Rothstein truly believed in the inevitability
of revolution in Britain; but he was less convinced of its imminence.
Following his conversations with Lansbury Lenin also came to this
conclusion and spoke out in favour of parliamentarianism as a
means of preparing Britain for communism, and opposed any
adventurist attempts by revolutionaries in the industrial
organisations to make a bid for power.

On 22 January 1920, *The Call* published an article from Tom
Quelch[3] entitled 'Parliamentarianism, Lenin and the BSP', which

claimed Lenin's support for the BSP's pro-Parliamentary stand. In this article, Quelch referred to a letter from Lenin addressed to 'a leading English Communist' that had been published in the September 1919 edition of *Kommunisticheskii Internatsional*, extracts of which had appeared in the *Newcastle Daily Journal*, favouring participation in parliamentary elections by a revolutionary party.[4] Rothstein, too, contributed a lengthy article on 'Revolutionary Perspectives in England' to the *Kommunisticheskii Internatsional*, which addressed many of the issues Lenin would later raise in *Left-Wing Communism* concerning the British communist movement and affiliation to the Labour Party. Rothstein's article suggested that Britain had reached the same political stage of historical development within the Marxist scheme of history as Russia had on the eve of the 1917 February Revolution. All sections of society, Rothstein argued, expected a Labour Government to be formed in the near future. The reactionary nature of this Government, he asserted, would force the working-class movement further and further towards the left. The bourgeoisie, finding itself unable to resume political power, would stage a coup d'état along the lines of Kornilov or Kapp in Germany, leading to Britain's October Revolution. The proper place for British communists, therefore, was inside the Labour Party struggling for a communist programme and preparing the ground for the second Soviet stage of the British revolution, which would follow inevitably the demise of the Labour Government.[5] In short Lenin needed his trade agreement with Britain and was prepared to compromise. The British Revolution could wait; the historical conditions were those of February not October 1917; 'Comrade History' was not so different from 'Citizen History'; both counselled caution.

While Lloyd George and Lenin were engaged in moderating their positions, however, other dangerous trends came to the surface. On 8 February 1920 Churchill published an article in the *Illustrated Sunday Herald* entitled 'Zionism versus Bolshevism' which suggested that the Jews had been, and remained, the mainstay of the October Revolution; while on 22 April Grigorii

Zinoviev, President of the Comintern, issued a wild statement on behalf of the Executive Committee of the Communist International (ECCI) on the British situation which drew a distinction between 'parliamentarism, which sought to change the present system constitutionally through Parliament, and Sovietism which sought to use parliamentarism for overthrowing Parliament'.[6]

Churchill's article pitting Zionism against Bolshevism was provocative and anti-Semitic in tone and sought to set Jew against Jew, ostensibly West End Jewry against East End Jewry:

> it may well be that this same astonishing race [the Jews] may at the present time be in the actual process of producing another system of morals and philosophy, as malevolent as Christianity was benevolent, which, if not arrested, would shatter irretrievably all that Christianity has rendered possible. It would almost seem as if the gospel of Christ were destined to originate among the same people; and that this mystic and mysterious race had been chosen for the supreme manifestations, both of the divine and the diabolical.[7]

In this article Churchill's view of world Jewry divided the Jews into three political types: one 'good', one 'bad' and the other 'indifferent'.[8] The 'good' Jew was the national Jew, an Englishman who practised the Jewish faith and responded with undivided loyalty to the host nation. He contributed positively to finance and industry and played his part in progressive politics and military service. In stark contrast was the 'bad' Jew – the 'international Jew', 'the revolutionary Jew', in particular the 'Marxist revolutionary Jew'. This type of Jew was 'destructive and dangerous', witness the Russian Revolution:

> With the notable exception of Lenin, the majority of the leading figures are Jews. Moreover, the principal inspiration and driving power comes from the Jewish leaders. Thus Tchitcherin, a pure Russian, is eclipsed by his nominal subordinate Litvinoff, and the Russians like Bukharin and

Lunacharski cannot be compared with the power of Trotsky, or of Zinovieff, the Dictator of the Red Citadel (Petrograd), or of Krasin or Radek – all Jews [...] although [...] there are many non-Jews every whit as bad as the worst of the Jewish revolutionaries, the part played by the latter in proportion to their numbers in the population is astonishing.[9]

In opposing any form of agreement with Soviet Russia, Churchill praised the idealism of the 'Zionist Jew', which he promoted as an antidote to the 'Bolshevik Jew'. According to Churchill the creation of a Jewish homeland in Palestine, under British auspices, would serve not only as 'a refuge for the oppressed' but would embody 'a national idea of a commanding character' for the benefit of world Jewry. Not only would it 'be especially in harmony with the truest interests of the British Empire', but it would be in the interest of Europe as a whole. The crux of Churchill's message 'was that a Jewish centre in the Middle East would syphon Jewish energies away from radical politics in the west.'[10]

No less alarming was the statement issued by the Jewish Bolshevik Zinoviev, 'Dictator of the Red Citadel of Petrograd', on behalf of the ECCI calling for a Communist Revolution in Britain. 'We have to state again', Zinoviev wrote, 'that the most vital part of the struggle must be outside of Parliament – on the street. It is clear that the most effective weapons of the workers against capitalism are the strike, the revolt, armed insurrection. Comrades have to keep in mind the following: organisation of the Party, instalment of Party groups in the trade unions, leadership of the masses, revolutionary agitation among the masses, etc. Parliamentary activities and participation in elections must be used only as a secondary measure – no more.'[11]

All three tendencies – the normalisation of relations and the signing of an Anglo-Soviet trade agreement; Zionism versus Bolshevism; and 'direct action' versus 'parliamentarism' – sprang directly from the October Revolution and had a profound effect on Anglo-Soviet relations in 1920. All three sat uncomfortably alongside Bolshevik idealism, and sowed divisions among British revolutionaries. The formal Polish declaration of war on Soviet Russia on 26 April 1920 changed the dynamics dramatically.[12] Churchill persuaded Lloyd George to send military aid to the Poles while a new wave of pogroms carried out by anti-Bolshevik forces incensed the East End's Jewish population; West End Jewry no less so. Lucien Woolf, 'the *de facto* "Foreign Secretary" of British Jewry',[13] remarked in his diary:

> I was convinced that doctrinally the overwhelming mass of Jews of all classes, were opposed to Bolshevism; but what could these poor people do when the anti-Bolshevik forces – the Poles, the Ukrainians, the Roumanians, the armies of Kolchak and Denikin, the Siberian armies and now even the British Expeditionary Forces – were insisting that they were all Bolshevists; and were making war on them as such?
>
> They were, in fact, being driven into Bolshevism whether they liked it or not.[14]

On the second anniversary of the October Revolution the liberal progressive *Jewish Guardian* claimed that 'about half the Jews in Russia were now pro-Bolshevik'; while the *Jewish World* defended Bolshevism:

> Bolshevism, however crazy as a form of government, however [. . .] undemocratic – and Lenin himself had had to make vast concessions of his communistic theories – is not necessarily a creed of bloodshed and slaughter [. . .] such as it has been represented doubtless with some substratum of truth, but equally doubtlessly, with immense exaggeration. The stand that Bolshevism has made rather goes to show that it has a great hold upon the Russian people and [. . .] it is surely for the Russian people only to determine the form of Government they themselves wish.[15]

Lenin, unlike Churchill, rarely visited the Jewish question but during the war of intervention he recorded a gramophone record in which he defined anti-Semitism 'as the spreading of enmity against the Jews', and regarded the pogroms against the Jews during the war as reminiscent of the 'last hours' of the 'damnable Tsarist monarchy' when attempts were made 'to divert the illiterate workers and peasants into pogroms against the Jews.' Capital, he observed, in its last hours was peddling the same vice: 'Even in other countries one often experiences that the capitalists stir up enmity against the Jews, in order to divert the attention of the workers from the real enemy of the working masses, capital.'[16]

The occupation of Kiev by Polish forces on 8 May made military defeat of the Bolsheviks likely. For Lenin the formation of a Communist Party in Britain able to put domestic pressure on the British Government to stop the war became an urgent priority. On 10 May London dockers refused to load a ship with ammunition bound for Danzig in what became known as the *Jolly George* incident'. This was 'Direct Action' in keeping with Zinoviev's wilder statements on behalf of the Executive Committee of the Communist International calling for industrial action for political purposes. As such, it was a new and dangerous departure from the norm, and certain to give rise to claims that the interests of the State were being endangered. The *Jolly George* incident' coincided with the arrival of the Soviet Trade Delegation in London headed by Leonid Krasin, whose secretary, Nikolai Klishko, an OGPU agent, had a covert agenda of a more political nature. In August, a national conference of Labour set up Councils of Action to enforce a general ban on the movement of munitions intended for Russia.

Thirteen days after the *Jolly George* incident' Basil Thomson informed the Home Secretary, Herbert Samuel, that the 'agitation against the Polish offensive is undoubtedly spreading from the Labour Press to the Trade Union officials and is meeting with a certain response from the rank and file.

> It is not unlikely that the railwaymen will come into line with the dockers and refuse to handle material. This action appears entirely to be conducted by the 'Daily Herald.' The 'Daily

Herald' is causing considerable mischief by its incessant agitation on behalf of Soviet Russia. On May 26th it published a facsimile of a label taken from a railway wagon at Stockport and alleged that the shells destined for Roumania were designed for use against Russia. Following upon the dockers' conference to which I referred in my last report, the Executive Committee of the Miners' Federation of Great Britain has decided to exert pressure on the Government to 'cease support of Polish intervention'. The officials of the National Union of Railwaymen have also resolved to instruct their members to refuse to handle any material which is intended to assist Poland. The congress of the National Union of General Workers indicated that its members would be similarly advised. Members of the Russian Trading Delegation, except Krasin, who elected to be bound by an honourable undertaking, have all signed promises to abstain from interference in political questions in this country. Klishko, who is acting as Secretary, has already broken his undertaking. It is believed that Krasin himself may be trusted but there is definite evidence that Nogin and Rosovsky, to say nothing of the others, have agreed to get in touch with the Sinn Fein organization if an opportunity occurs.[17]

Nevertheless, despite the subversive activities of his colleagues Krasin continued to make good progress and a trade agreement looked likely. The All-Russian Co-operative Society (Arcos), a private British company but under ultimate Russian control, was registered on the London Stock Exchange on 11 June 1920. It quickly entered into negotiations with various firms and some contracts were signed for the eventual supply of goods.[18] *The Times* newspaper, following a survey of business leaders, admitted that there was a 'growing volume of opinion in favour of trade being resumed.' The Soviet Trade Delegation, however, had descended upon Britain with an agenda other than trade. In June the talks faltered on the British demand that propaganda directed against the British Empire and the governments of the *Entente* should stop. Moscow, on the other hand, insisted on a comprehensive peace treaty before any agreement to end anti-British activities by communists could be concluded. On 16 June Krasin issued a veiled threat to Lloyd George that Soviet foreign policy operated on two levels, dominated by two opposing groups – the one seeking trade and the normalisation of relations while the other, 'a minority [...] preferred world revolution to world peace'.[19]

To maintain pressure on Lloyd George the formation of a united communist party in Britain affiliated to the Labour Party and shorn of its wilder revolutionary elements was now a matter of some urgency; Lenin's overall design to isolate this 'minority' in his own party informed Krasin's negotiating strategy. A trade agreement with Britain would not merely undermine 'Left Communism'[20] in Russia; but would also help secure full diplomatic recognition, and the protection of the Soviet State in the world system of States. A Communist Party in Britain affiliated to the Labour Party would be in a position to exploit the parliamentary system in order to both promote communist ideals and guarantee the diplomatic status of Soviet Russia. A combative Communist Party concentrating solely on revolutionary propaganda and extra-parliamentary activity would have the opposite effect. At one last meeting on 29 June before his return to Russia on 1 July Krasin told Lloyd George that his Government was ready to give up communist propaganda in Western countries in exchange for a trade agreement.[21]

In July 1920, however, the Red Army went on the offensive and after a series of decisive victories against the Polish Army in Ukraine threatened to occupy Warsaw. At the Second Congress of the Comintern there were renewed calls for a European revolutionary war and for the Red Army to support an anticipated communist uprising in Germany. Although Lenin was less enthusiastic than many in his Party he saw in this situation an opportunity to put additional pressure on Lloyd George. By the end of July Krasin was on his way back to London from Moscow accompanied by a member of the Politburo, Lev Kamenev,[22] who took over as head of the Soviet delegation in what amounted to a 'good cop – bad cop' routine. According to Thomson after 'the arrival of Kameneff they conducted their campaign for secretly undermining the morale of the country with consummate ability.'[23] An intercepted cypher message from Litvinov to Chicherin at this time informed British intelligence that Litvinov was insisting that Rothstein must be included on the new Delegation:

> July 12th LITVINOFF to TCHITCHERIN (003314) 'I am herewith transmitting extracts from cyphered messages received from MOTSART (i.e. ROTHSTEIN)'. Then follows the latter's criticism of KRASIN's negotiations which ends with:- 'after having worked for 20 years in the Socialist movement and for 2 years as your (?unofficial receiver), having given up my literary work and connections, I now find myself with nothing to do. Ask Moscow to re-call me without fail'. LITVINOFF then adds 'I insist that MOTSART [Rothstein] be included in the new Delegation'.

And again:

> July 22nd LIVINOFF to TCHITCHERINE 003519 'Is ROTHSTEIN included in the Delegation for if not he can be arrested and deported?'[24]

Litvinov's persistence paid off and by the end of the month the trade delegation was made up of Krasin, Kamenev, Miliutin and Rothstein. At this time all of Rothstein's cyphered messages to Litvinov, and those from Litvinov to Chicherin were being intercepted and decrypted.[25] Bolshevik codes had been broken as early as November 1919 by Ernst K. Fetterlein, the Tsar's chief codebreaker, who had fled to England in May 1918. He had joined Room 40 housed in the Admiralty Old Building in Whitehall before moving to Watergate House and the newly created Government Code and Cypher School (GC&CS) on the 1 November 1919, where he began working on the Russian codes.

Throughout 1920, therefore, the British Government enjoyed an invaluable insight into the covert acts of the Soviet Trade Delegation and Rothstein's activities in promoting Communist Unity. On 23 September Thomson 'estimated that at least £100,000 of Russian money has been spent on revolutionary propaganda in England during the last nine months.'[26] The most ambitious plan for Soviet financial intervention in British politics was the scheme to subsidise the *Daily Herald*, which was monitored closely by Thomson's sleuths. In 1920 the paper was confronted with a near embargo on supplies from British paper merchants, and was experiencing difficulty in obtaining the necessary supplies of paper from Scandinavia. A cable was intercepted from Litvinov to the Soviet Trade Delegation on 22 July instructing the Delegation to 'Hand over money or papers (? securities) to FRANCIS through MOTSART [Rothstein] who should immediately inform FRANCIS of the reception of the papers for him.'

FRANCIS was Francis Meynell, a long-standing friend of Wilfrid Scawen Blunt, a director of the *Daily Herald* and the youngest child of poet Alice Meynell. Meynell had approached Rothstein privately asking for his help in securing the *Herald*'s future. Rothstein introduced him to members of the Soviet Trade Delegation at a dinner party at the fashionable Floral Frascati's restaurant in Oxford Street. Frascati, celebrated for its cosmopolitanism, luxury and excellent cuisine, prided itself on its floral displays and its wonderful orchestra accompanying the dancers on a wooden dance floor shaped like a banjo. The *Daily Herald* was losing £1,000 a week when Meynell raised the question of a subsidy over dinner.[27]

It was agreed that Meynell should visit Litvinov, who was then in Copenhagen negotiating an exchange of prisoners taken in the War of Intervention with Jim O'Grady (the British representative). The British Government had refused Ivy Litvinov permission to join her husband in Denmark and an elaborate plot was entered into at Frascati's to secure funding for the *Daily Herald* involving Meynell's sister, Viola Meynell, a close friend of

Ivy Litvinov's. Viola was to call on Ivy and collect a gift for her husband that her brother would legitimately carry in his luggage on a trip to Copenhagen. The gift, a spotted necktie, would contain a secret 'note from Rothstein:

> When I reached Copenhagen I telephoned Litvinoff in his hotel and was bidden to visit him. He left his sitting-room door open when I arrived, saying loudly that he always did this when he had visitors. He wanted to reassure the window-cleaner and the bannister-polisher on the landing (who, oddly, enough, always arrived at the same time as the visitors) that no funny business was afoot.
>
> I said, 'Here, dear Maxim, is a present from Ivy', and gave him a carefully parcelled new tie in which was sewn a note from Rothstein, who was substituting for Litvinoff in London. Maxim thanked me with an understanding glance and went into his bed-room. In a few minutes he returned, wearing the new tie. When we were seated, and chatting, the door open all the time, he said, 'You English, are great pipe smokers. Here is some Russian tobacco to try and he tossed me a tobacco pouch. I knew that he knew that I never smoked a pipe, so I guessed that the pouch contained an answer to Rothstein. It did – a practical one; for when I got back to my hotel I opened the pouch and found two strings of pearls.[28]

Meynell made a number of such trips to Copenhagen, each time transporting jewels back to Rothstein for sale on London's black market. On one such trip he posted a large and expensive box of chocolate creams, each containing a pearl or diamond, to his friend the philosopher and future broadcaster Cyril Joad.[29] Once back in London Meynell was taken to Scotland Yard and searched but nothing was found. Two days later Meynell and his wife recovered their chocolates from Joad and 'spent a sickly hour sucking the chocolates and so retrieving the jewels.'[30] On another occasion, he was stopped on his return and his baggage searched. 'The sleuths', he later recalled 'were helpful in repacking, but I found it difficult to thank them and at the same time prevent three large diamonds in my mouth from rattling.'[31]

The importance of Meynell's trips to Copenhagen cannot be understated. The *Daily Herald* was widely read by the working classes, and was the only daily newspaper to consistently support the Comintern and Russian government. An intercepted telegram, signed by Rozovsky, Rothstein and Klishko, sent to Moscow on 14 July stated that 'we are making use of the "Daily Herald" for purposes of information and agitation'.[32] Since there was little chance of establishing a daily communist newspaper in Britain Litvinov believed that the *Daily Herald* should be supported whatever the cost. Fearing that unless the *Herald* resolved its financial difficulties it would have to turn sharply to the right thereby depriving the Comintern of a newspaper which 'in Russian questions acts as if it were our organ'[33] there followed a whole series of cable exchanges between Litvinov and Chicherin regarding the possibilities of subsidizing the *Daily Herald*', all of which were intercepted and decoded by GC&CS:

> Among the remittances received by Rothstein from Russia was a packet of diamonds. Some of these now adorn the persons of Mrs. Rothstein and her daughter, but the rest have been converted into money [...] Besides the Bolshevik code, of which the Authorities possess a copy, Rothstein has a password, which is confided to very few persons.[34]

Basil Thomson knew from agents placed inside the labour movement and from cable intercepts that Rothstein's codename was MOTSART (Mozart), and that MOTSART was working closely with Meynell. He also knew, from the same source, that the Soviet Trading Delegation was financing the *Daily Herald*:

> The Russian Delegation [...] appear to have felt it safer to communicate Soviet Government news to the 'Herald' than to deliver money from hand to hand. For this purpose they appointed an intermediary, one Mozart, who was to receive the

money from the delegation and to deliver it to Francis Meynell. It has now been pretty conclusively proved that this Mozart is no other than Theodore Rothstein, and the name Mozart is an anagram of the Yiddish Dmsart = Red-stone = German: Rothstein.[35]

It was now only a matter of time before the authorities closed down the Rothstein network and curtailed the activities of the Russian Trading Delegation. When Klishko was summoned to Scotland Yard on 28 May 1920 to be interviewed by Thomson, it was made clear to him that Rothstein's secret agent career in London was all but over:

> Ques. We know a good deal more than you think we do. There is no object in telling you all I do know. But it is rather a dangerous game from your point of view. You all agreed that you came over only on this question of trade. Our complaint is that you are not playing the game by us.
> Ans. You consider that I, personally, have not played the game on this matter.
>
> Ques. [...] I will tell you what you probably already know; Mr. Theodore ROTHSTEIN has been acting as an agent of the Soviet Government for many months in this country, with my full knowledge. Our policy here is that when we know a thing we can easily deal with it when the time comes. [...] Yes. You understand [...] I think you will be well advised to cut off relations with Mr. Rothstein until we settle about him. He has for a long time been interfering in politics here. We do not think it important enough to take any action, but there comes a time when it may be expedient to act. After all, he is a Russian.
> Ans. I quite see that.[36]

Klishko, who was apparently visibly unsettled by this encounter, immediately made contact with Meynell and asked him to look after a number of platinum bars for the Russian Trade Delegation:

'There is danger' he [Klishko] told me, 'that we shall be expelled. We have here a large quantity of platinum. We do not want to take it with us. Will you guard it for us till our return?' I agreed, and struggled down the stairs with a barely portable suitcase in each hand. In the street I hailed a taxi. The first suitcase went safely in. When I lifted the second its handle came off and several wrapped bars of platinum fell on the pavement. A policeman helped me lift them on to the taxi's floor. 'Heavy, ain't they?' he said.[37]

Rothstein was less fortunate. Thomson's agents followed him to a converted Pullman car at Top Hill, Cunsey Back, Windermere, where he was known to be co-ordinating the secret negotiations for the formation of a Communist Party in Great Britain.[38] A Unity Convention was due to be held in London on the 31 July although two of the main factions, the executive of the SLP and Pankhurst's WSF, were refusing to attend; leaving the BSP and the SLP's Communist Unity Group the dominant groups. Rothstein's BSP vastly outnumbered the SLP; 'three-fifths of the delegates represented branches of the BSP, as against only one-sixth from SLP branches. The remainder were accredited by local independent Socialist societies, Shop Stewards and Workers' committees, Guild Socialist groups, and so on.'[39] The question of affiliation to the Labour Party was discussed on the second day; despite Rothstein's activities behind the scenes, and the publication of Lenin's *Left-Wing Communism* the resolution in favour of affiliation was passed by only a small majority – 100 to 85. Full unity had yet to be achieved and an eight-member committee (four BSP, four SLP) was set up with an additional six persons elected by the Convention to finalise proceedings.

In the meantime, Sylvia Pankhurst had tried to seize the initiative from Rothstein by declaring the WSF the Communist Party (British Section of the Third International) in June 1920. To distance itself from Pankhurst the newly formed BSP-SLP committee declared itself the Communist Party of Great Britain, and under that name it applied for affiliation to the Labour Party on the 10 August, which was rejected unanimously by the Labour Party National Executive. Pankhurst, at this time, was in Moscow attending the Second Congress of the Communist International where she complained to Lenin that she had been denied funding by Rothstein. As a consequence, Rothstein returned to Russia apparently on Chicherin's orders[40] to report on the progress being made towards Communist Unity in Britain. Thomson triumphantly observed: 'Rothstein's recall to Moscow is connected with Miss Pankhurst's presence in that city. She claims Rothstein has appropriated for his personal use money given him for propaganda and that he has mismanaged propaganda in this country. Orders have been issued that Rothstein shall be refused leave to land if he should return to this country.'[41]

An alternative version of these events is given by Andrew Rothstein who in a 1981 letter to the author stated that his father returned to Moscow simply as a result of his own request. He asked to accompany Miliutin of the Russian Trading Delegation who was returning 'to report on progress in the peace talks with Lloyd George [. . .] TR specifically asked to be allowed to go, not having been back for 29 years. In fact there is a letter from Lenin which missed him, pressing him not to go, because the British Government might play some dirty trick on him!'[42] Lenin's letter to Theodore Rothstein dated 15 July 1920 reads: ' I am not against your coming "to take a look" at Russia, but I am afraid that to quit Britain is harmful for the work'.[43] Moreover, an intercepted telegram from Rothstein to Chicherin dated 19 July advising him 'to allow Pankhurst to enter Russia' had referred 'to money and valuables received by her from him and his dealings with her in January 1920.'[44] Thomson may well have got it wrong.

On 10 August Rothstein left with Miluitin for Reval, present-day Tallinn, on a destroyer. Not missing a trick he attempted to subvert the British crew on the way.[45] The following day R. F., a MI5 agent, sent a letter to Thomson informing him that

Andrew ROTHSTEIN, a British born subject, son of Theodore ROTHSTEIN [...] has applied for a visa to visit Russia. In view of the fact', R. F. continued, 'that you consider his father to be the Bolshevik secret agent here, I would be greatly obliged if you would let me have your views on the desirability of granting him any facilities.'[46] His reply to R.F.'s letter was addressed to Kell and was quite pointed: 'I have to inform you that the Passport Office has been acquainted by the Director of Intelligence that it would be unwise to with-hold a passport in this case.'[47]

Rothstein had been grooming his son as his successor for some time. Thomson knew by this time that Theodore Rothstein was not going to be allowed back in the country and wanted to keep tabs on Andrew. On his visit to Russia in November he was accompanied by one of Thomson's agents who reported on his every move in Moscow. Kell and Thomson, at this time, were engaged in a fierce struggle for control over British intelligence, and the Rothstein deportation saga appears to have been part of this 'turf war' with Thomson wanting to monitor the chief Bolshevik agent [and his son] in London; while Kell simply wanted to deport him. On the sixteenth Kamenev wired to Chicherin, intercepted by GC&CS, 'to send ROTHSTEIN back immediately'.[48]

As soon as he was out of the country the government declared Rothstein *persona non grata* and took the necessary steps to deny him a re-entry visa, dispatching a Foreign Office cypher telegram on 31 August, classified SECRET, to the British Embassies in Christiana (present day Oslo), Helsingfors (Helsinki), Reval (Tallinn), Riga and Stockholm:

> Pending a Cabinet decision on the subject of the Russian Delegation in London. Messrs. Milutin and Rothstein now in Russia are not to be permitted to return to this country. Should they apply for visas, you should refuse on the ground that no instructions to visa their passports have been received from England. You should report by telegraph if any such application is made.[49]

A further telegram dated 11 September reported that the 'Cabinet have now declared that persons named therein [Miliutin and Rothstein] are not permitted to return to this country. You should therefore definitely refuse visas on this ground.'[50] The long-standing saga over whether or not Rothstein should be dismissed from MI7 and deported to Russia had finally come to an end. His brother Albert, a naturalized British citizen remained in Leeds.[51]

10

Prising Open the Lion's Jaws

Perhaps I am too much of an 'Easterner' nowadays, and you are less optimistic. Would it be too much to ask you to write down your views, in any form or length you please, for the young men I speak of? They asked me the other day whether there was reasonable hope of obtaining an article from you on Egypt: pointing out that a really critical stage in Anglo-Egyptian relations has again arrived. And I agree with them that today, when there are greater possibilities than ever there were before for prising open the lion's jaws – with the new social lever of the proletariat – the observations of one of the oldest enemies of imperialism must obviously be of very great value.[1]

> Andrew Rothstein to Wifred Scawen Blunt,
> 19 November 1921

This kind of mosquito bite won't scare the British elephant.
Jan A. Berzin to Maxim Litvinov, May 1923

Leave the mosquito alone and go after the elephant.
Unknown MI5 officer, 22.xi.22

With Theodore Rothstein back in Russia[2] his communist activities in Britain devolved to his son, Andrew. Born in Hackney on 26 September 1898 Andrew Rothstein had received an excellent, progressive education at the prestigious Owen's School, Goswell Road, Islington. Founded by Dame Alice Owen and the Worshipful Company of Brewers in 1613, Owen's School was then a prestigious, mixed, partially selective secondary school. Entrance was based on examination, and places were offered on the basis of academic and musical ability. Andrew was a gifted scholar, and in 1916 he won a Brackenbury Scholarship to read History at Balliol College, Oxford. His studies, however, were interrupted by World War I when he was called up in 1917 to serve with the Hampshire Yeomanry. In 1918 he was transferred to the Meteorological Section of the Royal Engineers and stationed at Stonehenge, Wiltshire. He served in Ireland and was by all accounts a good soldier earning promotion to the rank of Lance Corporal. Between January and February 1919 he played a minor role in the soldiers' strikes calling for the immediate demobilisation of troops and an end to the policy of military intervention in Russia. He returned to Balliol College in October 1919 where he was placed under MI5 surveillance; their reports identifying him as the 'leader of the Communist set at Oxford and an extremely active propagator of intellectual Bolshevism.'[3]

During World War I and the 1920s Balliol College, which had long enjoyed a reputation as a 'reforming college,'[4] educated a number of radical students who were openly communist and who went on to have distinguished academic and political careers. Among them Rajane Palme Dutt, Tom Wintringham (also a Brackenbury Scholar), David Platts-Mills and Christopher Hill; under the expert guidance of G. D. H. Cole, Balliol pioneered the academic study of labour history.

A particularly able student, Andrew Rothstein 'just missed getting a first in Schools in June, 1920, because he could not keep his opinions [Marxist] out of his answers'; subsequently the authorities of Balliol refused him permission to continue in residence.[5] His own and his father's communist activities were strongly condemned by the Chancellor of the University of Oxford, the then Secretary of State at the F.O. and former Balliol College student, Lord Curzon, who denounced Andrew Rothstein as 'a very dangerous Communist' who 'must not be allowed to stay'. His army grant-funding was withdrawn, and his application for postgraduate study refused. At the time his activities on behalf of his father in 'Hands Off Russia' and the newly formed Councils of Action[6] were being closely monitored by the Government Code & Cypher School (GC&CS) who were intercepting and deciphering most, if not all, of the cable traffic between Moscow and London. It was clear, as this wire from Chicherin to Litvinov despatched on the 9 September 1920 made plain, that almost a month after his father's arrival in Moscow, Andrew Rothstein was being groomed to take over his father's propaganda activities and he was now working closely with Kamenev of the Russian Trade Delegation:

> ROTHSTEIN desires me to transmit to you the following: 'I notice in the papers an inclination on the part of the Council of Action towards the side of agreement with adaptability to the policy of the British Government. This is unavoidable, having regard to the present composition of the Council, and therefore I should consider necessary the energetic continuation of the agitation among the masses themselves through the Committees of "Hands off Russia" and the ruthless exposure of the traitorous tendencies of the Council through the Communist Party. Communicate this view of mine to KAMENEFF for transmission to my son and instruct KAMENEFF to offer £500 for the use of the Committee indicated.'[7]

Kamenev was deported from Britain two days after this wire was intercepted. At this time MI5 were taking a particular interest in the political activities of the entire Rothstein family and it was noted in Andrew Rothstein's file that the Zionist Organisation had recommended his uncle, Samuel Rothstein, along with Morris Meyer, a leading figure in Poale Zion ('Workers of Zion')[8] to travel to Palestine. At the end of the year the Director of National Intelligence (DNI), Basil Thomson, approved the issue of a passport to Andrew Rothstein enabling him to visit his father in Russia, despite Kell's reservations.[9] He travelled to Moscow in December with two Oxford undergraduate friends, according to MI5 files, and there achieved some notoriety at a Moscow dinner party by claiming to be 'primarily responsible for the preparation of the list of persons to be shot in England when the Red revolution dawned. When asked by another diner how he selected persons for inclusion on this list, he refused to give any understandable answer.'[10] On his return to London in December 1920 he joined the Soviet Trade Delegation as Press Surveyor in the Trade Delegation's Information Bureau and served as the main link between the Soviet Government and the CPGB. On 11 December, MI5 remarked on his connection with Klishko, the secretary of the Soviet Trade Delegation, reporting that the two men had attended the first annual dinner of the Hampstead Communist Party along with one of the Dutts.[11] This was an interesting trio. The two Dutt brothers, Clemens and Rajani, were founder members of the CPGB.[12] Clemens, the older of the two, had graduated in botany from Queen's College, Cambridge; while Rajani took a double first from Balliol College, Oxford, despite being expelled from the university in 1917 for disseminating Marxist propaganda. Rajani's future wife, the Estonian communist Salme Murrik, arrived in Britain in 1920 as a representative of the Comintern; while Clemens Dutt married Violet Lansbury, the youngest daughter of George Lansbury. In October 1920 a Home Office Warrant (HOW) was taken out on the Dutt's correspondence largely as a result of their meetings with Klishko.

Klishko, who had first arrived in England as a political refugee in 1907, had a history of subversive activity in Britain dating back to 1910. In that year he had been investigated by MO5(g) who noted that he was 'on friendly terms with well-known Russian nihilists, including Boris Kahan, the brother-in-law of Theodore Rothstein' and was a member of the Bolshevik faction of the Russian Social-Democratic Labour Party.[13] He was also known to have struck up a friendship with the Russian owner of a small engineering firm in Hoxton, in London's East End, called Belinsky, who Scotland Yard believed was involved in smuggling arms to Russian revolutionaries. Klishko was then working as a draughtsman and a translator in the Foreign Department of the armaments' firm Vickers.[14] Following his wife and son's return to Moscow in 1912 he rented a house with Litvinov in Kentish Town and began courting Phyllis

Frood, a manageress of a dressmaking business in London's West End. Early in 1916, when Litvinov was suspected by the authorities of being a German agent, Klishko went to live with Frood. His association with Litvinov, however, led to him being labelled a security risk by MI5 who questioned his continued employment at Vickers on the grounds that 'he was in possession of facts relating to the supply of munitions to Russia.'[15] Nevertheless, Vickers regarded Klishko favourably and refused to part with his services, arguing that he 'would cause less trouble' if he was permitted to remain. In October 1916, however, the Labour Department at Vickers raised concerns about Klishko's considerable influence over other Russian employees who held dangerous 'nihilist sympathies'. Following the February Revolution and the decision to extend the Military Services Act to Russians living in Britain Klishko extended his influence over Russians employed by Vickers after he successfully applied for exemption certificates for three Russians employed by Vickers (all of whom were under investigation by MI5) on the grounds that 'he [Klishko] personally had an exemption certificate from the Russian Army, granted to him by the Russian [presumably Revolutionary] Government.'[16] It was then decided to cancel his permit to work on munitions but on 16 October he was issued with a Russian diplomatic passport by the Russian Embassy in London, and the cancellation notice was withdrawn. He had been due to travel to Russia in November 1917 on behalf of Vickers, but because of the October Revolution the journey never took place.

Despite his pronounced Bolshevik sympathies he was allowed to continue working at Vickers but was kept under close surveillance. He was found to be working closely with Maxim Litvinov and Theodore Rothstein, MI5 reporting that he 'was receiving Press reports about developments in Russia and was acting as an unofficial agent of the Bolshevik regime in respect of their obtaining official recognition by the British Government and of the repatriation and support of political refugees in the U.K.'[17] MI5 now called for his deportation on the grounds that he was 'one of the most dangerous Bolsheviks in the U.K,' and

Special Branch raided the flat he shared with Phyllis Frood in search of incriminating evidence. Nothing was found, other than a copy of a letter Klishko had written to Sir Francis Barker, a director of Vickers, dated 27 December 1917, defending himself against charges that he had been engaged in subversive activities.[18] In July 1918 MI5 again advised his repatriation to Russia arguing 'that Bolshevism in the UK would suffer a distinct set-back through his departure.' As a result his permit to work on munitions was withdrawn; on 6 September he was interned in Brixton Prison under the Defence of the Realm Act and on 27 September, his name was added to the group of Russians to be expelled with Litvinov. He arrived back in Moscow on 2 February 1919 where he was appointed Assistant Director of the State Publishing House. He also worked closely with Krasin on the re-organisation of the Russian railways before returning to England in May 1920 as part of the Soviet Trade Delegation. He had been allowed to return after signing an undertaking that 'while in the United Kingdom [he] would not interfere in any way in the politics or internal affairs of the country'. Twelve days after his arrival he was interviewed by Basil Thomson who 'warned him not to associate with Theodore ROTHSTEIN, who was well-known to the Police as a Soviet Government agent.' Klishko, however, ignored Thomson's warning and maintained contact with Rothstein during the negotiations leading up to the creation of the CPGB in 1920. After the latter's expulsion he took over responsibility for propaganda and intelligence work among British Communists and well-wishers towards the Soviet Union. Andrew Rothstein was appointed his secretary and helped him in this work. It was later claimed, mistakenly, that Klishko had been the OGPU resident in the UK between 1920 and 1923, and that in May 1920 he had been attached to the Soviet trade delegation as the UK representative of the Comintern. However, Klishko was not a trained intelligence officer. His importance lay in his long experience of underground work in Britain in the pre-revolutionary period. The early work of Soviet intelligence in Britain was carried out by the Russian political émigré community who had gained considerable knowledge of conspiratorial work in the UK over a period of 25 years or more.

At the beginning of 1921 Andrew Rothstein was attached to the trade delegation as deputy correspondent to the Russian Telegraph Agency (Rosta), the state news agency of Soviet Russia.[19] He began writing for the Communist press in Britain using the pseudonyms Charles Roebuck and C. M. Roebuck. In April of that year he was appointed Manager of the Rosta office in London, he also worked closely with the Lansbury Group, which was then organising the unemployed in the East End London Borough of Poplar.[20]

George Lansbury and the *Daily Herald* had remained an influential propaganda outlet for the Bolsheviks since its solvency had been assured following Francis Meynell's visits to Litvinov in 1920 in search of funds. In 1921 the CPGB's newspaper *Communist*, edited by Meynell, reached a circulation of 60,000; while the *Daily Herald* enjoyed a circulation of between 200,000 and 300,000.[21] The Lansbury Group was an important contact for Andrew Rothstein and the Soviet Trade Delegation and kept them in touch with left-wing elements in the labour movement. In the autumn of 1921 with unemployment barely under 2 million the CPGB established the 'National Unemployed Workers' Committee Movement', and began recruiting among the unemployed. The Poplar Rates Revolt, or 'Poplarism' as the movement became widely known, became a *cause celebre* of the labour movement in 1921 when Lansbury and 30 councilors from Poplar Borough Council were jailed for six weeks for withholding contributions to the London County Council until the wealthier West End boroughs accepted a fairer share of relieving poverty in the East End. Selwyn Jackson of MI5's B Branch, Aliens division,[22] who had dealt with Samuel Rothstein's application to travel to Palestine, remarked in 1922 that: 'He [Andrew Rothstein] is now in intimate touch with the Soviet delegation and the Lansbury Group [...] the whole Rothstein family in this country [is] a constant and active danger. It may be noted that George Lansbury's son, Edgar, married one of the Rothstein girls, Minnie, who has recently died.'[23] A claim repeated by W. A. Phillips of MI5's A Branch to the passport office in May when dealing with Andrew Rothstein's application for a British passport to travel to Belgium, Holland, Germany, France and Italy; despite being a British citizen by birth Rothstein was told to travel on a Russian passport.[24] Minnie Lansbury, however, was never a Rothstein, she had been born in Stepney to Jewish parents, her father Isaac Glassman was a local coal merchant.[25]

Selwyn Jackson's coupling of Minnie Lansbury with the Rothstein family was disingenuous, and evidence of a growing tendency in MI5 to link legitimate labour protest with Bolshevik-inspired subversion. Kell's and Thomson's association with the Industrial Intelligence Bureau (IIB), the private industrial intelligence service of Sir George Makgill, a businessman with ultra-conservative views and a deep-rooted dislike of Trade Unionism, linked Britain's intelligence chiefs with what was referred to as 'the occult octopus' or what 'might today be called global capitalism.'[26]

The IIB was financed by the Federation of British Industries and the Coal Owners' and Shipowners' Associations to gather 'intelligence on industrial unrest arising from the activities of Communists, Anarchists, various secret societies in the UK and overseas, the Irish Republican Army and other "subversive" organisations'. From its inception Makgill's organisation established close ties with MI5, Special Branch officers and, through Churchill's future intelligence adviser Desmond Morton, MI1(c), the forerunner of MI6.[27] Although organised and financed by private interests, Makgill's intelligence service, therefore, had close official connections. It is clear that from an early stage Makgill had personal links with some members of MI5, and in particular with its head, Sir Vernon Kell; it was Kell who had introduced Makgill to Morton in 1920 or early 1921.

In a MI5 report discussing the CPGB's industrial strategy in the 1920s Theodore Rothstein was identified as the moving force behind the formation of Communist germ cells in British factories and the parliamentarian policy of the CPGB.[28] The two Communist tactics inside the labour movement that both the IIB and MI5 sought to counter:

The importance of the father [Theodore] may be gauged from the fact that the tactics laid down by Lenin for creating revolution in England, viz., through the formation of germ cells in factories etc., and the parliamentarian policy of the Communist Party in UK were based on Theodore Rothstein's reports and general views of the Labour movement and industrial conditions in this country.[29]

The creation of 'germ cells' in factories as a tactic was adopted by delegates to the Fourth Congress of the Communist International on 5 December 1922. 'No Communist Party', the 'Theses on Comintern Tactics' proclaimed, 'can consider itself a serious and well-organised mass Communist Party unless it has strong Communist cells in the factories, mills, mines, railways, etc.'[30] However, by definition, 'germ cells' were divisive and encouraged covert activity within the labour movement; not surprisingly, the Communists were regarded as an unwelcome threat by many labour officials. They also appeared to contradict recent Comintern directives calling for a temporary alliance between Communist and non-Communist workers to achieve short-term, immediate goals. The Comintern's United Front Tactic, ushered in under Zinoviev's guidance, had called upon Communists 'to join with all workers belonging to other parties and groups and all unaligned workers in a common struggle to defend the immediate, basic interests of the working class against the bourgeoisie.'[31] By these tactics Zinoviev had hoped to achieve the Bolsheviks' strategic goal of working class unity under Communist leadership. The United Front, however, was from the outset prone to disunity. The existence of 'germ cells' operating independently of the official labour movement led to the creation of two distinct factions – the United Front 'from below' and the United Front 'from above'. The supporters of the latter sought temporary rapprochements with non-Communist leaders of the labour movement and proved the more resilient; while the former, which aimed to separate non-communist workers from their socialist, social democratic or anarcho-syndicalist leaderships, struggled to make headway. The comparative success of the United

Front 'from above' interlaced communists with the official labour movement and encouraged Thomson, Kell and Makgill in their joint defence of 'the occult octopus' to target all sections of the British labour movement. That the 'Theses on Comintern Tactics' was indisputably an incendiary document, calling for civil war between the proletariat and the bourgeoisie, was never in doubt. It could only help legitimise the Thomson-Kell-Makgill intelligence alliance and prepare Special Branch, MI5 and the IIB for the class struggles that would define British society between 1922 and 1930.

Class politics dominated 1920s Britain and after the fall of Lloyd George's coalition government in November 1922, a genuine fear of a Labour Government manifested itself in the popular press. The outcome of the general election, a Conservative Government under Bonar Law, prompted a Conservative backlash against Lloyd George's policy of accommodation with the Soviets. The newly appointed Foreign Secretary, Lord Curzon, now demanded the curtailment of communist-backed anti-British propaganda in various parts of Asia in exchange for a trade agreement. A curious array of Conservative and Liberal political forces, 'a sort of three-sided tug-of-war between Lloyd George, Curzon and Churchill',[32] now came together to formulate a policy towards Soviet Russia that would eventuate in the signing of an Anglo-Soviet Trade Agreement on 16 March 1921, two days before the Peace of Riga ended the Polish-Soviet War. As a result the Soviet trade mission became a permanent presence in London, and a British Commercial Mission, headed by Robert M. Hodgson, opened in Moscow.[33]

According to Curzon, who had earlier personally intervened to get Rajani Palme Dutt and Andrew Rothstein expelled from Balliol College,[34] Anglo-Soviet relations hinged upon two crucial factors. Firstly, the knowledge that Russia critically needed trade with Britain and would 'pay almost any price for the assistance which we – more than anyone else – are in a position to give'; and, secondly, that an ending to communist subversion in the East, in India and Persia, was the price to be demanded.[35]

Following the Red Army's evacuation of Poland the Bolsheviks' First Deputy Commissar for Foreign Affairs, Lev Karakhan, had 'pressed for the invasion and occupation of Persia, so that, in his words, 'we become for England a serious and immediate menace and that we place our aggression in the East in direct dependence on England's policy toward us: we respond blow for blow.'[36] Curzon had long held the belief that the Russians were determined to one day take the whole of Persia and establish another point of pressure on India. The appointment of Theodore Rothstein as Soviet Ambassador to Persia[37] on 28 November 1920, who would prove so violently anti-British that Curzon would insist on his withdrawal, was regarded by the British Government as a provocation. In a letter to Wilfrid Scawen Blunt setting out the noble purpose of his mission, Theodore Rothstein, was dismissive of British intentions in the region:

I am preparing to leave for Persia as Minister Plenipotentiary. I shall come there armed with a treaty by which we give up all that has been stolen from the Persian people by the old Tsarist regime, including all concessions, banks, roads, buildings, mortgages, etc., without any compensation whatsoever. We are also prepared to withdraw from Persian territory our troops simultaneously with the British[38] as soon as the British Government accepts our proposal for a mixed commission. We do all this not as a matter of policy, but as one of principle.[39]

The enormous expenditure involved in this enterprise showed the importance Lenin was then attaching to communist propaganda in the East while the trade negotiations with Britain were continuing in London. The tactics adopted by the Soviet Trade Delegation, with Krasin promising an end to hostile propaganda in exchange for a trade agreement, linked the two intrinsically. Rothstein's Persian mission was accompanied by an elaborate radio deception plan carried out by the Bolsheviks to harm British interests in the East. From as early as January 1920 the Bolsheviks had known that a former Tsarist World War I codebreaker, Ernst

Fetterlein, had defected to London and had broken their codes. In response they began releasing double cross messages that played on fears of communist subversion across the British Empire in the knowledge that they would be intercepted and read by British intelligence. In order to wrest concessions from the British in the diplomatic arena – to 'nudge Lloyd George's Cabinet towards the negotiations Russia so desperately needed'[40] – Chicherin cabled Litvinov in Copenhagen in February 1920 informing him that the option of renouncing a hostile policy towards Britain in East Asia was on the table, once 'peace with England' had been concluded:

> The Afghan mission in Tashkent is secretly working out [...] with our (representatives?) a draft [...] offensive and defensive alliance, but we [...] decided not to bind ourselves in view of [possible] peace with England, in which case we would renounce in Asia a policy hostile to her. We are [...] as yet not concluding anything which [*sic*] would bind us.[41]

By 1921, however, Lenin was feeling confident enough to vacate the middle ground and initiate a more openly hostile policy towards British interests in Persia, which Rothstein would co-ordinate. The British Government now sought to counter Lenin's Eastern strategy by insisting that the Persians refuse Rothstein entry to Tehran 'on the ground that his mission was to foment revolution'.[42] Rothstein's protests, however, that if 'the Soviet Government really intended to precipitate a revolution it would have sent Budenny[43] with his cavalry instead of himself who came armed with Curzon's *Persia* as his Baedeker and Soviet declarations as his political guides' overcame Persian fears. The Premier, Zi ed Din, responsible for the delay in Rothstein's arrival, fled to Baghdad in a British automobile.[44] Lenin was perfectly aware that sending Rothstein to Tehran was a provocation, and, as the following intercepted letter from Theodore to Andrew Rothstein made clear, no expense was to be spared when it came to ensuring the mission's success:

As you see my journey is being delayed, the chief reason being that it is very difficult to get the necessary things together and we require an enormous amount of things. One is going to an uncivilized country and there is no real communication with it. One must procure lorries and automobiles, a radiographic station, telephonic appliances, a full equipment, house linen, even tablecloths and knives and forks, glasses, apart from all secretarial requisites and as well as a domestic staff; also chauffers, couriers, telegraph operators, a sentry, etc; a staff in the first instance of not less than 600 people. It is like a comet with a small head and a very long tail. For the transport of all this as far as Baku it will be necessary to have one's own trains and railway staff.[45]

Theodore Rothstein's opulent caravan eventually left Moscow for Persia on 17 February 1921 and after being delayed for a month at Ashabad, firstly by bad weather and secondly by a military *coup d'état* led by Reza Khan in Tehran, he crossed the Persian frontier on 6 April 1921.[46] He had been obliged to take the much longer 900-mile route along the Meshed Road because of the dangers of the Soviet-Azerbaijan Front across the much shorter Resht-Kazvin road.[47] It took him a further three weeks to reach Tehran, arriving in the capital on 25 May. On his arrival *The Times* reported that as there was no prospect of communism spreading to Persia, Rothstein's mission there was solely to destroy British interests: 'Persia is now at the mercy of the Bolshevists, who, entrenched in Transcaucasia and Turkestan, are extending their influence at our expense throughout the Middle East.'[48] A view shared by Theodore Rothstein who later confessed that 'the principal aim of the Russian representatives in Persia had been "to help Persia to rid herself from the clutches of Britain".'[49]

Despite the 'principled foreign policy' of the Soviets Rothstein soon found himself acting within the constraints of classical diplomacy. With revolutionary war no longer an immediate option in Europe and anti-colonialism spawning nationalist liberation movements in the East, the organization and pursuit of world revolution would be detached from day-to-day diplomacy and transferred to the Communist International. The People's Commissariat for Foreign Affairs (NKID or *Narkomindel*) had been given responsibility for classical diplomacy; while responsibility for promoting world revolution now rested with the Comintern. In Persia Rothstein worked for both outfits. Apart from his official posting to Tehran he had also been sent as a secret representative of the Comintern with instructions to take charge of propaganda work in Persia, Azerbaijan and Georgia; among his closest 'collaborators' in Persia was Avetis Sultanzade, a member of the executive committee of the Comintern.[50] Rothstein was to all intents and purposes Lenin's man in Persia, and was more than capable of playing both sides of the 'dual policy' with consummate skill.

After the Russo-Polish War Lenin had expressed serious doubts concerning the wisdom of setting up Soviet Republics in countries that were contiguous to Soviet Russia. Karakhan's policy of expansion in the East, however, was a serious challenge to this more cautious approach. Towards the end of the Russian Civil War Red Army troops had invaded Persia in pursuit of White units, Lenin now favoured their withdrawal in accordance with the February 1921 Soviet-Persian Treaty negotiated by Rothstein in Moscow. By that time, however, the Bolsheviks had driven the Menshevik government out of nearby Georgia by military force. Sergio Orjonikidze, the Bolshevik viceroy in Tiflis, along with his mentor in Moscow Joseph Stalin now thwarted Lenin's wishes by reinforcing the Red Army in the north Persian province of Ghilan. Rothstein, as Soviet Ambassador in Tehran, protested to Lenin arguing that Persia was a poor undeveloped, relatively backward country, lacked an organised working class, and was therefore unprepared for any sort of proletarian revolution.[51] To export one from Russia would only complicate matters both with the Shah and with the British, who had recently withdrawn from the south of the country and were threatening to return if Russian activities in the north didn't cease. 'It seems to me you are right', Lenin wrote to Rothstein, who then urged the Shah, Riza Khan, to march into Ghilan and suppress the uprising led by Stalin's protégé Kuchek Khan. Kuchek was quickly defeated and fled into the mountains, where he froze to death. His head was brought back to Tehran for display, and a number of Russian fighters were taken prisoner.

Stalin was furious [and] blamed Rothstein personally for the collapse of his efforts to sovietise – and thereby annex – northern Persia. He raised the matter with Lenin at a meeting of the Politburo. 'Good,' said Lenin, according to Chicherin who was present, with a gleam in his eye and dictated to the stenographer: 'A strict reprimand to Comrade Rothstein for killing Kuchik Khan.' 'No,' a Politburo member objected, 'it was Riza who killed Kuchik Khan not Rothstein.' 'Good,' Lenin said, 'a strict reprimand to Rhiza Khan for killing Kuchik Khan.' 'But we cannot reprimand Riza,' Stalin objected, 'he is not a Soviet citizen.' Whereupon Lenin burst into laughter and the matter was dropped.[52]

A GC&CS intercepted telegram clearly showed that trade had triumphed over the Bolshevik Red Flag in Persia:

Bolgov has arrived Teheran and has opened office in city with numerous staff. Bolgoff is Chief Commissar of Soviet Foreign Trade Dept. in Persia. He works direct under Moscow in liaison with Rothstein. Branch offices already function at Tabriz, Enzeil, Moss-I-Sar, Astara, Banderigaz and are to be opened shortly at Nishapur, Bunnurd and Moshed.[53]

Rothstein's activities now stretched far beyond Persia and into India. GC&CS intercepts detailing the Comintern activities of Samuel Epstein, supposedly a White Russian travelling in the East, pointed out that: 'On August 13th the undermentioned left Basrah by S.S. "Varcla" with French passport for Greece and Paris travelling via Bombay: Samuel EPSTEIN, [. . .] Facts about him are as follows:- [. . .] Though professedly anti-Bolshevik he had several secret interviews with ROTHSTEIN in Teheran. In Baghdad he flatly denied having spoken to him.'[54]

Throughout his posting in Persia Rothstein maintained correspondence with Scawen Blunt. However, MI5's Rothstein file fails to make any mention of Scawen Blunt after 1914 despite the fact that GC&CS were intercepting Theodore Rothstein's wireless and cable traffic along with his and Andrew Rothstein's private mail.[55] At this time Andrew Rothstein was also writing regularly to Scawen Blunt and had visited him on a number of occasions to discuss his father's activities in Persia. In July 1921 he sent him a letter thanking him for the 'two days of blissful rest' spent at his Southwater residence in Sussex, and asked if he might be allowed to visit him more regularly.[56] Both father and son placed great value on Scawen Blunt's friendship and saw him as a useful ally in the Bolshevik's campaign against British imperialism. On 19 November 1921 Andrew Rothstein wrote engagingly to Scawen Blunt requesting an article from him on Egypt for *Labour Monthly*, the communist theoretical journal edited by fellow Balliol College graduate, Rajani Palme Dutt. It was a clever move. By harnessing 'one of the oldest enemies of imperialism' to the anti-imperialist cause of a younger generation of intellectual communists, Andrew Rothstein hoped to demonstrate British communism's continuity with the anti-imperialist movement's Liberal Radical past:

Dear Mr. Blunt,

I do not know whether you are still seeing the 'Labour Monthly'. If you are, you probably know that it is a review published by a group of the younger men in the left wing of the British labour movement, who are some of them Communist, some Socialists, some bourgeois pacifist. All find a common ground in their detestation of the capitalist incubus upon the civilized and uncivilized world, although they differ occasionally about which people's fall under which category. In particular they have a great dislike of the British Empire [. . .] Perhaps I am too much of an 'Easterner' nowadays, and you are less optimistic. Would it be too much to ask you to write down your views, in any form or length you please, for the young men I speak of? They asked me the other day whether there was reasonable hope of obtaining an article from you on Egypt: pointing out that a really critical stage in Anglo-Egyptian relations has again arrived. And I agree with them that today, when there are greater possibilities than ever there were before for prising open the lion's jaws – with the new social lever of the proletariat – the observations of one of the oldest enemies of imperialism must obviously be of very great value.[57]

It is not known whether Scawen Blunt ever wrote the desired article on Egypt for *Labour Monthly*; but following his death in September 1922 Theodore Rothstein wrote an obituary describing him as a true sympathiser with the people of the East for the Communist journal, *Novii Vostock* (*New East*).[58] Theodore Rothstein's correspondence with Scawen Blunt and his son's visits to him between 1920 and 1922 are worth noting if only for Andrew Rothstein's later role as a recruiter of Soviet agents, and the future Cambridge spy Anthony Blunt's well-publicised reverence for his romantic kinsman.[59]

In June 1922 Theodore Rothstein was back in Moscow with the Persian Mission to negotiate a Trade Agreement. He now settled in Moscow and in October addressed a meeting of the Eastern Section of the Communist International. His proposals to establish a Near Eastern Bureau of the Comintern in Constantinople and to subsidise the Angora Communist Party were adopted. A cable intercepted and decoded by GC&CS shows that he was also taking an interest in Japan: 'The policy of the 3rd International in the Far East was discussed at a meeting of the Eastern Section of the Fourth Congress of the 3rd International, which was held in Moscow on 1.12.22. ROTHSTEIN, former Soviet representative in Persia, was present and his proposal that the Committee should convoke a Congress of workers of Eastern Asia, giving precedence to the question of Japan, was unanimously passed.'[60] Comintern funds were subsequently dispensed from Shanghai and a Japanese Communist Party was set up as a branch of the international communist movement.[61] According to MI5's Selwyn Jackson, Theodore Rothstein was at this time 'one of the most important directors of IIIrd International propaganda and agitation in the East.'[62] Later that month he was included in a strong Soviet delegation to The

Hague Peace Conference organised by the Amsterdam Trade Union International that included Karl Radek and Alexandra Kollontai to discuss ways of preventing war. Lenin drafted their position:

> I think the greatest difficulty lies in overcoming the prejudice that this question is a simple, clear and comparatively easy one. [. . .] It must be explained to the people how great is the secrecy with which war arises, and how helpless the ordinary workers' organisations are in the face of war that is really impending, even if these organisations call themselves revolutionary.[63]

Lenin's pessimism – 'when it comes to "the defence of the fatherland the overwhelming majority of the toilers will settle in favour of their bourgeoisie"' – was in stark contrast to the revolutionary optimism evident in Rothstein's anti-war activities in Britain dating back to the Boer War. In 1922 Rothstein remained convinced that British imperialism was a danger to world peace; as Leeper had predicted in 1920, Theodore Rothstein in Tehran and Moscow had become a significant threat to the interests of the British government.

On 30 March 1923 the British Government presented an appeal to the Soviet Government to remit the death sentence passed upon Monseigneur Butkevich, Vicar-General of the Roman Catholic Church in Russia. The reply came the following day in a note signed 'G. Weinstein', the chief of the Anglo-American section of the Commissariat for Foreign Affairs, in which the appeal of the British Government was stated to be 'an unfriendly act and a renewal of the intervention which has been successfully repulsed by the Russian people.' Weinstein also found it 'necessary to mention' they had received a message on the same subject from the Irish Free State referring to 'the hypocritical intervention of the British Government, which is responsible for the assassination in cold blood of political prisoners in Ireland, where 14,000 men, women and young girls are treated in a barbarous and inhuman fashion in conformity with the will of Great Britain, while British control over cables prevents the civilized world from learning the horrible details of these atrocities.' Weinstein's concluding paragraph was even more pointed:

> If similar facts which have taken place under British rule in India and Egypt are taken into consideration, it is hardly possible to regard an appeal in the name of humanity and sacredness of life as very convincing.[64]

Was the Weinstein note a deliberate provocation? Or an opportunity not to be missed to remind the British Government that it remained susceptible to propaganda and subversion throughout its Empire? Or was it simply bad, or inexperienced, diplomacy? On 1 April 1923 the British representative at Moscow, Hodgson, sent his reply: 'I am sorry to say that I cannot accept the note of the 31 March, bearing your signature, in its present form.'

Weinstein responded by despatching a further note in the name of *Sovnarkom*[65] accusing Hodgson of deliberately withholding his (Weinstein's) protest note from the British Government and threatening to by-pass the Hodgson Mission altogether:

> The People's Commissariat for Foreign Affairs regrets that you do not find it possible to transmit to your Government the note handed to you but intended for it and that, consequently, it only remains for it to find other means for acquainting the British Government with its contents.[66]

The Soviet Government then published the entire correspondence. An outraged Curzon reacted by issuing a sharply worded note on 8 May, the Curzon Ultimatum, giving Moscow ten days to settle a number of British grievances concerning propaganda in Asia, especially in India and the Near East, fishing rights and outrages on British citizens; otherwise the trade agreement would be at an end. Curzon also insisted on 'the unequivocal withdrawal of the two communications signed by M. Weinstein.' The Soviet Government, by now genuinely alarmed at the possibility of a complete breakdown in relations, acceded to Curzons demands and Weinstein disappeared from the diplomatic scene along with his notes.

Soviet diplomacy had opted for a more conciliatory approach. Weinstein, who never existed, was later revealed by an MI5 informant inside the CPGB to be Theodore Rothstein.[67] On 25 May 1923 *The Times* reported on Soviet peace overtures and Weinstein's replacement by Weinstein, that is, Rothstein:

> The Soviet Press declares that Moscow's reply to Great Britain demonstrates the Soviet Government's unbounded love for peace, for which cause they are making great sacrifices in order to appease capitalist cupidity and preserve the international proletariat from the war desired by the militarists.
>
> *Izvestia* warns Imperialists against regarding the Soviet's compliance as weakness. The danger of conflict is not past, but if war results, the Soviet has shown the whole world where the responsibility will rest.[68]
>
> Weinstein has been transferred to the Finance Commissariat. [Weinstein was the subordinate official of the Foreign Commissariat who wrote the insulting letters to the British Agent at Moscow.] Rothstein, notorious for his activity in Asia, has been appointed to the Foreign Office staff, evidently replacing Weinstein.[69]

Curzon, believing that he had outwitted the Soviets, now demanded that the agents responsible for anti-British propaganda across Asia be 'disowned and recalled from the scene of their maleficent labours'. He pressed home his advantage by publishing in *The Times* intercepted Soviet messages highlighting the subversive activities of Fyodor E. Raskolnikov, Plenipotentiary Representative to Afghanistan.[70] As a result Jan A. Berzin, a member of the Soviet Trade Delegation to Britain, wrote to Litvinov in late May suggesting that Raskolnikov 'be transferred immediately and Moscow revise its Oriental strategy.' Raskolnikov's plans to incite Indian rebellions, he remarked, were 'a childish attempt to lead serious policy without appropriate conditions. [...]

This kind of mosquito bite won't scare the British elephant'.[71] An interesting observation, and one that was reminiscent of an earlier phrase used by MI5 when investigating the possibility that Andrew Rothstein had a penetration agent working inside the War Office connected to MI1(c).

In September 1922 delivery of Andrew Rothstein's *Pravda* to his London address had mysteriously stopped and he had written to *Pravda* in Moscow to discover the reason why. Their reply, sent on 29 September, was addressed to Andrew Rothstein, MI1(c) War Office, London, which was the address of the British Secret Intelligence Service. This letter informed Rothstein that his copies of *Pravda* were still being dispatched to the address he had given them, which for some inexplicable reason was the address of MI1(c). 'I am at a loss', wrote the head of MI5's B Branch, Captain Harker, 'to explain why copies of the Bolshevik paper should be sent to the War Office for M.I.1.c. and why, when the office of the paper wish to inform Rothstein that they were sending "Pravda" to the address he gave, they should address their letter to him at the War Office. I suggest that some enquiry should be made at W.O. "post room".'[72] Apparently, they had been receiving these papers for some time:

[Redacted] rang me up to say that they had been getting these papers for some time and had wondered who had ordered them. They are addressed to M.I.1.c., War Office. Meanwhile Rothstein has apparently asked the publishers for an explanation for the stoppage of their delivery; they replied that "Pravda" is being sent regularly to the address he gave.

Now, [...] M.I.3.c.[73] say they have enquired, but the paper does not appear to be coming through the post room at the W.O.[74]

This last sentence gave rise to the unwelcome suspicion that someone working for MI1(c) was receiving Rothstein's paper directly from Moscow, and the prospect that Rothstein was running an agent inside MI1(c) could not be ruled out. 'Does Rothstein hope his correspondence will be forwarded to him by W.O.?' Harker asked. 'He would have to give the Bolos [Bolsheviks] a very good reason for daring to give MI1(c) as his London address. Had Rothstein an agent in the "post-room at the War Office" whose duty was to pick out anything for Rothstein?'[75] On 17 November MI5's Major Ball had a different explanation. 'Is it possible', he wrote, 'that the "Pravda" people are pulling M.I.1.c's leg?'[76] 'This is serious', another officer noted, 'but the experts have failed to discover anything strange about the newspapers! Shall we ask Fleming to make enquiries in "R" [*sic*]?'[77] prompting the comment: 'Leave the mosquito alone and go after the elephant.'[78]

That Andrew Rothstein had an agent or 'sympathiser' in MI1(c) in 1922 was not beyond the realms of possibility. At this time he was wooing his future wife, Edith Lunn, a Russian political émigré with Bolshevik views who had left Russia with her family shortly after the October Revolution in 1917. Edith had three sisters, two of whom, Helen and Lucy, were employed by British intelligence, in GC&CS and MI1c respectively. Edith's third sister, Margaret, had also worked with MI1(c) in Helsingfors (Helsinki) for one month in 1919 before being dismissed for going 'red'. Despite being Russian born the Lunn's family background was British. Their paternal grandfather, Michael Lunn had been born in Slouthwaite, Yorkshire, in 1820 and had emigrated to Russia in 1845 where their father had been born in March 1855; his birth was registered at the Anglican Church, Moscow. Edith and Helen were born in Balashicha, near Moscow on 21 March 1887 and 12 August 1895 respectively. Lucy was born in Moscow on 27 December 1891; while Margaret's birth date and description were not included in MI5's file on the family. Both parents were described as having 'anti-Bolshevik tendencies'.[79]

MI5 had first taken an interest in Edith Lunn as early as December 1917 when she applied for employment in wartime Postal Censorship. She had been turned down owing to her association with an army officer, Cyril Marsh Roberts, who had been wounded at Ypres and had become 'an out & out anti-war Socialist.' MI1(c) advised MI5 on 3 December: 'From the tone of Miss Lunn's correspondence we consider her a very doubtful candidate for work in the postal censorship.'[80] Edith was then living in West Kirby and often visited an aunt in Hampstead with whom she occasionally stayed. Confident that she would be accepted by Postal Censorship she had moved to London and lived with her parents and two of her sisters, Margaret and Lucy, at 85 York Mansions, Prince of Wales Road, Battersea. The family later moved to no. 67 with the exception of Helen who, according to the Passport Office, listed her address as The School, Market-Bosworth, Leicester.[81] Lucy always stayed at 67 York Mansions when on leave from MI1(c) and considered the address to be her main home. In November 1920 George Lansbury took an interest in the family and recommended Margaret Lunn to Klishko for translation work with the Soviet Trade Delegation:

> There is also a young woman here who formerly lived in Moscow. She is a middle class woman and her people were pretty well off, but, of course, they lost their money in the Revolution. She has not, however, become bitter and soured towards you and the Bolsheviks. Her name is LUNN. I met her first in Helsingfors where she was working in the British Embassy. She is now I believe doing work here, but very much wants to get back to Russia when peace is signed and would like to work for you. I believe she is thoroughly straightforward. She is very well educated and can speak two or three languages.
>
> It seems to me that if you do get settled down you might be glad of a person like her for translations and so on. I should say she was rather an exceptional person altogether.[82]

By now Edith Lunn was moving in select communist circles and was working as secretary to Mary Rhodes Pekkala, the English-born wife of the Finnish Communist Eino Pekkala, then running an Information Bureau for the Comintern in Moscow. On 25 March 1921 a H.O.W. was taken out on Edith at the Lunn's family residence at 85 York Mansions, on the grounds that 'it is extremely possible that Miss Lunn's address is being used by Madame Pekkala for purposes of correspondence.'[83] However, despite being employed by ARCOS since the end of May (along with her sister Margaret) the H.O.W. on Edith was suspended on 6 September.[84]

The Lunn sisters, despite their political differences, remained very close. Between 1918 and August 1925, Edith, Lucy and Margaret, lived together with their parents at 85 and 67 York Mansions, before Edith was 'thrown out' by her father, apparently for 'her Bolshevik sympathies'.[85] The real reason for her father's displeasure, however, appears to have been that she was three months pregnant with Andrew Rothstein's child and had arranged for an abortion through Russian friends of the Rothstein family.[86] Helen Lunn, who worked on Russian codes and cyphers with Fetterlein at GC&CS, does not appear to have moved into 67 York Mansions until November 1925, three months after Edith's departure.[87] Nevertheless, in August 1925 MI1(c)'s Desmond Morton had his suspicions and requested information from MI5 on the Lunn family and a H.O.W. was issued for the sisters' correspondence. On 25 August it was reported that 'One of the daughters, who is described "as the fair one" was recently actually seen in conversation with the notorious Palme Dutt, who is living at No. 51 York Mansions.'[88] MI5 described Edith as having brown eyes and auburn-coloured hair; Lucy was described as having hazel eyes, auburn hair and a fair complexion; while Helen had brown eyes, a clear complexion and brown hair; no description of Margaret appeared to be available. Who 'the fair one' was is not stated; but from MI5's descriptions of the three women Lucy appears to be the best fit.[89] The Lunn sisters, Lucy, Margaret and Edith all appeared to enjoy the company of the three notorious diners who had attended the Hampstead Communist Party's annual dinner in 1920 – Dutt, Klishko and Rothstein – this would have given them access to Russian intelligence.

On 3 November 1925, however, MI5 reported back to Morton that they had 'discovered nothing to the detriment of Miss Lucy Lunn, secretary since 1919 in S.I.S., Near Eastern Organisation, nor of Miss H.C. Lunn, of the Government Code & Cypher School, now believed to be living at 67, York Mansions with her parents'; but Edith Lunn was said to be 'very red indeed' while Margaret

Lunn was 'receiving letters from an individual who writes on ARCOS notepaper.'[90] An intercepted letter from Mrs Lunn to Edith signed simply 'Mother', dated 13 November and postmarked 16 November, scolded Edith for not visiting the family at weekends as agreed, and gave news of Helen. In January 1926 it was decided to wind up the investigation, MI5's Major Ball advising Morton that while Edith was 'on very intimate terms' with Andrew Rothstein, and 'on quite friendly terms with her family [. . .] this case may be dropped' (Minute Sheet No. 43). Communication between the four sisters remained ongoing, however, with Margaret sharing Edith's flat in Highgate, and dividing her time between there and Battersea. Nevertheless, on 19 March Morton concurred with Major Ball, informing him that 'no further action' was 'to be taken in this case as he is satisfied that the two LUNN girls who are employed under S.I.S. are quite sound from a security standpoint.'[91] Was this a wise decision? The possibility of Edith gaining information on the nature of Helen and Lucy's intelligence work, either directly or through Margaret, and relaying it to the Soviets through Andrew Rothstein remained. Given the fact that Curzon's ultimatum to Moscow issued in May 1923 had been based on GC&CS intercepts of Soviet messages, and that their publication in *The Times* had made it clear to the Soviets that their codes had been broken any information from this source would have been extremely valuable. Moscow's response to *The Times* articles, while denying that the intercepted quotes were genuine, 'tacitly recognized' that Britain 'had compromised Soviet traffic.'[92] Nevertheless, Moscow did not introduce a new cryptographic system until late 1923; in the interim the Soviets were happy to continue releasing messages that played on fears of communist subversion in the sure knowledge that they were being read by British intelligence. An intelligence strategy was being developed among the Soviet trade negotiators in London centred upon deception and agent penetration of British institutions, including the official labour movement. Andrew Rothstein's position in the latter made him an invaluable Soviet intelligence asset.

On 22 May 1923 Andrew Rothstein was listed on the staff of the Soviet Trade Delegation along with Krasin, Chief Official Agent, Jan Berzin and Klishko, Assistant Official Agents.[93] The withdrawal of Klishko in 1923 following Curzon's ultimatum gave notice of a significant change in Soviet intelligence practice in Britain linking the pre-revolutionary Russian political émigré community with a new professional breed of agent. Threats to security arising from the operations of the Soviet intelligence service and the CPGB gave rise to skillful and extensive infiltration measures in government, intelligence, media circles and the labour movement.

The arrival of David A. Petrovsky[94] in 1924 as the permanent representative of the Executive Committee of the Comintern in Britain – in effect, Comintern Ambassador[95] – concealed under the alias Alfred John Bennett, coincided with the appointment of Andrew Rothstein as Chief Commissar of Mestkom. This was a Trade Union or Employees' Soviet 770-strong, into which the staff of ARCOS, Russian Oil Products (ROP), the Soviet Trade Delegation and Embassy of the Soviet Union and Centrosoyuz were organised; without Mestkom's consent no employee could be engaged. That same year Rothstein was also admitted to the inner circle of the Russian-British section of the Communist 'underground' movement, the organisation with responsibility for coordinating clandestine intelligence operations in the UK. Working closely with the Soviet Embassy and the Soviet Trade Delegation the underground section of the British Communist Party had been given four main tasks. Firstly, the acquisition of naval and military secrets; secondly, the spreading of propaganda among the Armed Forces; thirdly, the control of agents and the running of a courier system; and fourthly, the quarterly transmission of Russian money from the Soviet Embassy to the CPGB and the National Minority Movement (NMM). The latter an organisation set up by the Party in 1924 to create communist groups inside existing trade unions, in keeping with the Comintern's United Front Tactic 'from below'.

11

The Anglo-Russian Committee and the Zinoviev Letter

There is a document in London which you ought to have. It shows the relations between the Bolsheviks and the British Labour leaders. The Prime Minister knows all about it, but is trying to avoid publication. It has been circulated today to Foreign Office, Home Office, Admiralty and War Office.

Vice-Admiral Sir Reginald 'Blinker' Hall
to Thomas Marlowe, editor *Daily Mail*

The Comintern's United Front Tactic, ushered in under Zinoviev's guidance, called upon Communists 'to join with all workers belonging to other parties and groups and all unaligned workers in a common struggle to defend the immediate, basic interests of the working class against the bourgeoisie.'[1] The 'United Front' was a dramatic departure from hitherto accepted Comintern practice in respect of international trade unionism. The young Russian trade union movement had originally intended to join the Comintern in March 1919 but with the creation of the reformist Social-Democratic 'International Federation of Trade Unions' (IFTU) in Amsterdam in August 1919, Lenin had begun to favour the creation of a rival revolutionary trade union International in Moscow. An interim propaganda body called the International Council of Trade and Industrial Unions was set up in June 1920, the progenitor of the Red International of Labour Unions (RILU) or Profintern. The Profintern's view of the IFTU was encapsulated in Lenin's dismissal of the Amsterdam International as 'yellow' – '"yellow," in trade union jargon, implying that the IFTU and its member unions were paid agents of international capitalism'.[2] National Bureaus of the new organisation were organised and a British Bureau of the RILU was established in December 1920 and in July 1921 delegates attended the Profintern's Russian sponsored inaugural conference. Two years later the British Bureau of the RILU was summoned to Moscow to have the general tactic of the United Front explained to them:

> [they were told] not to organise independent revolutionary unions or to split the revolutionary elements away from the existing organisations affiliated to the T.U.C. and through it to the Amsterdam International, but to convert the revolutionary minorities existing in the various industries, into revolutionary majorities. Hence the British Bureau is not an organisation of unions but only of revolutionary minorities of unions. [...] Where separate districts break away from the main body and form independent revolutionary unions, the Bureau does its utmost to liquidate the split and get the seceded group to return to its parent organisation.[3]

In June the British Bureau of the RILU dissolved itself and amalgamated with the National Minority Movement (NMM). Steps were now taken to establish an alliance between the NMM and the All Russian Central Council of Trades Unions. Andrew Rothstein's appointment as Chief Commissar of Mestkom now provided an opening for the Russian trade unions, albeit coached by the OGPU, to play a more direct role in organising British trade union affairs. In September 1924 Rothstein accompanied a delegation of the All-Russian Central Council of Trade Unions led by a member of the Central Committee of the CPSU, Mikhail Tomsky, to the TUC Congress at Hull where he acted as his interpreter. In keeping with the Comintern's United Front tactic the formation of an Anglo-Russian Committee was accepted by Congress to work for trade union unity; although from the outset it was clear that this was to be a unity of trade union leaderships not of the rank and file.[4] On 5 September, a day after his speech to Congress, Tomsky appeared before the General Council of the TUC to discuss a proposal from the Russians, first made in July, that a British delegation should visit the Soviet Union. 'He was asked to indicate "precisely" the Soviet intention in urging such a visit.'[5] His answer came as something of a surprise. 'Not a word was said, on this occasion, about any formal ties between the two trade union organizations. The purpose of the English visit [was to be] purely educational. The Soviets wanted their British colleagues to acquire firsthand information on the real situation inside Russia. That was all he had in mind, Tomsky said. The councilors questioned him intensively, but his story remained the same.'[6] The resolution that was finally passed 'reflected the Council's meticulous vigilance. It recommended accepting the Russian invitation but only on the clear understanding that the express purpose of the trip was to investigate conditions in the USSR and submit a report. The delegates were not to be charged with any other responsibility.'[7]

Between 1920 and 1924 the activities of the CPGB's rank and file had been dominated by major industrial confrontations, most of them centred upon the coal industry. It had been no coincidence that the Federation of British Industries and the Coal Owners' and Shipowners' Associations had put up the finance for the intelligence alliance between Thomson, Kell and Makgill. Britain's economic strategy after World War I had been to strengthen sterling against the dollar to compete effectively in world money markets. As this relied chiefly upon cheap energy and the export of coal (the UK's largest single export), the government's attack on organised labour was concentrated largely upon the mining industry; their only practical method of lowering fuel costs was to make the miners endure longer hours for less pay. As a consequence the Miners Federation of Great Britain were drawn into repeated defensive battles to protect their members' basic standards, and called on the sympathetic support of fellow trade unionists to strengthen their position.

Between the arrival of the Russian trade delegation in May 1920 and the formal inauguration of the Anglo-Russian Unity Committee at the Scarborough Conference of the TUC in September 1925 labour unrest, reminiscent of pre-war Syndicalism, spread fear of the 'Red Menace' in British society. Within the framework of Lenin's 'dual policy' this had its uses; but it could not be allowed to spin out of control. Since 'Black Friday', 15 April 1921, when the railway and transport workers' leaders reneged on their commitment to assist the planned miners' strike against drastic wage reductions British Communists had been condemning the treachery of British trade union leaders. Anglo-Russian trade union unity and the 'United Front' were intended to reverse this trend and control labour militancy in Britain in pursuit of Russian foreign policy objectives.

The formation of a Labour Government in January 1924 and the recognition on 2 February 1924 of the Soviet government as the *de jure* government in those territories of the former Russian Empire acknowledging its authority, was regarded by British and Russian Communists as a vindication of the 'United Front' tactic and Lenin's policy first espoused in *Left Wing Communism: an Infantile Disease*.[8] The Labour Party's election manifesto had included a proposal for the 'resumption of free economic and diplomatic relations with Russia'.[9] At the Party's victory rally held in the Albert Hall on 8 January 1924 MacDonald had told his audience that the 'pompous folly of standing aloof from the Russian Government'[10] would be ended.

During the latter part of 1922 and the early part of 1923 Curzon's 'uncompromising attitude' towards the Soviet Union had been widely supported in business and financial circles; by 1924, however, it was largely confined to a declining aristocratic, landowning coterie of Tory 'Diehards' and F.O. officials who shared Curzon's fears of Russian encroachment on the British Empire in the East. Differences within the Conservative Party had been exposed during the crisis that followed the 'Curzon Ultimatum' by the lobbying of 'an amalgamation of engineering firms with a close interest in Russian trade', the 'Becos' group, with a share capital in excess of 50 million pounds.[11] They had circulated a memorandum among MPs strongly opposing the threatened rupture in relations with Russia; while the major banks called on the government to restore European trade by promoting the development of the Russian market as a 'reasonable substitute' for the collapse of foreign trade with Germany. The only significant obstacle to this trade was Russia's lack of credits held up by the absence of full diplomatic recognition. J. D. Gregory, Head of the Foreign Office's Northern Department, complained bitterly of a 'persistent campaign' being waged against the F.O. by business and mercantile interests on the question of Russian trade.[12]

However, at the beginning of 1924 with registered unemployment in Britain standing at 10.3 per cent of the working population it was widely believed that the Russian market offered limitless opportunities for the sale of British goods.[13] By increasing the volume of trade with Russia it was expected that the level of unemployment would be significantly reduced; Curzon and Gregory at the F.O., however, supported by the 'colonial-agrarian-finance' wing of the Conservative Party, persisted in their 'pompous folly' of standing 'aloof' and now looked to break off relations with Russia entirely. Consequently, the Curzon group found itself increasingly outside mainstream political thinking on Russia across the political spectrum, and in relative decline within the Conservative Party. The communists and socialists were quick to seize the initiative. In 1923 the *Socialist Review* had depicted Curzon as an 'Elder Statesman [of 'The Great Game'] whose feet are washed by the Persian Gulf, while his head is still in the Pamirs';[14] while Kamenev, who became a member of the ruling triumvirate in Russia after Lenin's death in 1924, offered an interesting appraisal of the comparative world views of Lloyd George and Curzon. Lloyd George, he thought, 'realized that he was living in the twentieth century, though he had not always the courage to make the necessary deductions and act on them'; Curzon, on the other hand, 'is determined that, if this is not the nineteenth century, he will behave as if it were'.[15] The Communist MP for Motherwell, Walton Newbold, summed up the dramatic shift that had taken place in international relations since World War I when he dismissed Curzon as 'representative of those interests, which looked away from the Dominions and the Democracy of the US to the autocratic Empire in India'.[16] Philips Price, writing in the *Communist*, connected those interests with 'outspoken militarists and [...] certain powerful families of the aristocracy which have regarded the War Office, the Admiralty and the India Office for years past as their special preserve.'[17] That they were in relative decline within the Conservative Party there can be little doubt.[18]

The impact that these changes had on the social composition of MI5 was not negligible, and the intelligence alliance between Kell's MI5 and Makgill's IIB began to reflect both the backward-looking aspects of Curzon's foreign policy and the strategical demands of British industry. MI5 from its inception had been dominated by the 'colonial-agrarian-finance' sector of traditional conservatism, and the 'outspoken militarists' from the India Office. Many MI5 officers shared the views of the die-hard conservatives, and opposed the Labour Government's *de jure* recognition of the Soviet Union on 2 February. Individual members of MI5 were recruited from a section of the social elite who were in decline, and they were eager to be deployed against those classes of society who, in the wake of World War I and the Russian Revolution, were challenging their values and economic position. Many drifted towards the recently formed British Fascisti while Makgill's IIB spearheaded the attack on the CPGB.

As early as 1921 Makgill had successfully infiltrated an IIB agent, 'Jim Finney', inside the CPGB, and had created a mechanism whereby he could place spies inside the Communist Party to monitor potential labour unrest. Finney worked closely with a fellow IIB agent, Captain Herbert Boddington, who joined MI5 the following year. Boddington, on Kell's instructions, joined the CPGB in 1923; his experiences as an actor apparently helping him pass himself off as a Communist.[19] The mastermind behind this plan to penetrate the CPGB was a young self-taught agent-runner, Maxwell Knight, a member of the IIB who would later join MI5. In 1924, at the behest of Makgill, who was then running agents on behalf of Kell, Knight joined the British Fascisti (BF),[20] and remained a member until 1930. He was no ordinary member. In the same year that he joined the organisation he became their assistant chief of staff as well as their director of intelligence. The BF at the time claimed a membership of about 100,000. Knight was a committed fascist and an admirer of the Italian dictator Benito Mussolini, as was Churchill, the 'first of his three wives, Miss G. E. A. Poole, whom he married in 1925, was the director of the BF Women Units. In the mid-1920s, on Knight's instructions, six British Fascists posing as Communists succeeded in joining the CPGB to work as penetration agents for Makgill's IIB. Knight's most important recruit while working for the British Fascists, a Communist student, continued to work for him (and later for MI5) for over thirty years.'[21]

Throughout this period the lead role in domestic intelligence gathering on revolutionary organisations in the United Kingdom belonged to Scotland Yard[22] and Kell's MI5 was restricted to counter-espionage and counter-subversion in the armed forces. However, Kell was able to make good this deficit by making common cause with Makgill's IIB whose principal concern was the Bolshevik threat to British Imperial capitalism, which was regarded as jeopardising Britain's postwar return to profitability.[23]

Following the formation of Ramsay MacDonald's Labour Government the communists had been confident that police supervision of their activities would be relaxed. They were soon disappointed. Arthur Henderson as Home Secretary defended the Special Branch in the Commons against attacks by his own backbenchers and 'continued to authorize Home Office Warrants on the correspondence of leading Communists.'[24] Within a few days of coming to power MacDonald was confronted with a strike by 110,000 dock workers and he wasted no time in making it known that he would use troops to ensure the movement of essential supplies if necessary.[25] A few weeks later a strike by London tram workers persuaded him to consider taking action under the Emergency Powers Act, whose enactment the Labour Party had bitterly opposed in 1920.[26]

MacDonald's Cabinet was not as radical as many had either hoped or feared and included the ex-Liberal, Lord Haldane who, as Lord Chancellor, had been instrumental in setting up the Secret Service Bureau in 1909, and two ex-Tories, Lord Chelmsford at the Admiralty and Lord Parmoor, Lord President of the Council. On the day the new Cabinet was announced the Stock Exchange rallied and *The Economist* reported 'sweeping rises' across all markets.[27] Full diplomatic recognition of the Soviet Union had not strengthened communism in Britain; on the contrary it had softened it.[28]

MacDonald's recognition of the Soviet Government, nine days after taking office, was to be followed by a conference to settle all the outstanding differences between the two countries, including compensation for British owners of Russian property sequestered after the revolution and the ending of propaganda and subversion of institutions. The conference on the Anglo-Soviet Treaties was scheduled to open in London on 14 April 1924. The inclusion of Maxim Litvinov and Theodore Rothstein in the Soviet delegation was regarded by the British Government as a deliberate provocation. Litvinov, who was to have led the delegation, had been expelled from Britain in 1918; while Rothstein, who had been declared *person non granta* in 1920, was intended as his secretary. At this point MacDonald requested information on Rothstein from MI5, which he received from Miss S. (Jane Sissmore).[29] He had recently been elected a member of the Collegium of the Commissariat of Foreign Affairs as a result of the 'Curzon Ultimatum' in May 1923, and had recently been appointed Head of the Foreign Commissariat's Press Bureau; a position, MI5 commented, 'for which his former experience in London qualifies him.'[30]

On 31 March a letter appeared in the *Financial Times* from an outraged member of the Travellers' Club, Pall Mall, on Rothstein's unsuitability for the role of trade negotiator arguing that he should not be allowed into Britain:

Neither the past record of M. Litvinov nor that of M. Rothstein suggests their suitability as delegates to a conference designed to place our relations with Russia on a more normal footing.

As for Mr. Rothstein, in the course of twenty years during which he found asylum in this country as a political refugee he developed a violent hostility to it, which bore fruit in his anti-British propaganda in Persia, where he was Russian Minister until Lord Curzon felt called upon to demand his withdrawal. Shortly before his appointment as secretary to the Russian delegation at the London conference M. Rothstein delivered himself as follows regarding the de jure recognition of the Soviet Government by the British Government:-

"The bourgeois world has confessed its helplessness in face of our world revolution, and now finds itself constrained to adopt an attitude towards us which it hitherto only accorded to respectable States recognizing the sacredness of territorial and capitalist institutions, the bourgeois electoral law, the bourgeois freedom of the Press, freedom of religious profession, legal conscience, and other exploiting and high sounding institutions".[31]

The following week Andrew Rothstein came to his father's defence, and in a letter to the *Financial Times* claimed that the Curzon Note, which the outraged letter writer of the previous week, L. G. M. Gall, had claimed had led to Theodore Rothstein's withdrawal from Persia, was not only based on 'forgeries foisted upon the Foreign Office by a German agency' but was despatched in October 1921 and could have had little bearing on the decision to recall Theodore Rothstein to Moscow.[32]

On 7 April the *Daily Mail* reported that neither Litvinov nor Rothstein would be included in 'the delegation which is to discuss treaty and debt positions between Britain and Russia and the restoration of Russia's credit.' 'Their absence', the paper continued, 'leaves the delegation handicapped, since only one of the 18 delegates here today speaks English.'[33] There was, however, some confusion over the reasons behind their exclusion. The *Daily Mail* claimed that both 'were objected to by the British Government' and were refused 'the much coveted visa.' However, the paper also reported that Preobazhensky, the leader of the delegation, had issued a statement denying that the British Government had refused the visas, stating that Rothstein had been taken seriously ill on the eve of his departure, while 'Litvinoff was busy and would probably join the delegation in London later.'[34] The conference, which was expected to last several months, opened in London on 14 April 1924. The Russian negotiating team included four prominent trade unionists; among them, Tomsky, the powerful chairman of the All-Russian Central Council of Trade Unions. His inclusion meant that those British leftist trade union leaders, sympathetic to the Soviet experiment while by no means revolutionaries themselves, might be prevailed upon to support Russian foreign policy objectives.

Despite being excluded from the delegation to attend the conference on the Anglo-Soviet Treaties Theodore Rothstein was apparently admitted to London in July as a member of the Soviet Peace Delegation to the London Conference,[35] a fact commented upon in an exchange of memos between MI1(c)'s S. G. Menzies and MI5's Major W. A. Alexander in September 1924: 'The ROTHSTEIN whose family is said to play an important part in Soviet foreign affairs, is evidently THEODORE A. ROTHSTEIN. [. . .] In May 1923, he was appointed a member of the Collegium of the Commissariat of Foreign Affairs. He was a member of the recent Soviet Peace Delegation in London.'[36] However, there is no secondary evidence to support this latter claim, and it is unlikely that Rothstein would have been admitted to Britain in 1923. At this time Major Alexander appeared to be running an agent in the CPGB, Minnie Birch, who was passing information on the activities of the Rothstein family, but her information was confused:

> According to Minnie BIRCH the ROTHSTEIN family plays an important part in Soviet Foreign Affaires. All of them hold important positions in the Foreign Office. One of the sons has changed his name to REINSTEIN, sometimes WEINSTEIN. BIRCH does not know the reason for this.

The ROTHSTEIN in the London Trade Delegation is
another son who, himself has a son in the London branch of the
Y.C.L.[37]

The son mentioned as a member of the London Trade Delegation
was Andrew; while the son who had changed his name to
Reinstein or Weinstein was never identified.[38] Weinstein had
earlier been involved in the exchange of notes with Curzon that
had threatened the Anglo-Soviet trade agreement in 1923, which
had borne all the hallmarks of a Rothstein family diplomatic
manoeuvre.

The conference on the Anglo-Soviet Treaties opened in London
on 14 April 1924 and coincided with the interception of the
following message by MI1(c) from Moscow: '[Andrew] ROTHS-
TEIN is to hand over to 'PAULI' a subsidy of £5,000 from
ZINOVIEV.' They added that 'PAULI' appeared to be identical
either with William Paul,[39] the well-known member of the CPGB,
or with Eden Paul, the writer of Communist pamphlets in London.
Zinoviev who was then at the height of his political powers would
soon fall foul of a forged document purporting to be seditious
instructions from the President of the Comintern to the CPGB, the
famous 'Zinoviev Letter' published in the *Daily Mail*, during the
general election campaign later that year.

Nevertheless, the mood during the talks was conciliatory; the
Russians, for their part, making it known that they would
consider settling pre-revolutionary debts if they were advanced a
large loan. The leader of the negotiating team, Christian
Rakovsky, in an interview with *Izvestia* on 30 July, suggested
that the 'central question is the loan.'[40] The City, however,
remained aloof making it inevitable that any loan would have to
be guaranteed by the Labour Government. On 5 August, the
negotiations broke down and the Conservative newspapers went
on the offensive. The collapse of the Labour Party's Russian
policy, it was expected, would lead to the downfall of the Labour
Government. The same thought had struck the Liberal Party and
the maverick Lloyd George:

By now he [Lloyd George] was obsessed with the domestic political scene and his own chances of making a comeback. Unlike Asquith, the official Party leader, he recognized that the Liberals could have no future if the Labour Party made a good showing in office. He was anxious for action and a quick annihilation of Labour before people got too used to the idea of Labour government. The treaty with Russia gave him his chance.[41]

With the Conservative leaders constantly on the look-out for any tendency on the part of the Labour Party to be 'soft' towards Communism; the Russian loan was an issue on which they could be sure of Liberal support.[42] Their opportunity came on 25 July 1924 when the acting editor of the *Workers' Weekly*, J. R. Campbell, published a 'Don't Shoot' appeal to the troops. He was arrested on 5 August under the Incitement to Mutiny Act 1795.[43] The Attorney General, Sir Patrick Hastings, however, withdrew the prosecution following protests from Labour backbenchers that Campbell's article was merely an appeal to the Army not to carry out strike-breaking orders. When Parliament reconvened on 30 September the Attorney-General defended his decision by stating that 'Campbell was a man of excellent character' who 'had served in the forces during the war, had been decorated for gallantry and was now permanently disabled by wounds' received in battle.[44] The Conservatives countered his arguments by accusing the Labour Government of political bias in favour of a communist.

On the back foot, MacDonald refused the Liberal Party's demand for a Select Committee of the House to re-examine the case, and called on the Liberals to withdraw or bring down the Government. On 8 October a combined Liberal and Conservative vote defeated the Government by 364 votes to 198, and MacDonald called for the dissolution of Parliament.

The following day copies of a document, initially received by MI1(c) from their Riga station, were transmitted to the F.O., as well as to four other ministries with a covering note saying that the document contained 'strong incitement to armed revolution' and 'evidence of intention to contaminate the Armed Forces [. . .] a flagrant violation' of 'the Anglo-Russian Treaty signed on the 8th August'.[45] This document, the notorious Zinoviev Letter was dated 15 March 1924, and called upon the CPGB to pressurise the labour movement to ensure ratification of the Anglo-Soviet Treaty by organising mass demonstrations on 1 May. Such pressure, it was argued, 'would assist the success of the work of the Soviet Delegation in England, [and] be a powerful step forward on the road of the development of the revolutionary movement in Great Britain.' Tomsky, who had attended the recent TUC Congress along with Andrew Rothstein, was to be the custodian of money allocated by the Comintern for this purpose.

The F.O. received the document on the 10 October. They never doubted the authenticity of the letter[46] although the original was never seen by anyone in authority and 'was mistakenly assumed' to be in the hands of the CPGB; 'an accusation easily believed but never objectively substantiated.'[47] What now unfolded has been described by one historian as 'a most extraordinary and mysterious business'[48] involving MI5, MI1(c), Conservative Central Office, Makgill's IIB, past and present intelligence personnel, one of the principals of an obscure White Russian trading company in the City and the editor of the *Daily Mail*.

The 'role of the Occult Octopus' and MI1(c)'s Desmond Morton, who was at the time overseeing the case of Rothstein's missing copies of *Pravda*, would prove central to this 'mystery'. Morton, who had responsibility for evaluating the Letter's authenticity, immediately accepted it as genuine and authorised its circulation; according to F.O. historian Gill Bennett there was nothing unusual about this:

> The source cited in the Riga report was FR3/K, and the FR network, operating out of Riga, had been producing consistently good reports for the previous two years, with well-placed and enterprising agents in Moscow. These agents had secured copies of minutes of key Soviet bodies such as the *Sovnarkom* (Council of People's Commissars, the executive arm of the Central

Committee of the CPSU), and of the Executive Committee of the Comintern, [and] similarly inflammatory letters written by Zinoviev to the Communist parties of other countries. [. . .] This one looked, at first glance much like the others.[49]

That the F.O. attached great importance to the Letter was apparent in the fact that it was handed personally to the Permanent Under-Secretary for Foreign Affairs, Sir Eyre Crowe, who asked Morton for 'corroborative proofs' of the authenticity of the letter before putting it to the Prime Minister. MacDonald was then out of London campaigning for the forthcoming general election.[50] At this time Morton was still working on the Lunn-Rothstein case and was sharing an agent, Jim Finney, inside the CPGB with Makgill's IIB. On the evening of the tenth Morton met with Finney who informed him that the Central Committee of the CPGB had held a meeting during the week of 29 September – 4 October to consider a letter of instruction from Moscow concerning 'action which the CPGB was to take with regard to making the proletariat force Parliament to ratify the Anglo-Soviet Treaty'. Finney went into great detail outlining how the Communists intended to infiltrate the armed forces, spread propaganda, orchestrate strikes and create a revolutionary situation. The armed forces would be won over to Communism and they would then either refuse to quell the unrest or join the rioters.[51] Morton concluded that Finney's information was confirmation that the Zinoviev Letter had been received by the Central Committee of the CPGB and acted upon.

However, SIS records show that in his original written report, Finney did not mention the Zinoviev Letter nor, indeed, did he make any reference to letters from Moscow. He had merely stated that at a recent meeting of the CPGB Executive it had been decided once more 'to do all in their power to make whatever government was in power to be the promoters of the Revolution. This was to be brought about by the Communist Party taking more effective action in promoting strikes and incitement, so that the Government in office would be compelled to bring out troops to quell disturbances.'[52]

On 11 October Morton sent Crowe a report based on the information he had received from Finney which, he suggested, provided the 'corroborative proof' Crowe desired. The letter was now submitted to the F.O.'s Northern Department for further comment where it was examined by a junior clerk, William Strang. Strang did not consider the Letter 'to be "out of the ordinary run of things" and was about to pass it on with a short minute when, learning from Crowe's secretary, Sir Neville Bland, that the Permanent Under-Secretary attached extraordinary importance to the letter and favoured its publication, he substituted a long and detailed minute.'[53] On 13 October Crowe told MacDonald that he had heard on 'absolutely reliable authority' that the Letter had been discussed by the CPGB's Executive Committee.

News of the document's existence, somewhat mysteriously, now reached a former MI5 officer Donald im Thurn, who tried to sell a copy of this letter (which he did not possess) to the *Daily Mail*. Although im Thurn had left MI5 for the City in 1919 to become a director of the London Steamship & Trading Corporation he had kept up his contacts with the secret world, and continued to lunch regularly in the grill-room of the Hyde Park Hotel with Major William Alexander of MI5's B Branch. He was also well acquainted with the Chief of SIS, Admiral Hugh 'Quex' Sinclair, who listed 'food' among his greatest passions.[54] Im Thurn had first got wind of the Zinoviev Letter, 48 hours before the Permanent Secretary at the F.O., courtesy of Morton and Makgill's spy in the Communist Party, Finney.[55] On 15 October, he telephoned an old friend, Major Guy Kindersley, the Conservative MP for Hitchin, asking him to come round to his office where he informed him of the existence of the 'Zinoviev Letter'. On hearing of the contents of the letter Kindersley contacted the Treasurer of the Conservative Party, Lord Younger, who agreed to pay im Thurn £7,500 for a copy of the letter. Later that day im Thurn lunched with Alexander but was told that MI5 'had no photo of original and could not discover where it was.'[56] On 16 October im Thurn noted in his diary that he again met with Alexander who told him that K (Kell) was waiting to hear from 'C'

(Sinclair). Alexander thought that the letter 'should be more public but would not commit himself. A [Alexander] offered publish it through me in a perfectly safe manner. K [Kell] interested.'[57]

That same day MacDonald, who had first heard about the Zinoviev Letter while campaigning in Manchester, composed a short note of protest to be sent to the Soviet *charge d'affaires* in London, Rakovsky, counselling Crowe 'that a despatch to the Soviet would only be damaging unless the authenticity of the letter were established and the accusations well founded.'[58] Utterly convinced of authenticity, however, Crowe instructed J. D. Gregory of the Northern Department to prepare a draft Note of protest to Rakovsky, which he altered extensively before sending to MacDonald. He also advised MacDonald that both the Note and the Letter should be published as soon as they reached Rakovsky. MacDonald, however, was not free to examine the draft until the early hours of 23 October when he redrafted those parts which did not appear to him 'to be strong enough or pointed enough to meet the circumstances.' However, he did not initial the draft and instructed the F.O. to first verify the authenticity of the letter and to send him back the 'final form' before it was despatched. His instructions were ignored. On 24 October Crowe, aware that the *Daily Mail* now had a copy of the Letter and was about to publish its contents, authorised its despatch and official publication.[59]

The formal involvement of the security service MI5 in all of this has never been proven; but there seems little doubt that a number of leading intelligence officials, past and present, either through serendipity or collusion, were responsible for the publication of the Letter in the Press. The editor of the *Daily Mail*, Thomas Marlowe, had first got wind of the Letter on the morning of the twenty-third courtesy of Vice-Admiral Sir Reginald 'Blinker' Hall. A telephone message from 'an old and trusted friend', which had arrived late the night before, was waiting for him on his desk:

> There is a document in London which you ought to have. It
> shows the relations between the Bolsheviks and the British

Labour leaders. The Prime Minister knows all about it, but is trying to avoid publication. It has been circulated today to Foreign Office, Home Office, Admiralty and War Office.[60]

The 'old and trusted friend' was 'Blinker' Hall, the legendary wartime Director of Naval Intelligence, and architect of the Zimmerman Telegram.[61] During the war Sinclair, the head of MI1(c), had been a subordinate officer of 'Blinker' Hall's and the two men had remained in close contact. According to im Thurn Sinclair had been coaching Kell on the subject of the Zinoviev Letter. 'Blinker' Hall, who had been elected Conservative MP for Liverpool West Derby in 1919, was also in close contact with Conservative Central Office despite losing his seat in the 1923 election to the Liberal candidate, Charles Sydney Jones. Conservative Central Office was also liaising with the head of MI5's B Branch, Joseph Ball, who appears to have obtained a copy of the Zinoviev Letter on or around 22 October. Hall's intelligence contacts extended much further and included 'the Occult Octopus'. He was a founder member of National Propaganda, a group of industrialists belonging to the British Empire Union set up to counter communist activity in British industry; like Kell, he was closely associated with Makgill's IIB.[62] Kell's interest in publicising the Letter, however, was said by im Thurn 'to have waned, as it became increasingly clear that Sinclair was intent on masterminding the operation himself.'[63] On 20 October Kell became ill and took to his bed. According to Christopher Andrew, MI5's 'authorised historian':

> MI5 had little to do with the official handling of the Zinoviev letter, apart from distributing copies to army commands on 22 October 1924, no doubt to alert them to its call for subversion to the armed forces. Possible unofficial role of a few MI5 officers past and present in publicising the Zinoviev letter with the aim of ensuring Labour's defeat at the polls remains a murky area [...] A wartime MI5 officer, Donald Im Thurn [...] who had served in MI5 from December 1917 to June 1919, made

strenuous attempts to ensure the publication of the Zinoviev letter and may well have alerted the *Mail* and Conservative Central Office to its existence. [...] Though he was not shown the actual text of the Zinoviev letter before publication, one or more of his intelligence contacts briefed him on its contents. Alexander appears to have informed Im Thurn on 21 October that the text was about to be circulated to army commands. Suspicion also attaches to the role of the head of B Branch, Joseph Ball. Conservative Central Office, with which Ball had close contacts, probably had a copy of the Zinoviev letter by 22 October, three days before publication. Ball's subsequent lack of scruples in using intelligence for party-political advantage while at Central Office in the later 1920s strongly suggests, but does not prove, that he was willing to do so during the election campaign of October 1924.[64]

On 23 October Marlowe was visited by another 'old and trusted friend' from wartime intelligence, Lieutenant-Colonel Frederick Browning, with a copy of the 'Zinoviev Letter' in his pocket. An old boyhood friend of Marlowe and 'Blinker' Hall's,[65] Browning had been promoted to second-in-command of MI1C during World War I. The Zinoviev Letter was published in the *Daily Mail* at the height of the election campaign and was seen to be a contributory factor in the defeat of Ramsay MacDonald's Labour Government. Its impact on future relations with the Soviet Union was nothing short of disastrous, and led not only to the breaking off of relations with the Russians but to the expulsion of the Russian representatives from Britain altogether. The curious thing is that the People's Commissar for Foreign Affairs, Chicherin, in a report to *Sovnarkom* appeared to admit the existence of the Letter and used it to weaken Zinoviev and the Comintern, which, he complained, was undermining his efforts to normalise Anglo-Soviet relations, and to place Soviet diplomacy on a firmer basis.[66]

12

The 1926 General Strike and the Anglo-Russian Committee

The methods used in the world war against the 'external enemy' are now being used against the 'internal enemy', that is, the working class defending its rights.

Executive Committee of the Communist International Manifesto On The General Strike In Britain, 7 May 1926

The question of whether or not the Zinoviev Letter was genuine or fabricated – the result of a right-wing conspiracy involving members of Britain's intelligence and security services, Conservative Party Central Office and the *Daily Mail* – continues to provoke controversy. But, as the *Daily News* remarked on the 6 March 1928 if the document was a forgery, the creation of White Russians in Berlin, 'it so closely resembles the speeches Zinoviev was making at the time, and the various manifestoes he was framing, that he need not have been greatly ashamed of the falsely ascribed authorship.' For this reason the Zinoviev Letter had a profound impact on the left, both in Britain and the Soviet Union, and marked the beginning of the Stalinist takeover of the Communist International. Despite being partly engineered by the Comintern's adoption of United Front tactics, Soviet attempts to steer revolutionary propaganda among militant British trade unionists into calmer waters were scuttled by the Zinoviev Letter.[1] The Letter was seized upon by Chicherin to complain about the impossibility of conducting diplomatic negotiations with Britain while the threat of revolutionary propaganda emanating from the Comintern was continuing to disrupt Anglo-Russian relations. His report to the *Sovnarkom* on 25 October 1924[2] following receipt of the F.O. Note to Rakovsky was evidence of a sea change in the attitude of the Politburo towards Zinoviev's leadership of the Comintern:

> With the permission of the Politburo I approached comrade Zinoviev with the request that he should give explanations on the accusations levelled against us contained in the above-mentioned Note.
>
> Comrade Zinoviev categorically declared that the copy of the communication of the ECCI is a deliberately distorted version of a letter from the Presidium of the ECCI to the Central Committee of the British Communist Party, drawn up by comrade MacManus[3] and despatched to its destination, but owing to the criminal negligence of certain workers of the ECCI, or the treachery of some one of the British Communists, became known to the British police. [...] Undoubtedly we have to deal here with an instance of carefully planned provocation, directed simultaneously against the Labour Party and the U.S.S.R.[4]

The first step of the People's Commissariat for Foreign Affairs (NKID), Chicherin continued, would be 'to deny the accusations levelled against us, especially as the British Government is hardly likely to possess any direct proof that the letter was actually signed by Zinoviev, sent from Moscow, and actually received by the British Communist Party.'[5] He also called for an investigation to be carried out by the Foreign Section of the OGPU 'to ascertain the sources from which the British Government obtains its news and secret information about the SSSR, and also to ascertain by what means the data regarding the letter of the ECCI came into the hands of the British Foreign Office.'[6]

On the 29 October 1924 Theodore Rothstein attended an Extraordinary sitting of the NKID to consider the subject of the

'Zinoviev Letter' along with Stalin, Zinoviev, Chicherin, Litvinov, Yoffe and Molotov.[7] The previous day, at a session of the Collegium of the Soviet Foreign Office, Zinoviev had sounded a belligerent note:

> Speaking plainly, an apology from the British Government in the affair of my letter, even if one is forthcoming, is really of no importance to us at all.
>
> Everyone knows that we are conducting propaganda, and will continue to do so in the future, until either we win or ourselves are crushed.
>
> This is a matter of fighting for our existence.
>
> The only question is whether British bankers wish to risk this, in the hopes of securing huge profits through entering into trade relations with us.[8]

On 29 October, however, Zinoviev's proposal, supported by Molotov, 'that the NKID should break off all diplomatic relations with Britain until the question of the letter was settled' met with strong opposition from Chicherin, Yoffe and Litvinov. They counselled caution until a British Government Commission, headed by Conservative Foreign Secretary, Austen Chamberlain, had looked into the authenticity of the document. Stalin, who had been kept up to date on the negotiations to set up an Anglo-Russian Committee by Tomsky, now pressed for a Commission of International Trade Unions from both the right and left wings of the trade union movement to investigate the Letter; it was agreed that the Delegation of British Trade Unions due to arrive in Moscow in December 'should acquaint themselves with the position of affairs on the spot, carry out a non-party investigation, and adopt a resolution in accordance with their findings'. Although the TUC, when accepting the invitation to send a delegation to Russia had specified that they would 'not be charged with any other responsibility,' Stalin ignored their protestations.

Towards the end of 1924 Stalin began to develop the international implications of 'socialism in one country', attacking both Trotsky and Zinoviev for their 'infatuation' with the idea of the necessity for revolutions in the West. Initially, the tensions between Stalin and Zinoviev had been concealed by their joint desire to keep Trotsky out of the succession. By October, however, the vilification of Trotsky had taken such a toll on his health that the scene was set for a direct confrontation between Zinoviev and Stalin.

There is no record suggesting that Theodore Rothstein spoke at this meeting of the NKID, and his views on Stalin's call for a Commission of International Trade Unions to investigate the Zinoviev Letter are not known. However, Andrew Rothstein was invited to attend the Moscow conference of the All-Russian Union of Soviet Employees (Mestkom)[9] as the representative of the London Committee of this body in December 1924. Before his departure he addressed the vexed question of increasing the 'responsibilities' of the delegation in the wake of the Zinoviev Letter by sending a telegram from the Rosta Press Agency to the delegation's leader A. A. Purcell, asking 'his opinion of Zinoviev's proposal [it was actually Stalin's] that the delegation while in Russia should investigate the affair.' Purcell's reply: 'In my opinion the offer is a generous one and in the interests of all should be accepted' was then published in the *Daily Herald*.[10] Purcell, General Secretary of the Furnishing Trades' Federation, as president of the Amsterdam-based International Federation of Trade Unions (IFTU) was well placed to push forward Stalin's 'proposal' for an international commission of trade unions to investigate the Letter.

The trade union delegation's official report: *Russia Today. The Official Report of the British Trade Union Delegation Visiting Soviet Russia and the Caucasus* was issued in February 1925 and ran to 272 pages with a nine-page report on the 'Zinoviev' Letter published both separately and as an appendix. It began with a summary of the results of their investigation into the Comintern which, in keeping with the United Front from above, the authors defended as a bastion of 'moderation' 'in respect of English affairs':

The Comintern, like other Internationals, is a co-ordinating and controlling authority – not a world-wide conspiracy. It enables a central Communist organization to discuss and direct a common policy with national organizations; which on the whole, tends rather to prevent local extremists from disturbing the peace in futile intrigues and insurrections. Further, they have good evidence that the influence of the Comintern in respect of England is at present exercised for moderation and for action on constitutional lines. They are satisfied that the Commissariat for Foreign Affairs has both a position and a policy that would prevent any action by the Comintern in breach of Treaty engagements; and that the Comintern has not committed or even contemplated any such breach. Finally, that the Comintern so far as Great Britain is concerned is not the formidable affair that both its opponents and officials might like it to be thought.[11]

This last sentence was a direct challenge both to Zinoviev's leadership of the Comintern as well as the anti-Soviet foreign policy of the Conservative government. Before their departure from Moscow the British trade union delegation had agreed to press ahead with the Anglo-Russian Committee and create a political role for the international communist trade union movement through penetration of the IFTU.[12] Power in the International sphere was shifting from Zinoviev to Stalin who now sought to win over the All-Russian Central Council of Trades Unions in his power struggle with Trotsky and Zinoviev, and manage the international implications of 'socialism in one country'.[13]

The IFTU, however, looked upon Moscow's desire for affiliation and international trade unity with some trepidation and called upon the Russians to repudiate the Red International of Labour Unions, the Profintern, as a precondition for talks. Shmidt, the Soviet Labour Commissar, urged an early Anglo-Soviet conference on Anglo-Soviet trade union unity, and called upon the British General Council to arrange Amsterdam-Moscow talks. An invitation inviting the Russians to confer 'about the difficulties that stand in the way of your becoming affiliated to the

Amsterdam International' was sent to Shmidt on the 26 February 1925, and a Russian delegation arrived in London in April. In an intercepted document from the Soviet ambassador in London to Chicherin, a message from Michael (identified by MI5 as Tomsky) to Stalin dated 8 April, 1925, reported on a recent conference of British and Russian trade unionists that had 'ended well.' Tomsky informed Stalin that an announcement would follow on 'the actual creation of an Anglo-Russian Committee' at the weekend but that he was not to publish anything until he had heard from Andrew Rothstein:

> At least 75 per cent of the programme has been carried out. The Committee is composed as follows:-
>
> The presidents and Secretaries of the General Council [TUC] and of the All-Russian Central Union of Trades Unions[14] and three more persons from either Organisation. The Committee is called 'Conciliatory'. Do not publish anything until you hear from ANDREW [Rothstein.][15]

Tomsky was due to leave for Moscow on the Saturday and had arranged for an OGPU agent, BASIL ('Jarotsky or Shmidt'?), from the All Russian Central Union of Trades Unions to remain behind until the end of April to ensure Russian influence on the joint proclamation announcing the setting-up of the Anglo-Russian Committee:

> From MICHAEL for STALIN
>
> We earnestly request you to refrain from making any (? favourable) comments in the press on the Conference which has just concluded until our return. The danger of the mobilization of the forces of the "Right" at the meeting of the General Council is not excluded. With regard to the ZINOVIEV letter nothing can be published until after the holidays. We are leaving on Saturday. BASIL [Jarotsky or Shmidt?] is remaining until the end of April. This will ensure our influence on the data to be published.[16]

The Russian delegation departed from Victoria Station on the 10 April 'carrying bouquets of red roses courtesy of their British colleagues, well-satisfied with what they had achieved.'[17] According to an MI5 report Andrew Rothstein played a key role in these negotiations 'to pave the way for a fusion of the Red International of Labour Unions and the Amsterdam Trade Union International.'[18] Three months later, Walter Citrine wrote to Rothstein thanking him for 'a proof copy of the Anglo-Russian Conference, held in April 1925, and inviting him to call in at Ecclestone Square (headquarters of the TUC) so that certain paragraphs might be omitted.'[19]

High-ranking Tories and right-wing Trade Union officials were genuinely alarmed by these developments. Speaking out at a London meeting of the National Association of Trade Protection Societies on 13 May, F. E. Smith (Lord Birkenhead) claimed that the unions were 'now undertaking responsibilities very alien to their original purposes. We might contemplate them with less anxiety if we saw any signs that the older and trusted leaders of trade unionism were at the helm today.'[20] Zinoviev, he said, had declared Britain to be his next target, and the General Council leaders seemed only too willing to assist him. The trade unions had to decide, and decide quickly, 'whether they are going to march along the common road side by side as Englishmen, or whether they are going to accept the orders [. . .] of men who care nothing for England but whose whole philosophy of life is the insane campaign of [. . .] the world's revolution.'[21]

In Moscow Tomsky wasted little time in explaining the work of the London conference to Russian trade unionists; while Zinoviev, addressing the 14th Conference of the CPSU, presented the Anglo-Russian Committee as a triumph for both the Comintern and the Communist Party of the Soviet Union (CPSU). England, he suggested, 'presented good prospects for Communist exploitation over the longer period.' The trade union movement there had swung decidedly to the left, slowly but surely, he claimed, a revolutionary situation was 'beginning to evolve'. The Anglo-Russian Committee was a way of 'advancing to meet this clearly expressed tendency in the historical development of

England [...] towards the revolutionisation of England and its labour movement.'[22]

Stalin also seized upon the formation of the Anglo-Russian Committee but for very different reasons. Disagreeing with Zinoviev's belligerent revolutionary optimism he maintained that British trade unionism, as it stood, was an unlikely instrument for Communist revolution. In an article reminiscent of Theodore Rothstein's turn of the century lament, 'Why is Socialism in England at a Discount?' he noted that in Russia 'the Party had founded the trade unions, and had been able to keep them under control. In the west, it was different. Trade unionism there came first. The Party only appeared later. The worker's primary allegiance, therefore, was to his union. To create a mass Communist organization, it was necessary for the Party to penetrate the unions, take them over, and enlist their members. Trade union unity would facilitate the process. When a mass party had been built, it could be used as an instrument of insurrection.'[23]

For Stalin, however, insurrection was to be expected in decades not years. As the new standard bearer of Lenin's 'dual policy', Stalin was 'more concerned with brandishing the revolutionary stick than with actually bashing anybody with it.'[24] Following the Zinoviev Letter and the Conservative government's decision to break off relations with the Soviet, he became convinced that Britain was making preparations for a new war of intervention. The threat of Communist-inspired revolutions would be the Soviet Union's strongest defence against a generally hostile outside world. The workers, he believed, were the Soviet Union's natural allies and would back her in the event of war. If an attack came, he warned, 'we shall take all measures to unleash the revolutionary lion in every country on earth. The leaders of the capitalist countries must realise that we have some experience in such matters.'[25] The Anglo-Russian Committee was to be a vehicle for the mobilisation of the British proletariat in defence of the Soviet Union, 'their class fatherland.'[26]

It was a shrewd calculation on Stalin's behalf and could not be lightly dismissed. On 18 May 1925 the *Daily Herald* accused the

British Government of 'taking steps' which, if successful, can end only in disaster for the whole world. 'Ever since the incident of the "Red Letter" there has been a steadily growing campaign in the Tory Press, fostered and fed by members of the Government, for the breaking off of all relations with the Soviet Republic. The re-isolation of the Russian people and active encouragement of the anti-Russian forces in Europe, the *Herald* concluded, may easily light again the fires of war.'[27] Those in the Conservative Government calling upon Russia to censure the Comintern and to expel the Communist International from Moscow were dismissed as intriguers who knew full well that the Soviet Government's refusal to act against the Comintern would lead to the 'withdrawal of recognition [...] and the end of all attempts at reviving trade and renewing friendships.'[28]

The Anglo-Russian Committee had been Stalin and Tomsky's invention and, with the help of Andrew Rothstein, had been pressed into service in the interests of 'Socialism in One Country.' Most members of the TUC General Council appeared happier with the role Stalin set for them as peacekeepers than with the revolutionary role envisaged by Zinoviev. Committed to supporting the normalisation of diplomatic relations with the USSR, the exchange of ambassadors, and the expansion of trade, the TUC maintained that world peace required that Russia be accepted as part of the family of nations. The next step would be to formally establish the Anglo-Russian Committee at the TUC's Scarborough Congress in September.

In the intervening months Special Branch and MI5 monitored the developing relationship between the Russian and British trade unions closely, and took a particular interest in the activities of Rosta and Andrew Rothstein:

ROSTA, for some considerable time, has been suspected as a cover for:-

(a) Russian Espionage.
(b) The transmission of revolutionary funds in this country.

The principal employees at ROSTA appear to be
Andrew ROTHSTEIN,
Charles ASHLEIGH and
TAYLOR, Fred[29]
all of whom are known to be prominent members of the
Communist Underground Organisation.[30]

MI5 suspected that Rosta formed part of the Communist
Intelligence Organization controlled by the Federated Press of
America (FPA), and requested the General Post Office to 'institute
a supervising check' on Rosta's telephone calls and issued a H.O.
W. on their correspondence: 'In connection with the check on the
correspondence of "Rosta" (Russian Telegraph Agency) you
should also know that the subject of the check is believed to be
acting as paymaster and report centre for secret agents of a
foreign power engaged in espionage in this country and is in
constant communication with the subject of H.O.W. No.3058.'[31]
(W. N. Ewer[32] and the FPA)

As a result, it became clear that not only was the FPA engaged
in diplomatic and military espionage; but was also engaged in
spying on Russians resident in Britain, prominent British
Communists, and British intelligence officials. Laborious efforts
were made to identify and trace to their homes officers and
members of the secretarial staffs of MI5, MI6, the Code and
Cypher School,[33] and other departments of the Government. It
was also revealed that FPA was in close contact with ARCOS, the
Soviet Embassy, the *Daily Herald* and an organisation known as
the Vigilance Detective Agency (VDA), set up in London in 1920
by Klishko. The VDA's nominal head was the *Daily Herald*'s
editor W. N. Ewer, who had travelled to Moscow in 1920 with
Andrew Rothstein. Ewer's activities meant that communist
agents, forewarned of action to be taken against them, were often
one step ahead of their British counterparts.

The Comintern's United Front tactics and the setting up of the
Anglo-Russian Committee introduced Russian methods into the
British trade union movement; a tendency noted by Beatrice

Webb in her *Diaries* when she denounced Communist influence at the Hull and Scarborough Trades Union Congresses. The 'communistic trade union leaders', she wrote, 'have taken over the General Council and are plunging head over ears into grandiose schemes of immediate and revolutionary changes.'[34] An organised strike threat against a drastic reduction in mining wages, she thought, 'savoured of emotional syndicalism'.[35]

During World War I the mines had been placed under total government control; but they had not been nationalised. At the end of the war the Government had prepared to hand back the mines to the coal-owners who threatened to impose wage reductions across the board. The response of the British labour movement was swift and effective. In 1919 the Triple Industrial Alliance of miners, railwaymen and transport workers had threatened widespread industrial action to protect miners' living standards if the government didn't back down. Cabinet ministers, fearing widespread social and industrial unrest if not revolution, agreed to the setting up of a Royal Commission to investigate wages and conditions in the mining industry. Lloyd George's appeal to the leaders of the Triple Alliance was both true and memorable:

> You will defeat us. But if you do so have you weighed the consequences? The strike will be in defiance of the government of the country and by its very success will precipitate a constitutional crisis of the first importance. For, if a force arises in the state which is stronger than the state itself, then it must be ready to take on the functions of the state, or withdraw and accept the authority of the state. Gentlemen – have you considered, and if you have, are you ready?[36]

The Commissioners reported wholly in favour of the miners, recommending a seven-instead of an eight-hour day, wage increases of 2s a shift and a system of public ownership for the coal industry; the threatened strike never happened.[37] By 1921, however, once the threat of revolutionary upheaval in Europe had passed, the government felt strong enough to face down the Triple Alliance, and announced that control of the mines would be terminated by the end of March. While the Decontrol Bill was still being debated in Parliament the coal owners seized the initiative announcing sweeping wage reductions, while lockout notices were posted at all collieries. The Triple Alliance responded on 8 April giving notice of a railway and transport strike to begin in four days' time. The government reacted promptly and decisively. A state of emergency was declared, reservists were called to the colours, machine-guns were posted at pitheads, and troops in battle order were sent into many working-class areas.[38] The Triple Alliance, later dubbed the Cripple Alliance, backed down on Friday 15 April. This was 'Black Friday'.

The collapse of the Triple Industrial Alliance opened the door for any other body that could claim to speak for the mass of trade unionists. The formation of the TUC General Council was a direct result of 'Black Friday' and coincided with an improvement in the miners' standard of living. Following the French occupation of the Ruhr and the subsequent crisis in the French and German coal industries British coal exports to Europe increased substantially and the miners were able to secure a substantial wage increase. A Labour government was in power and the coal owners, 'notable even among postwar British capitalists for their inert stupidity', had made 'no plans whatever for the disappearance of the temporary boom due to the Ruhr adventure of the French.'[39] Hard on the heels of the Zinoviev Letter and the election of a Conservative Government the Chancellor of the Exchequer, Winston Churchill, put the British currency back on the gold standard at the pre-War level. It was an ill-conceived decision, the equivalent of an automatic tax on every export. Markets shrank and profits fell producing what the eminent economist J. M. Keynes described as 'an atmosphere favourable to the reduction of wages.'[40] The coal owners gave notice that they were terminating the National Wages Agreement of 1924, wages were to be cut very considerably and the minimum wage in the mining industry abolished altogether. The miners appealed to the General Council for support and instructions were issued for a complete stoppage of the movement of coal to begin on 31 July to be backed up, if necessary, by strike action. Unlike 1921 the Government was ill-prepared for major industrial action and backed down agreeing to pay a subsidy to coal-owners to maintain miners' wages at the old rates until 1 May 1926. This was Red Friday.

In the celebrations that followed, warnings from the Communists that the capitalist class would spend the next nine months organising to smash both miners and the General Council went unheeded. 'If the workers are doped by the peace talks and do not make effective counter preparations then they are doomed to shattering defeat', commented the *Workers' Weekly*.[41] 'The warnings were repeated in subsequent editions with a growing sense of urgency. Both the CPGB and the Russian-dominated Red International of Trade Unions (RILU), the Profintern, continued to demand that the TUC prepare for the test in May.[42] Less than two months' after the July settlement the state was ready to assert its authority over the TUC General Council.

The setting up of the Organization for the Maintenance of Supplies (OMS) with ex-viceroys and ex-admirals[43] placed at the head of a voluntary strike-breaking organisation, gave notice that the social elite that had emerged from World War I economically unscathed, was preparing to smash the labour movement.[44] Large reserves of coal were piled up; special constables (under 45 years of age) were recruited; a call went out for volunteers to maintain public services, to work as transport drivers,[45] messengers, cyclists and clerical workers. 'All the machinery was ready by April 1926, to move on receipt of the one telegraphed word: "Action." '[46] MI5 was wheeled into place and a new body MI(B), composed of ex-MI5 officers, was given responsibility for intelligence during the strike:

Kell kept a reserve list of former members of MI5 for use in emergencies. In order to keep in touch with retirees and other former members of MI5 Kell founded the IP (Intelligence and Police) dining club, which continued to meet until the Second

World War. During the General Strike, called by the TUC on 3 May 1926 'in defence of miners' wages and hours', the War Office department MI(B),[47] which was given a major role in both intelligence co-ordination and intelligence collection during the strike consisted entirely of (mostly retired) MI5 officers under Kell's deputy Holt-Wilson.[48]

During the strike both Special Branch and MI5 looked to exploit divisions within the labour movement, targeting British Communists and raising the spectre of Russian agents operating freely in Britain. They played on the fears of the General Council, which had changed dramatically since the triumph of the left at the Scarborough TUC,[49] in much the same way that Lloyd George had played on the fears of the Triple Alliance in 1919. In the two days between the posting of the lock-out notices and the onset of the strike they made frantic efforts to call off the strike. In last minute talks with the Cabinet they called for a suspension of the lock-out notices to allow negotiations to continue. It seemed an agreement was at hand when the intervention of the editor of the *Daily Mail*, Thomas Marlowe, made it all but certain that a strike would take place. "'Something has happened at the *Daily Mail*," Baldwin informed the General Council during a lull in the talks, "and the Cabinet has empowered me to hand you this letter'".[50]

The Cabinet letter referred to a telephone message they had received from Marlowe that the National Society of Operative Printers and Assistants had refused to print an editorial that claimed foreign revolutionaries were fomenting unrest in Britain. The spectre of the Zinoviev Letter hovered menacingly over Marlowe's message:

> We do not wish to say anything hard about the miners themselves. As to their leaders, all we need to say at this moment is that some of them are (and have openly declared themselves) under the influence of people who mean no good to this country.
>
> A general strike[51] is not an industrial dispute. It is a revolutionary movement intended to inflict suffering upon the

great mass of innocent persons in the community and thereby to put forcible constraint upon the Government.

It is a movement which can only succeed by destroying the Government and subverting the rights and liberties of the people.

This being the case, it cannot be tolerated by any civilized Government and it must be dealt with by every resource at the disposal of the community.

A state of emergency and national danger has been proclaimed to resist the attack.

We call upon all law-abiding men and women to hold themselves at the service of King and Country.[52]

'And now', Baldwin scolded them, the Cabinet 'ask immediately for a repudiation of this action.' The General Council immediately withdrew to discuss the ultimatum, drafted a formal repudiation and sent a deputation downstairs to the Prime Minister's room to present it. To their astonishment they found the Cabinet room in darkness. A servant told them that the Prime Minister had already gone to bed. The Conservative Government, to all appearances, had decided on class war. On Tuesday morning an eerie silence greeted the country:

> When the bells rang at midnight on Monday over the silent cities, they announced the beginning of a stillness which nobody had ever known before in English history. The Council had said that all activities should cease, in the trades that it named,[53] and cease they did. There were no trains, no bus services, no trams, no papers, no building, no power.[54]

Had Baldwin been right to force the moment to a crisis? Was it necessary to give MI5 a lead intelligence role in MI(B)? Who was 'the enemy within' – foreign communists, British communists, the trade union movement or the British working class itself? There can be little doubt that the Communists played a significant part in the strike; but it was also obvious that they were not in a position to lead a revolution, as the Government and both MI5 and Special Branch knew only too well: 'Theoretically they [the Communists]', Special Branch concluded, 'should have turned the general strike into a struggle for the seizure of power, but actually events had marched much more rapidly than they had anticipated and the general strike was declared when they were considering measures for preventing the transport of coal in the event of the miners' strike.'[55]

Foreign influences on the strike, however, were a different question. On 6 May a H.O.W. was taken out on the London offices of the Russian trade union journal *Trud* to prevent British Communists sending reports to communist papers abroad. Andrew Rothstein as TASS[56] representative in Great Britain during the strike was reporting events on a daily basis, and he was singled out by MI5 as an important individual keeping Moscow abreast of developments. It was later claimed that while working alongside a number of 'expert economists' from the Labour Research Bureau, he had acted 'half in an "intelligence" and half in an advisory capacity to the miners during the strike'.[57] He was also known to be 'in the closest contact with the Russian Embassy at Chesham House and the Russian Trade Delegation at 49, Moorgate'.[58] In this way he was able to oversee the payment of Russian funds to certain individuals; although claims that he was in a position to foment a revolution were far-fetched:

> He probably knows as well as any other single individual the many channels through which directions and subsidies have been reaching the prime movers in the business of creating a situation from which revolution might spring.[59]

However, as it turned out 'Moscow Gold' played little, if any, part in the actual General Strike; although it did much to alleviate hardship during the six-month miners' strike that followed. 'When the crisis came', New Scotland Yard reported, 'subsidies from Russia do not appear to have been there to meet it.'[60] The strike was two days old before the All Russian Council of Trades

Unions voted the first instalment of £25,000, and three days old before it was actually transferred to London with orders to pay it to the General Council. They, in any case, refused to accept any Soviet money. A second instalment of £175,000 and £25,000 was transferred on 8 May via Berlin and New York respectively but the London bank[61] involved in these transactions was prohibited from dealing with the foreign banks involved except by licence of the Secretary State, under 13A of the Emergency Regulations put in place at the onset of the strike. On 13 May the strike was called off and Baldwin managed to stay awake long enough to talk about 'unconditional surrender' on the wireless.[62] The miners, sustained by subsidies from the Central Union of Russian Trades Unions to the Miners Federation of Great Britain amounting to £380,000 by the middle of June, fought on until November.[63] In the 1927 Trade Disputes and Trade Unions Act that followed general strikes and sympathetic strikes were forbidden and fresh restrictions on picketing enacted. The Conservative Government also launched an attack on the unemployed 'worsening their condition by wholesale deprival of benefit on the ground that applicants were "not genuinely seeking work." [. . .] little money was saved by these tactics, though the suffering and humiliation caused were unmeasured.'[64] The workers' movement had effectively been smashed, the political left disabled for a generation, and as one American historian pessimistically concluded 'much that was imaginative, thoughtful, humane and good in British life and thought did not again get a serious hearing until after the Second World War.'[65]

13

The ARCOS Raid and 'Class Against Class'

I desire to thank all Officers and their Staffs, also the Ladies of the Office, for their splendid work and co-operation during the General Strike. The manner in which all hands have put their shoulders to the wheel shows that the ancient war-traditions of M.I.5 remained unimpaired.

Vernon Kell, letter to staff, 16 May 1926[1]

Was the involvement of Britain's security service MI5 in countering the labour movement during the General Strike a welcome departure from its original purpose of protecting Britain's secrets against a backdrop of intense imperial competition between Germany and Great Britain? The creation of a secret political police force during World War I may well have defeated pacifism but it led directly to an attack on democracy during the affair of the Zinoviev Letter in 1924. Moreover, by proclaiming a Civil Emergency and putting the country on a quasi-military footing during the General Strike the Conservative Government had created a role for MI5 that encouraged involvement in an industrial dispute for the first time in its history. It had political implications, counter-subversion was no longer solely concerned with Russian intrigue and the activities of the CPGB during the General Strike it had strayed into the area of trade unionism and, as the Zinoviev Letter had earlier demonstrated, the Parliamentary Labour Party and the Foreign Office. Was this justified?

Throughout the dispute MI5 agents had noted that the miners' leader, Arthur Cook, had been in close contact with Andrew Rothstein. During the strike both men were known to be staying at the National Hotel in Russell Square where, it was reported, Rothstein had arranged for Cook to meet 'with people' from Chesham House:

> Agent confirms that Cook's room is No. 129. [...] It has now been ascertained that ROTHSTEIN is staying there. His room is No. 39. He is accompanied by a woman delegate, believed to be either wife or daughter. The chambermaid stated that COOK has stayed at the National for years and that during the last strike, four years ago, he was also frequently visited by ROTHSTEIN. Agent also received information that COOK had been visited at the hotel by people from Chesham House recently, but he could not obtain the names.[2]

Of the Russians in London in 1926 the Soviet Counsellor at Chesham House, Ivan Maisky, was interviewed by MI5 agents on at least two separate occasions.[3] Maisky, who had arrived in England in May 1925, had known Theodore Rothstein in emigration before the October Revolution,[4] and during the strike he had been working closely with Andrew Rothstein and other members of the Rothstein family, including W. P. Coates and Zelda Kahan, who were then employed as English assistants to his Press Bureau.[5] That Maisky had some knowledge of the attempted distribution of 'Moscow Gold' to British strikers seems certain:

> He said that the number of workers on strike was not much over ?3,500,000 but that of course he knew very little about the conditions as the Soviet Government did not wish to be accused of interfering in England's internal troubles. When pressed, however, he said 'it is a mistake to think that there is a uniform strike pay. The strike pay depends on the individual Unions strike funds. In some cases it is 10/- per week, in some 20/- per week.' This means that the Moscow Narodin [Narodny] Bank

has been instructed to bring up the 10/- Union pay of the poorer Unions to the uniform strike pay of 20/- per week.[6]

Other Russians connected with Chesham House involved in the 'financial support' of strikers identified by an agent with close ties to the Embassy were the First Secretary to the Embassy, Dimitri Bogomolov, the Director of Moscow Narodny Bank, N. V. Gavrilov, and the charge d'affaires, Christian Rosengoltz:

> Previous to my seeing Maisky I had asked to see Bogomoloff but the Russian porter told me that Bogomoloff had gone out early in the little grey car and would not be back till late, if he came back at all today.
>
> I then asked for Rosengoltz and waited in their waiting drawing room for about 5 minutes when I saw the Moscow bank car arrive in the courtyard with Gavrilovitch [Gavrilov] and a woman.[7] They were shown into Rosengoltz' room at once and then Goldfad appeared saying that Maisky would be back in 5 minutes and would then see me as R. begged to be excused owing to a conference. She was unwell with flu and looked as if she had been kept at work all night. I gave her some aspirin and began to put her through a questionnaire. She mentioned Coate's wife [Zelda Kahan] and that Coate's telephone number was Regent 5032. Coates acts as English assistant to Maisky's Press Bureau and is a confirmed communist propagandist.[8]

The MI5 agent who compiled the above report appears to have been on extremely good terms with Maisky's principal secretary, Madame Goldfad: 'A very intelligent White Russian Jewess whose husband is retained in Moscow as a kind of hostage for her loyalty over here.'[9]

The economics behind Russian financial activity in Britain during the strike were complex and involved three different Russian institutions, ARCOS, the Moscow Narodny Bank and the Russian Trade Delegation, all of whom were targets for MI5.

The importance that the Russians attached to this activity and the sense of urgency, if not panic, among officials, was demonstrated by the intervention of the Soviet Politburo; pressure was undoubtedly put on both Maisky and Gavrilov to free up the Moscow Narodny Bank's funds for political purposes:

> A meeting took place (Thursday) yesterday [6 May] at 12.30 at Arcos at which CHOLIAMPKIN and MAISKY as well as all the other Directors of Soviet organisations in London were present. The whole party numbered 12 members. The servants were not allowed under any circumstances to enter the Council chamber. GAVRILOVITCH and MAUTUCHI, Directors of the Moscow Co-operatives Bank (Holborn) were brought to the meeting at 1.30 by special car. At 4.15 pm the conference was still sitting but Maisky was fetched urgently at 3 pm.
>
> This means undoubtedly that MAISKY has ordered the funds of the Moscow Bank to be made liquid; that a census of these funds has been taken, that the Directors did not willingly consent to their funds being used for political purposes; that Maisky must have been armed with full powers from the Moscow Executive of the Collequim of the Presidium, that these funds are about to be moved.[10]

The industry of the Trade Delegation and ARCOS during the General Strike led to a concerted campaign by the Government and intelligence agencies to curtail their activities, with a view to closing them down altogether. Scotland Yard's June 1926 report, 'Aspects of the General Strike,' began by listing the various 'communist influences at work in this country'; these included ARCOS and a number of other bodies (12 in number) which relied to some extent on the guiding hand of Rothstein. All were closely monitored by MI5 and New Scotland Yard with Guy Liddell submitting a particularly acute observation regarding Rothstein and the 'Society for the Promotion of Cultural

Relations' that doesn't appear to have been followed through by Kell. In a 1925 memo on the Society Liddell added, almost as an afterthought,[11] the following brief paragraph:

> Recent information shows that Andrew Rothstein takes a very active part in the meetings of the Society for the Promotion of Cultural Relations between Great Britain and Soviet Russia – one of the subtler propaganda organizations recently established by the Soviet Government in this country.[12]

According to a later report Rothstein not only took 'a very active part' in the meetings of this Society; but also attached great importance to the Society's work among academics, writers and scientists which anticipated the recruitment of secret agents in the universities in the 1930s.[13]

It soon became clear that Rothstein was expecting trouble in the aftermath of the General Strike, and it is a credit to his tradecraft that he always managed to keep one step ahead of his watchers. On 9 June 1926 MI6 sent New Scotland Yard's Captain Miller an extract 'from the stenograph report of a Protocol of a session of the Collegia of the NKID' that gave advance warning of a decision taken to remove secret documents from the Soviet Embassy following a report on Anglo-Soviet relations by Theodore Rothstein:[14]

Protocol of a session of the Collegia of the NKID.

Agenda	Decision
'Report by Rothstein on Anglo-Soviet relations.	In view of the complications manifest in the relations between the USSR and England, which might lead to surprises, to instruct BOGOMOLOV to take in hand at once the despatch of the more secret documents in London to Berlin and further to Moscow.'

The significance of the above is not very clear, but I take it to be
that ROTHSTEIN has reported the rising British feeling about
the continuance of diplomatic relations with Soviet Russia, and
that the NKID, in view of the possibility that extra-territorial
powers might be abrogated, is anxious to remove the more
incriminating documents from the Soviet Embassy.[15]

In July 1926 an added precaution was taken when Andrew
Rothstein was withdrawn from TASS[16] to take up employment as
the London correspondent to *Trud* and *Pravda*. Instructions were
received that he was 'to keep more in the background so that there
would be less risk of his secret communist activities compromising official Russian concerns in this country.'[17] There can be little
doubt that in the aftermath of the General Strike the Russians
were extremely worried by the implications of the strike for
its covert activities in Britain and Anglo-Soviet relations in
general. These concerns reflected the power struggle then taking
place in the Soviet Union between Stalin and the recently
resurrected triumvirate of Trotsky-Kamenev-Zinoviev organised
in the United Opposition.[18]

It was by no means clear that the Stalinists were unhappy with the
strike being called off. Tomsky, in fact, had 'wired the Central Trade
Union Council the day the strike ended suggesting that the TUC
really had no choice but to capitulate.'[19] It had ironically been the
Stalinist-controlled Politburo's[20] decision to ensure the continued
existence of the Anglo-Russian Committee that had led to the
formation of the United Opposition both within the Comintern and
the CPSU. Zinoviev now used the TUC General Council's 'betrayal'
of the General Strike to demolish Stalin's argument that the Anglo-
Russian Committee was an effective defence against British
imperialist military intervention. They had betrayed the proletarian
cause during the General Strike; they would do so again in the event
of war.[21] The CPGB shared this sentiment. The decision to call off
the strike was 'the greatest crime that has ever been permitted [. . .]
against the working class of [. . .] the whole world,' an act of 'abject
and unforgivable cowardice.'[22] The Russian trade unions issued a

statement on 7 June dubbing the General Council members as traitors and cowards.[23] By now, it was only the 'die-hard' triumvirate in Baldwin's cabinet, Joynson-Hicks, Churchill and Birkenhead, who held firmly to the belief that the General Council was working 'hand in glove' with the Russians, and they were determined to prove it with the help of the intelligence services. 'As they saw it, the Russians were trying to buy themselves a revolution in Britain, and they were not going to stand for it.'[24]

In a memorandum on 'Russian Money' produced by the Cabinet on 11 June 1926 Joynson-Hicks announced that capturing the TUC 'had been the major goal of Soviet strategists for two whole years now. The Minority Movement had been organized to help achieve that end, and so had the Anglo-Russian Committee, an instrument "for maintaining permanent and close contact between the extremists of the two countries."'[25]

There was undoubtedly some truth in this; only the Anglo-Russian Committee was not plotting revolution but pursuing Stalin's foreign policy strategy, aimed at normalizing relations and preventing British military intervention in the Soviet Union. Russian intelligence work in Britain was not, as Joynson-Hicks, Birkenhead and Churchill believed, based upon 'maintaining permanent and close contact between the extremists of the two countries' to guide the British revolution forward; but had, for some time now, diversified into the collection of state and military secrets.

By the end of September 1926 MI5 had drawn up a pretty comprehensive picture of the activities of the Secret Communist Organisation in Britain, and Rothstein's role in its proceedings was confirmed. A Committee of five was believed to be responsible for organising and directing the Party's 'underground' activity in the armed forces, and was in turn 'controlled by an inner circle of the British section of the Communist "underground" organization'. This inner circle, referred to by MI5 as B. group, received instructions from and passed its reports 'to a higher authority viz., an inner organization of the Russian-British section of the Communist "underground" movement', referred to as A. group. This 'higher authority' was 'in close touch with the Soviet Embassy and the Russian Trade Delegation.'[26] The members of this group were Andrew Rothstein (who topped the list), two English employees from Tass, Fred Taylor and Allen Hutt; while Fred Quelch, Allen Squair and Schichoff were employed by ARCOS; both Quelch and Squair were members of Rothstein's Mestkom. Andrew Rothstein, himself, was described as 'a freelance engaged on secret work for the Russians under cover of being a special correspondent of the newspaper "Trud".' An eighth member, Tom Walsh, was also believed to be working freelance. 'Both the A group and B group', it was reported, 'concern themselves mainly with the more secret side of Communist activity viz:-

(a) Acquisition of Naval and Military Information.
(b) Propaganda in H. M. Forces – independently of YCL activity and Press propaganda emanating from 16 King Street.
(c) Smuggling foreign agents into and out of this country.
(d) Secret courier system to and from abroad.'[27]

Informed by MI5 that Russian intelligence had developed a highly sophisticated outfit Joynson-Hicks saw in the General Strike an opportunity to prove direct Soviet support for subversive activities in Britain and to take the requisite steps to close down all Soviet intelligence activity. Leading up to the strike Joynson-Hicks maintained

the Soviets had involved themselves in intensive preparations for the decisive confrontation' exploiting the 'intimate and uninterrupted' connection with the General Council they had achieved via the Committee.[28] When direct contact had proved to be impossible or embarrassing, Rothstein, through the Soviet Embassy, had acted as go-between. The most urgent exchanges, Joynson-Hicks claimed, involved arrangements for financing the coming confrontation. On 4 May, he reported, 'the Bank for Russian Trade, Arcos, had paid in three cheques of

£100,000 each to the Westminster bank, to the credit of an organization the Home Secretary identified as the Wholesale Cooperative Society. The Society drew the money out again within 24 hours, £14,000 of it in silver and the rest in bills, 'and the Cooperative representative quite openly referred to it as strike pay'.

Thus, Joynson-Hicks could announce triumphantly, a Russian governmental agency – Arcos – 'was without doubt providing money *on the first day of the General Strike* for the financing of the strike.' Such damning evidence (which of course could not be made public since it was based on 'most secret information') demanded the cabinet discuss two urgent issues. Firstly, should Britain cut diplomatic ties with the USSR immediately and order all Russian representatives out of the country forthwith. Second, should the Home Secretary ban all donations from abroad for the miners' strike.[29]

Joynson-Hicks, however, had got it all terribly wrong; not for the first time and certainly not for the last. But it was interesting that the *Daily Mail*, that old Tory war horse from the Zinoviev Letter campaign, had its hooves all over the affair:

it must have been terribly humiliating for him [Joynson-Hicks] to discover, a day or so later, that the most formidable piece of evidence he had collected on the Russian gold was in fact a casual bit of ill-considered Fleet Street gossip. Those Soviet cheques (actually made out not to the 'Wholesale Cooperative Society,' which did not exist, but to the Cooperative Wholesale Society) represented in fact normal repayments on short-term loans; the funds drawn out by the trade unions at the same time and in about the same amounts were legitimate trade union reserves left on deposit with the Society; and the source of the 'most secret information,' apparently, was a representative of the *Daily Mail!*[30]

The Foreign Office now took it upon itself to rein in the Home Office for the simple reason that 'maintaining diplomatic relations with the Soviets did facilitate trade with them, trade which was not "negligible".[31] The moment was not opportune for a rupture and Joynson-Hicks had to bide his time. The rhetoric, however, remained bellicose and in June Chicherin was complaining to Chamberlain that Churchill – the architect of the 1918–19 war of intervention – 'was still determined to bring the Soviet government down'.[32] To offset the threat Stalin readied the Anglo-Russian Committee's aim to defend the Soviet Union; while in Moscow the war scare would be called upon to ensure the final defeat of the triumvirate Trotsky, Kamenev and Zinoviev. 'At the meeting of the Central Committee of the CPSU on 15 July Stalin defined the tasks of the committee as, *inter alia*, to "widen the fissure between Amsterdam and the British trade union movement", to create conditions favourable to removing the reformist leadership of the unions, and replacing them with communists, to organize a movement against British intervention in the Soviet Union. Those who were trying to torpedo the committee', he argued, 'were playing into the hands of the interventionists.'[33] On 23 July 1926 Zinoviev was dropped from the Politburo, the United Opposition being charged with trying to establish an illegal faction within the CPSU. Both the impact and importance of the General Strike on these events was made plain at a meeting of the ECCI presidium meeting on 7 August when Stalin suggested that the British side would be unwilling to break up the Anglo-Russian Committee because of the financial help coming from the Russian unions to the MFGB.[34] Soon afterwards Trotsky was dismissed from the Politburo and Kamenev from his position as candidate member of that body on 23 October; the following month Zinoviev was released from his office as President of the ECCI and from his work for the Comintern, and replaced by Bukharin.[35]

Rothstein's role as an interpreter and liaison between the CPGB and the Soviet Embassy had proved to be of greater benefit to the Stalinists than to the United Opposition, Rothstein effectively bringing the CPGB into the Stalinist fold. During this period MI5 continued to monitor Andrew Rothstein's movements and dealings with Chesham House. He was known to have attended a meeting of the Anglo-Russian Joint Advisory Council on 23 and 24 August, 1926, and a number of intercepted telegrams between London and Moscow, sent via an agent codenamed KOKOVTSEV, discussed the Anglo-Russian Committee, the TUC General Council, and the Miners' Strike; all bore Rothstein's imprint. MI5 identified KOKOVTSEV as ROTHSTEIN, and many of the telegrams were marked 'For Andrew, or for Andreev.'[36] There was some confusion here; Tomsky had recently been ordered to take two months' convalescence and had been replaced in July as head of the Russian delegation by Andrei Andreev, only just named a member of the Politburo. He met with British trade union leaders later that month. Kokovtsev's telegrams marked for Andrew or Andreev were, therefore, addressed to Tomsky's successor, Andrei Andreev. According to Rothstein, Tomsky's illness was more diplomatic than medical. He was regarded as being 'too close to the British leaders personally, and too genial and gregarious a soul [. . .] to make a convincing show of malevolence. Andreev, a hard, calculating *apparatchik* of the new breed, could do that sort of thing superbly.'[37] Andreev's appointment was designed to pull the rug from under the United Opposition's feet, and did so quite effectively.

MI5 now reported on Rothstein's very close co-operation with Radomsky, Rosengolts and Maisky[38] at Chesham House; noting that 'Maisky's wife, Agniya Aleksandrovna, an OGPU agent, was working in the secret department of the Russian Trade Delegation.[39] In this capacity she would have met Rothstein's future wife, Edith Lunn, as 'a member of the English cell of Mestkom'.[40] Edith was then living with Rothstein in Hampstead and engaged in secret work as an employee of The Arcos Company and worked closely with the Trade Delegation. The two organisations shared a number of rooms, including the cypher room, in their joint premises at 49 Moorgate.

Rothstein was a key figure in this set up. He was known to make periodical trips to Russia in Arcos steamers and was the only member of the CPGB in England who Moscow recognised as far as finance was concerned.[41] His journalism provided him with the perfect cover. An MI5 informant, known only as R.V. E., took a particular interest in both Rothstein and Edith Lunn,[42] reporting that Rothstein was in Moscow from 20 November until 7 December 1926, approximately.'[43] He was known to be in Berlin in November as a *Sunday Worker* correspondent reporting on a meeting of the British-Russian Miners' Delegation. From Berlin he travelled to Moscow to attend the Seventh Plenum of the ECCI held between November–December 1926.

Not surprisingly, given the recent collapse of the General Strike and its repercussions for the power struggle now unfolding in the Soviet Union, the British situation occupied much of the Seventh Plenum's agenda. The situation in respect of the Anglo-Russian Committee, with Trotsky commenting on 'the tendency in the Comintern to substitute diplomacy for policy', set the scene for the final showdown between the United Opposition and supporters of Stalin's 'socialism in one country'.[44]

The United Opposition's stand that the Russians should now withdraw from the Anglo-Russian Committee after the betrayal of the General Strike was opposed by Tomsky and Bukharin who argued that such an event would not only damage unity but would also put an end to Russian chances of entering the IFTU.[45] The Stalinists buoyed by the simple fact that the CPGB, despite recent membership gains, was not a mass movement had little difficulty defending the Anglo-Russian Committee.[46] The only remaining problem was the Profintern. While money earmarked for the CPGB was not compromised, significant funds were now set aside to tighten Stalinist control of the National Minority Movement (NMM).[47] Rothstein's 'secret duties' assumed even greater political significance:

> Up to the time of the raid on Arcos Ltd. on May 13th 1927 one of the principal secret duties carried out by ROTHSTEIN was the quarterly transmission of Russian money from the Soviet Embassy (where, in the form of American currency it used to arrive by diplomatic bag) to Albert INKPIN for CPGB funds and to Nat WATKINS for the funds of the NMM.[48]

When it came to the distribution of 'Russian Gold', however, Moscow distrusted the CPGB which was known to have been heavily penetrated by both MI5 and Special Branch agents. The *Sunday Worker*'s Charles Ashleigh was regarded as a safer pair of hands than anybody within the CPGB itself. In this respect, the SCR became Rothstein's 'greatest cover,' as MI5 came to appreciate, in the weeks leading up to the Arcos Raid in May 1927:

> ROTHSTEIN's greatest cover is the SCR. He is a Comintern Agent and is responsible for reporting to certain individuals employed by the USSR. Charles ASHLEIGH of the 'Sunday Worker' is also one of the few Englishman trusted by the Russian organization – more so than any of the King Street crowd. Fred TAYLOR is simply a stop-gap for the moment at TASS (Rosta).[49]

Rothstein returned from Moscow on the 10–11 January breaking his journey in Berlin to meet with Frederico Bach (Fritz Sulzbacher), the secretary of Willi Munzenburg's League Against Cruelties and Oppression in the Colonies. The two men discussed the arrangements for an anti-colonial congress to be held in Brussels, and the activities of the League in London. Special Branch working closely with their German counterparts passed intelligence to MI5 about this meeting, which included the date of the proposed congress, hitherto unknown:

12th Jan. 1927

> Dear Major Phillips,
>   We have just heard that Andrew Rothstein while in Berlin, presumably on his way back from Moscow, had a consultation with F Bach, secretary of the League Against Cruelties and Oppression in the Colonies, regarding its activities in London. This new connection is interesting. It appears that the International Conference at Brussels is now definitely fixed for February 10th.[50]

Muenzenberg could not guarantee communist domination of the International Conference and suggested a role for Rothstein and Workers' International Relief to the Secretariat of the Comintern in drawing up the guidelines for the congress.[51] Despite being turned down by the Comintern Rothstein's flirtation with Muenzenberg meant that his influence was becoming quite considerable, and independent of the Comintern. In April, MI5 had identified him as one of 'the ruling chiefs of the ARCOS Russian Norwegian Co., and the Russian Trade Delegation.'[52] In this capacity he was seen to be in personal contact with Jacob Kirchenstein, a director of the Russo-Norwegian Steamship Company,[53] and a secret agent of the Soviet Government and Comintern. Kirchenstein was ably assisted by Peter Miller of the Cypher Department of the Russian Trade Delegation, also an employee of the Russo-Norwegian Steam Navigation Company. Miller was described by MI5 as 'one of the worst members of the Delegation [. . .] the centre of all Russian intrigues.'[54]

It was the inability of Moscow Centre to guard against these intrigues that led to the ARCOS Raid and the expulsion of all Russian Embassy staff in 1927. In March the authorities got their breakthrough when they received intelligence from a Russian employee at Arcos, Dudkin, that the Russian Trade Delegation was conducting espionage in the UK. He handed to Sinclair, head of MI6, a photostat copy of a missing military intelligence document – 'Signal Training Vol III, Pamphlet No.11. Descriptions of and instructions for Wireless Telegraph' – informing him that the original document could be found in a safe at ARCOS Ltd. This was the long sought after smoking gun. On 10 May a further meeting between MI5's Captain Harker and Dudkin took place and the following day Dudkin handed Harker a number of documents which he claimed had been photo-stated or cyclostyled over a three-year period in the Photographic Room at Arcos House.[55] On 12 May the Commissioner of Police for the City of London armed with a search warrant raided the premises of Arcos Limited and the Russian Trade Delegation for the missing document based on 'information sworn by Captain Harker of the War Office'.

The search warrant was pretty comprehensive and permitted the search not only of the premises but of 'every person found therein', as well as 'the seizure of any sketch, plan, model, article, note or document, or thing of a like nature or anything whatsoever which is or may be evidence of an offence against the Official Secrets Acts 1911 & 1920'.[56]

During the raid a number of incriminating documents were found linking both Arcos and the Trade Delegation with covert activities. There was, however, surprisingly very little intelligence linking Rothstein with these activities other than a note claiming that he was personally known to Kirchenstein and a number of undated flyers instructing members of the Young Communist League to vote for a selected panel of candidates and officials at Mestkom meetings.[57] There were, however, a number of documents linking Rothstein, Edith Lunn and Maisky, with the Agitation Propaganda Commission of the London cell of the Russian Communist Party, the V.K.P. (b).[58]

> The London Cell has been proved to consist of members of the staff of Chesham House, the Russian Trade Delegation and of Arcos and its subsidiary companies. All members of the VKP (b) have the right to attend meetings of its Agitation and Propaganda Commission, which according to documents found during the raid take place at least twice a week. Certain specifically trusted British Communists have, by virtue of their position as members of the Russian and British Communist Parties also attended these meetings with the right to vote. Others who are not members of the Russian Party have on occasions been present in a consultative capacity. It is through these individuals that contact is made with the CPGB. The following are known to be concerned in this work: Andrew Rothstein, Edith Lunn, Leah Podolsky and Alexander Squair, Secretary of Mestkom.[59]

Maisky was also linked with the activities of Kirchenstein who was known to be operating a system of industrial and military espionage in Britain and America.[60] Rothstein, on the other hand, appears to have deliberately distanced himself from Kirchenstein's activities. The latter was particularly active in the NMM where he made good use of an older generation of communists, recruiting his main agents from ex-members of World War I Shop Stewards' Movement and the Socialist Labour Party. Many of them had worked closely with Theodore Rothstein in 1920, among them a Scottish engineer James Messer. All were well known to Andrew Rothstein. Messer received instructions ' "to build up a very secret organization to consist of specially trusted Comrades residing in certain districts". These "Comrades", working through the Shop Stewards in certain factories, were to obtain information on military and economic questions which they would transmit to MESSER who in turn would pass it on to KIRCHENSTEIN.'[61]

It was accepted practice for Russian intelligence to run parallel networks in Britain. Kirchenstein's network competed with, rather than complemented, Andrew Rothstein's. The two men appeared to distrust each other completely, and Rothstein not wanting to compromise his work with the NMM and the Anglo-Russian Committee complained on a number of occasions to Moscow 'Centre' about Kirchenstein's organisation, and put difficulties in the way of his operators. A letter sent to Kirchenstein in New York from one of his agents, Karlis, complained bitterly about Rothstein's activities:

> (10) ROTSTEIN & Co. are now wanting at all costs to clear me out and so is (11) the black one because you are not here, but the black one has received a hard knock and is now for the time being quiet. I am enormously worried about (10) Rot. & Co. as (12) B., who is standing by the black man has also been in correspondence to the centre along with (10) Rot. & Co. about me. They are using every means to try and get (me) out of the road, so then hasten over as quickly as you can. I am very worried about this clique and I am firmly convinced that they are responsible for your position. Other people are asking where you are. I say that I do not know but I am inclined to think that they think that you have gone off to the centre. (13) The little Russian

is also grumbling asking where you are all this time. A lot of fuss
(10) Rot. too has been asking (13) the Russian.

With greetings,
(14) Karlis.

10. Andrew ROTHSTEIN (son of Theodore ROTHSTEIN)
a member of the Soviet Delegation and of the CPGB. Has British
nationality. Is highly suspect.

11. C. Palme Dutt, an Indian half-caste. A member of the
Executive Committee of the Labour Research Dept. Head of the
Colonial Bureau of the CPGB and a member of the secret
executive of the Committee Pro-Hindou.

12. 'Comrade BENNETT', an envoy from the 3rd
International, whose identity has not yet been established.
[Petrovsky]

13. Could be a name KREENWINSCH or – in the new
Lettish spelling, KRIEVENS – KRIEVS – 'Russian' in Lettish.

14. Charles[62]

[Notes 10 – 14 are those of MI5]

Rothstein, along with Bogomolov, had been pre-warned by his
father that a raid on the Soviet Embassy was likely and to take
precautions. He had, for some time, been distancing himself from
Kirchenstein. When the 'ARCOS Raid' took place it had two
main targets: the missing Signals Training pamphlet and 'secret
documents' that could be used to wind up the Kirchenstein
organisation.[63] After the police entered the building they went
straight to two places: the Photostat Section, to search for the
missing military document and the Cipher Section, Room 5,
known also as 'the mystery room', so-called because a double set of
dark blinds were frequently pulled down during the day. There
was no handle on the door on the outside and it could only be
opened with a special key, the door locked automatically once
closed. There was a small sliding grid with a substantial bolt
through which papers were passed. Once inside the police found
the head of the cipher department, Anton Miller, brother of the

notorious Peter Miller, frantically burning documents.[64] A violent struggle took place during which a roll of papers fell from Miller's inside jacket pocket containing a list of legal and illegal addresses. Among the addresses were the headquarters of the Communist Parties throughout the British Empire and various foreign, mainly Latin American, countries. They were effectively 'the key to the underground movement of the Communist international', and to Kirchenstein's networks; Miller's legal work for ARCOS masked his illegal work for the Kirchenstein organisation.[65] The conclusion was drawn that the Head of the Trade Delegation, the entire staff at ARCOS and Chesham House, the Commissariat of Foreign Affairs in Moscow, and a former Charge d'Affaires were all engaged in supporting Kirchenstein and Miller's subversive and espionage activities. Despite strenuous Russian protests to the contrary a decision was taken to immediately expel the diplomats and members of the Trade Delegation.[66]

Rothstein, however, slipped into the shadows. Three days before the raid MI5's B.3. was still seeking clues to his identity: 'I am informed that a communist known as C. M. ROEBUCK is identical with Andrew ROTHSTEIN of Chesham House. I understand you have some record to this effect, but this confirmation may be useful.'[67] An earlier MI5 report described him as a 'Communist of the purest water' who avoided 'coming too prominently into the limelight'.[68]

In 1927 the Ninth Conference of the CPGB passed a resolution calling for a united working-class struggle to bring down the Conservative government, and its 'replacement by a Labour government pursuing a working-class policy under the control of the labour movement.' However, no sooner had this resolution been passed than a telegram arrived from the President of the Comintern, Bukharin, informing the CPGB's Executive Committee that the attitude of the communist parties to their respective social democratic parties was under review. The following year the Sixth World Congress of the Communist International adopted Stalin's policy of 'Class against Class', whereby all the social democratic parties were condemned as social fascist; the CPGB was ordered to stop supporting the Labour Party at elections and to drop its policy of affiliation to the Labour Party. Rothstein and other members of the National Executive Committee protested and argued that the British Labour Party was not yet a social democratic party in the accepted meaning of the term. They quoted from Lenin's *Left-wing communism: an infantile disorder* to argue that affiliation to the Labour Party gave the Communist Party a direct link to the masses. Rothstein was summoned to Berlin by ECCI to explain his support for a policy of 'class collaboration' and continued communist accommodation with the Labour Party. At the 11th National Congress of the CPGB, along with other leading members of the party, he was dismissed from the National Executive Committee on account of alleged 'right' deviation. The Central Committee of the CPGB even went so far as to conclude that he was a 'danger' to the British communist party and placed him at the disposal of the CPSU. In January 1930, on the brink of the purges, he left England to work with his father in Moscow who was then running the Anglo-American Press section at Narkomindel.[69] His activities in Moscow, and his subsequent career as a recruiter of NKVD agents opened up a new chapter in the Rothstein saga. In many respects the utopian idealism that had characterised the activities of father and son from 1890–1930 was subsumed by a more dystopian reality.

Epilogue

The activities of the Rothstein family in marrying a British Marxist tradition with Soviet Communism, and their contribution to the British labour movement, raises a number of important questions. The fact that Theodore Rothstein, the head of the family, learnt his Marxism in Britain and later adapted it to fit Soviet perceptions of communism is an indication that ideologies are never purely national. As such they can ensnare individuals regardless of their national, racial or class origin. They can, of course, be put to nationalist objectives as Stalin did with 'Socialism in One Country', and Churchill did when he tried to direct British working-class Jews away from Bolshevism towards Zionism, effectively subordinating East End to West End Jewry. The relationship between Russia and the British left over the period 1848 to 1928 and the role of the Russian political emigration in the British labour movement show that the status of an 'alien' in Britain belies the suggestion that an alien cannot play a full role in his adopted society and that an 'alien' is constantly in thrall to the culture he was born into, which determines his character.

For Britain's Special Branch and MI5 this caused a myriad of problems. The challenge thrown up by the revolutionary and anarchistic sympathies of many foreign Jews in British society was complicated not only by their involvement with the British left; but also by their support for a foreign power – Bolshevik and later Communist Russia – preaching the overthrow of capitalism. Kugelmann's 'police-tinged bourgeois mind' that saw the hidden hand of the International 'organising explosions' in various countries required a better understanding of native Marxism and communist ideology if it was to successfully counter subversion within labour movements and assimilate 'alien' groups. It is arguable that the British secret service MI5 and the intelligence service MI6 groped towards a partial understanding of this fact as the period under discussion in this book unfolded. Created initially to track down German spies in Britain before World War I, MI5 soon found its attention drawn towards curbing the activities of 'aliens' and militants inside the British labour movement. That this formed part of a global campaign to defend the British Empire pitted MI5 against sections of the 'alien' community allied to British anti-imperialists whether communist or progressive. In turn this led MI5 during World War I to monitor pacifists and anti-militarists, who were often portrayed as pro-German, alongside those members of the labour movement who opposed the war and industrial compulsion. 'The enemy within' broadened. The turf wars between Basil Thomson and Vernon Kell in the secret world had centred upon a rivalry between Special Branch, an old 'police-tinged' intelligence agency, set up in 1883 to combat Irish terrorism and MI5 established in 1909 to counter German espionage in Britain. Both strayed into the Russian political émigré community and labour activism, leading to a more sophisticated deployment of intelligence to combat both counter-subversion and counter-espionage post-October 1917. The Zinoviev Letter and the General Strike, however, showed that Britain's intelligence and security services were created to serve the interests of conservative elites. The ancient war-traditions of MI5 that Kell toasted following victory in the General Strike were invoked to defend 'the occult octopus' not the British working class. There was, however, a gentle sea change taking place.

In order to combat the Soviet Union's intelligence offensive during the 1920s MI5 needed the help of sympathetic elements within the British labour movement; if it was to succeed it needed to gain a more sophisticated understanding of the relationship between British and Russian Marxism, and to detach the aspirations of the British labour movement from those of the Soviet Union. Only that way could it combat extremism. MI5's obsession with Russian agents kicking the snow from their boots at labour meetings and the ever-present ' enemy within' served only to alienate the spooks from the British working class movement. Their unshakeable belief that British Communists and fellow travellers were seduced by 'Moscow Gold' or controlled by the hidden hand of 'aliens', undermined their effectiveness. MI5 took a long time to realise the fact that Britain's Communists had an uneasy relationship with the British labour movement. And yet the search for 'the enemy within' invariably took place within working-class institutions and communities. It is little wonder that they were so easily wrong-footed by the Cambridge spies Blunt, Burgess, Cairncross, Maclean and Philby, to say nothing of Oxford's elusive 'Homintern'.

The relationship between British and Russian Communists was always a two-sided affair simply because Marxism, as an ideology, existed in both countries; it was never imported from Russia, if anything, it was a British export. *The Communist Manifesto* and the first volume of *Das Kapital* were both written in Britain from close observation of industrial capitalism in the first nation to industrialise. The British class system and its inequalities that scarred the nineteenth and twentieth centuries, the revolutionary overthrow of feudalism in Russia, and the internationalism that emerged as an antidote to the warring-nationalisms of 1914–18 determined the symbiotic relationship between British and Russian Communism between 1920 and 1928. Henry Pelling's compelling statement – 'that there can be few topics more worthy of exploration than the problem of how it came to pass, that a band of British citizens could sacrifice themselves so completely [...] to the service of a dictatorship in another country' – is seductive because it probes the uneasy relationship between ideology and patriotic nationalism during the nineteenth and twentieth centuries. The failure to embrace 'my country right or wrong' cannot fully explain the motives of those British citizens for whom 'my ideology right or wrong' compelled them into 'the service of a dictatorship in another country'. Pelling's conundrum remains compelling.

Notes

Introduction

1. Henry Pelling, *The British Communist Party: A Historical Profile* (London: Black, 1958), p. 191.
2. Correspondence: Andrew Rothstein to David Burke, 15 January 1981.

Chapter 1   The Russian Political Emigration

1. Fyodor Dostoevsky, *The Idiot* (Penguin Books, 1955, p. 661 [1869]).
2. Zasulich shot and seriously wounded the St Petersburg police chief Colonel Fyodor Trepov, Figner and Perekovskaya were the main architects of Tsar Alexander II's assassination in 1881.
3. An unsuccessful rebellion of high-ranking officers in 1825 against the coronation of Tsar Nicholas I calling for the abolition of serfdom and a constitutional form of government.
4. Vera Broido, *Apostles Into Terrorists. Women and the Revolutionary Movement in the Russia of Alexander II* (New York: The Viking Press, 1977) p. 11.
5. Ibid.
6. Herzen's early political ideas derived their inspiration from French utopian socialism. The discovery of Saint-Simonianism, Herzen wrote in his memoirs was 'like a revelation.'
7. See E. Lampert, *Studies in Rebellion* (London: Routledge and Kegan Paul, 1957) p. 41.
8. Ibid., p. 176.
9. See ibid., p. 158.
10. A. J. P. Taylor, *The Struggle for Mastery in Europe* (Oxford: Clarendon Press, 1954) p. xix.
11. The June Days, 23–26 June, an uprising of French workers in response to plans to close the National Workshops, created by the Second Republic to provide work and a source of income for the unemployed.
12. Frederick C. Barghorn, 'Russian Radicals and the Western European Revolutions of 1848', *The Review of Politics*, Vol. 11, No. 3 (July 1949), p. 347.
13. Barghorn, 'Russian Radicals', p. 348.
14. Lampert, *Studies*, p. 247.

15. Quoted in Lampert, *Studies*, pp. 184–5.
16. E. H. Carr, *Romantic Exiles* (Middlesex: Penguin Books Ltd., 1933), p. 121.
17. See Richard Deacon, *A History of The Russian Secret Service* (London: Frederick Muller Ltd., 1972), p. 60.
18. Lampert, *Studies*, p. 186.
19. Ibid., pp. 186–7.
20. Ibid., p. 187.
21. Lampert, *Studies*, p. 233.
22. *To-Morrow: A Monthly Review*, No. 2 (Feb. 1896), pp. 101–2.
23. *Justice*, 6 May 1893.
24. *Labour Leader*, 28 December 1895.
25. Before the 1917 October Revolution the Russian Empire still used the Julian calendar as opposed to the Gregorian calendar adopted by the West in 1582, a difference of 12 days.
26. Sergius Stepniak, letter to his friends in Russia written in February 1882. Quoted from an archival source by E. A. Taratuta in her preface to S. M. Stepniak-Kravchinski, *Rossiya pod vlast'yu tsarei* (Moscow, 1965), p. 10, cited in Barry Hollingsworth, 'The Society of Friends of Russian Freedom: English Liberals and Russian Socialists, 1898–1917.' *Oxford Slavonic Papers*, Vol. 3, 1970, p. 48.
27. *Tomorrow*, No. 2 (February 1896), pp. 101–2; *Pall Mall Gazette*, 29 March 1886.
28. W. Earl Hodgson, *A Night with a Nihilist* (Cupar-Fife, 1886), p. 7.
29. Hyndman had been converted to socialism by reading a French edition of *Das Kapital* passed on to him for critical perusal by a Conservative Member of Parliament.
30. Before the October Revolution of 1917 the term 'Social-Democrat' (spelt with a hyphen) had none of the associations given to it in after years. 'It meant a Socialist who based his ideas on those of Marx – as distinct from those calling themselves Socialists who were in reality only impatient Radicals (in Russia) or preachers of Liberal or religious ideas in the labour movement (in Britain): and it distinguished the Socialist from the Anarchist.' Andrew Rothstein, *Lenin in Britain a communist party pamphlet* (Farleigh Press Ltd (T.U.), Watford, 1970) p. 3.
31. Stepniak, 'The Actual Position of Russia', *Commonweal*, I (March 1885).
32. Lev Alexandrovich Tikhomirov (1852–1923). The following year Tikhomirov repented his revolutionary activities. His book *Why I am No Longer a Revolutionary* was published in 1888 and he was granted an amnesty by Alexander III and allowed to return to Russia.
33. *To-Day*, June and July 1884; *The Times*, January to March 1884, esp. 9 January, 27 February, 26 March, and 18 April.
34. See J. W. Hulse, *Revolutionists in London* (Oxford: Oxford University Press, 1970), p. 35.
35. Ibid.

36. Pierre-Joseph Proudhon (1809–65) advocated only the reform, not the overthrow of capitalism.
37. *Dela I dni*, No. 2 (1921), pp. 90–1, cited in S. M. Baron, *Plekhanov, The Father of Russian Marxism* (California: Stanford University Press, 1963), p. 84.
38. Cited Baron, *Plekhanov*, p. 123.
39. See D. B. Saunders, 'Stepniak and the London Emigration: Letters to Robert Spence Watson (1887–1890)', *Oxford Slavonic Papers* new series L3 (1980).
40. Nikolai Vasileyevich Chaikovsky (1851–1926), revolutionary socialist and Narodnik, took up residence in England in 1878.
41. A. A. Titov (ed.), *Nikolai Vasil'evich Chaikovskii* (Paris, 1929) vol. 1, pp. 185–6, cited Saunders, 'Stepniak', p. 81.
42. The trial consisted of 193 students and 'revolutionaries'. The largest political trial in Tsarist Russia the trial ended in mass acquittals with only a small number sentenced to hard labour or prison.
43. Stepniak, S, *Chego Nam Nuzhno?* in Donald Senese, 'S. M. Stepniak-Kravchinskii and the National Front Against Autocracy', *Slavic Review*, 34 (1975), p. 508.
44. Eduard Bernstein, *Die Voraussetzungen des Sozialismus und die Aufgaben der Sozialdemokratie*, Stuttgart 1899. First published in English under the title *Evolutionary Sociaism* in 1907 by the ILP.
45. Senese, 'National Front', p. 509.
46. Baron, *Plekhanov*, pp. 140–1.
47. The Second International (1889–1916), an organisation of socialist and labour parties formed in Paris on 14 July 1884.
48. *Free Russia*, 1 October 1891; *Justice*, 19 September 1891.
49. *Justice*, 19 September 1891.
50. *Free Russia*, 1 October 1891.
51. Ibid. The 'enchanted flower' is an allusion to a widely spread popular superstition in Russia that the fern blooms on one night in the year known as Ivan Koupalo, and that whoever succeeds in discovering the flower will find a treasure, and be endowed with supernatural powers.
52. See Chapter 1 note 29.
53. *Justice*, 11 April 1891.
54. *Justice*, 10 September 1892.
55. *Labour Leader*, 11 May 1895.

Chapter 2   East End Jewish Marxist

1. Theodore, Albert and Samuel, see TNA Kew KV2/1575.
2. Nikolai Gavrilovich Chernishevskii (1828–89); Nikolai Aleksandrovich Dobroliubov (1836–61), among the Russian 'fore-runners of Marxism in Russia' (a Soviet phrase).

3. Correspondence: Andrew Rothstein to David Burke, 23 April 1983.
4. Father of future Home Secretary, Frank Soskice.
5. 'Platon. Evo zhizn' i filosofskaya deyatel'noct'. Biograficheskii ocherk. SPb., Tip. T-va 'Obshch. pol'za', 1896, 78 c., portr (*Zhizn zamechatel'nikh lyudei. Biograficheskaya biblioteka F. Pavlenkova*); Sokrat. Evo zhizn' i filosofskaya deyatel'noct'. Biograficheskii ocherk. SPb., Tip. T-va 'Obshch. pol'za', 1897, 75 c., portr (*Zhizn zamechatel'nikh lyudei. Biograficheskaya biblioteka F. Pavlenkova*); Aleksandr Makedonskii i Yulii Tsezar. Ikh zhizn' i voennaya deyatel'noct'. Biograficheskie ocherki. SPb., Tip. T-va 'Obshch. pol'za', 1898, 96 c., portr (*Zhizn zamechatel'nikh lyudei. Biograficheskaya biblioteka F. Pavlenkova*); Demosfen i Tsitseron. Ikh zhizn' i deyatel'noct'. Biograficheskie ocherki. SPb., Tip. T-va 'Obshch. pol'za', 1898, 88 c., portr (*Zhizn zamechatel'nikh lyudei. Biograficheskaya biblioteka F. Pavlenkova*); Osnovnie motivi rimsckoi poezii (Stranichka iz psikhologii rimskogo obshchestna). − *Zhizn*, 1901, T. 4, aprel, c. 101−102.
6. See *The Times*, 5 July 1890.
7. AN, F/7/12521/2: Angleterre (1887−1908), 12 July 1902 cited Robert Henderson, 'The Free Russian Library in Whitechapel' in Rebecca Beasley and Philip Ross Bullock (ed.), *Russia in Britain, 1880−1940: From Melodrama to Modernism* (Oxford University Press, 2013), p. 81.
8. Henderson, 'Free Russian', p. 81.
9. Followers of the French socialist Jean Allemane (1843−1935). Allemane, a disciple of Proudhon and a veteran of the Paris Commune of 1871, was a pioneer of syndicalism. In 1890 he formed the French Socialist-Revolutionary Workers' Party (*Parti Ouvrier Socialiste-Revolutionnaire*, (POSR)), which called for a general strike and direct action, acts of sabotage, strikes and factory occupations. The Allemanists worked closely with the trade union movement and rejected bourgeois parliamentary democracy as insufficiently democratic. Allemanism insisted on the autonomy of the trade unions and insisted that the proper function of the two French socialist parties, the Marxist French Workers' Party (*Parti Ouvrier Francais*) (POF) and the 'possibilist' or reformist Federation of the Socialist Workers of France (*Federation des travailleurs socialiistes de France* [FTSF], was to act as the political wing of the extra-parliamentary workers' movement.
10. *Justice*, 3 October 1896.
11. Ibid.
12. Th. Rothstein, 'The Russian Revolutionary Movement', *Justice*, 20 March and 1 May 1897. Chaikovskii described the members of his group, 'the Chaikovskii circle' as 'socialist-narodniks', which he claimed had been the dominant mode of revolutionary thought among the educated youth of Russia since the 1870s. He drew on Herzen's belief that the Russian masses possessed an immanent genius for revolutionary action and would create a better society free from the corrupting influences of an alien West.
13. Martin Crick, *The History of the Social-Democratic Federation* (Keele University Press, 1994), p. 97.

14. *Justice*, 22 May 1897.
15. *Justice*, 11 September 1897.
16. Ibid.
17. *Justice*, 13 November 1897.
18. *Justice*, 18 December 1897.
19. Ibid.
20. Ibid.
21. Ibid.
22. See W. H. G. Armytage, *A. J. Mundella 1825–1897. The Liberal Background to The Labour Movement* (London: Ernest Benn Limited, 1951).
23. *Justice*, 8 January 1898.
24. *The Social-Democrat*, March 1898.
25. Robert Blatchford, a charismatic figure in the labour movement, was the second son of John Glanville Blatchford, an alternative comedian, and Georgina Louisa Corri Blatchford, an actress. He had taken to writing whilst serving in the British Army where he rose to become a sergeant major with the Dublin Fusiliers. He launched his weekly newspaper *The Clarion* in December 1891, which was by far the most successful socialist newspaper in Britain before the World War I. By 1893 Blatchford was the leader of his own faction inside the ILP known as the Clarionettes, organising numerous choirs, Clarion Cycling Clubs, Socialist Scouts and what were happily known as Glee Clubs.
26. Crick, *Social-Democratic Movement*, p. 161.
27. The Stop-the-War Committee was established at a Conference of Friends of Peace summoned by the immensely popular late Victorian novelist, Rev. Silas K. Hocking on 11 January 1900.
28. TNA Kew KV2/1575 Precis of information regarding Theodore Aaranovich Rothstein.
29. 'Stop the War' activists and their jingoistic opponents were both susceptible to conspiracy theory, the jingoes tending to see the war hatched in Berlin to menace the vital sea route to India; while anti-war sentiment tended to see the South African war as a plot by cosmopolitan (almost invariably Jewish) financiers in search of cheap dividends. See Stephen Koss, *The Pro-Boers. The Anatomy of an Anti-War Movement* (London: The University of Chicago Press, Ltd., 1973), p. xxix.
30. *Justice*, 1 July 1899.
31. *Justice*, 9 September 1899.
32. *Justice*, 30 September 1899.
33. *Justice*, 7 October 1899.
34. Max Nordau, co-founder of the World Zionist Organisation with Theodor Herzl.
35. *Justice*, 7 October 1899.
36. *Justice*, 9 July 1898.
37. *Justice*, 21 October 1899.
38. Ibid.

39. J. A. Hobson, *The War In South Africa. Its Causes and Effects* (1900) (London: Create Space Independent Publishing Platform, 2103) p. 189. See also the discussion in (Colin Holmes, *Anti-Semitism in British Society, 1876–1939* (London: Hodder & Stoughton, 1979), pp. 66–70.

40. *Justice*, 28 October 1899.

41. *Justice*, 7 April 1900.

42. *Social-Democrat*, June 1900.

43. *Social-Democrat*, July 1900.

44. Ibid.

45. *Justice*, 29 June 1901.

46. *Justice*, 20 July 1901.

47. The Stop the War activists were disparagingly referred to as pro-Boers by their opponents.

48. The first-ever Socialist MP and the first president of the Scottish Labour Party.

49. *Justice*, 20 July 1901.

50. *Justice*, 27 July 1901.

51. *Justice*, 3 August 1901.

52. *Justice*, 10 August 1901.

53. *Justice*, 17 August 1901.

54. 'I have felt for some time past that I should like to offer criticism upon our proceedings from a more independent standpoint. Thus, a very able, enthusiastic and honest foreigner who does not fully understand the English language, or, of course, English affairs, has just been elected by the delegates at our Annual Conference at the head of the poll for the Executive Council of the SDF. If I had been elected at the same time, I should have been disinclined, perhaps, to comment on what seems to me a most absurd blunder.' Hyndman letter to the American land developer and socialist, Gaylord Wilshire, published in *The Challenge*, 11 September 1901.

55. C. Tsuzuki, *Hyndman and British Socialism* (Oxford, 1961), p. 132; SDF Conference Report, 4 and 5 August 1901.

56. V., Rabinovitch, 'British Marxist Socialism and Trade Unionism: The Attitudes, Experiences and Activities of the Social-Democratic Federation 1884–1901', unpublished PhD thesis, University of Sussex, 1977. Rabinovictch uses the term 'orthodox Marxist' to describe the group around Quelch; see also Crick, *Social-Democratic Movement*, p. 73.

57. The House of Lords decision upholding the Taff Vale Judgement between the Taff Vale Railway Co. v Amalgamated Society of Railway Servants (1901) held that, at common law, unions could be liable for loss of profits to employers that were caused by strike action.

58. The Labour Representation Committee was formed in 1900 by trade unionists and a number of socialist groups, including the SDF and the ILP, to secure representation for labour interests in Parliament.

Chapter 3 Socialist Unity, Revolution 1905, the London Congresses of the RSDLP and the Second International's Condemnation of Militarism

1. Kautsky endorsed the entrance of Millerand and two other socialists into the government of Waldeck-Rousseau where they sat alongside General Gallifet, the butcher of the Paris Commune. See J., Lenz, *The Rise and Fall of the Second International* (New York: International Publishers, 1932), p. 45.

2. This new party, formed in 1903, was anxious to avoid SDF accusations of slavishly following De Leon's American SLP. It, therefore, debated what was to be its new name: '"It doesn't matter what you call yourself"', James Connolly declared, '"you'll be dubbed the SLP anyway." And SLP we became.' Tom Bell, *Pioneering Days* (London: Lawrence & Wishart, 1941), pp. 40–1.

3. See Chapter 2 fn. 57.

4. *Justice*, 21 September 1901.

5. *Justice*, 30 August 1902.

6. Ibid. (Rothstein's emphasis).

7. *Justice*, 7 March 1903.

8. Ibid.

9. Ibid.

10. *Justice*, 9 May 1903.

11. The General Jewish Labour Bund in Lithuania, Poland and Russia, generally called the Bund, was a secular Jewish socialist party active between 1897 and 1920. The Bund had affiliated with the Russian Social-Democratic Labour Party (RSDLP) in 1898.

12. Bernard Porter, 'The British Government And Political refugees, c. 1880–1914', in John Slatter, *From The Other Shore, Russian Political Emigrants in Britain, 1880–1917* (London: Frank Cass, 1984), pp. 23–45.

13. The first edition of *Iskra*, a four-page journal printed on the thinnest paper imaginable so that it might be smuggled across the Russian border, had appeared on 24 December, 1900 in Leipzig, numbers 2 to 21 were published in Munich.

14. The other three members were Plekhanov, Axelrod and Potresov.

15. William Melville (1850–1918) retired as head of Scotland Yard's Special Branch in 1902 to become head of the intelligence section WO3 in the War Office responsible for counter-intelligence.

16. Porter, 'British Government', p. 35.

17. TNA Kew HO 144/545/A55176 item 44, 'Memorandum by E. R. Bradford, 24 May 1902; See also Porter, 'British Government', p. 35.

18. See Nadezhda Krupskaya, *Memories of Lenin* (London: Lawrence & Wishart, 1970), pp. 64–90.

19. This article formed the basis of Lenin's system later set out in his pamphlet *What is to be Done?* published in March 1902. In this essay Lenin argued the case for a

centralised, disciplined party, which would lead the workers' movement, and not follow in its wake; 'it provoked the criticism that such a book owed more to the terrorists of Russian agrarian socialism than to conventional contemporary Marxism', Robert Service, *A History of Twentieth-Century Russia* (Cambridge, MA: Harvard University Press, 1997), p. 71.

20. James William Long, 'Organized protest against the 1906 Russian loan', *Cahiers du monde russe et sovietique*, Vol. 13, Numero 13−1 (1972), pp. 24−5, 28.

21. Ibid., p. 28.

22. Long, 'Organized protest' p. 28n.1; 'Hoover Institute on War, Peace and Revolution, Okhrana Archives, VIj, 15C. Although somewhat sketchy in places the reports of the secret police agents give a fairly good account of the activities of those opposing the loan. One reason for this was Witte's desire to obtain the names of these so-called "traitors." ' See Okhrana Archives, XIIIe, folder 4.

23. Long, 'Organized protest', p. 26.

24. The Duma met for the first time on 27 April 1906.

25. Witte had been appointed Russia's first President of the Council of Ministers, i.e., Prime Minister on 1 November 1905; Pyotr Durnovo Russian Minister of the Interior. Witte resigned on 27 April 1906, and his resignation was accepted by the Tsar on 5 May 1906. He was replaced by Pyotr Stolypin who was later assassinated.

26. Olga Crisp, 'The Russian Liberals and the 1906 Anglo-French Loan to Russia', *The Slavonic and East European Review*, Vol. 39 (June 1961), p. 497.

27. Set up in the Russian embassy in Paris in 1885 to keep an eye on revolutionaries abroad, satellite offices existed in Berlin and the Balkans.

28. Richard, J. Johnson, '*Zagranichnaia agentura*: the Tsarist political police in Europe', *Journal of Contemporary History* 6 (1971), p. 222.

29. Johnson, 'Zagranichnaia', p. 231.

30. Second Duma: 5 March − 16 June 1907 (Dissolved by Nicholas II).

31. Rothstein, *Lenin*, p. 22. There were 105 Bolsheviks, 97 Mensheviks, 57 Bundists, 44 Polish Social-Democrats, 29 Lettish Social-Democrats and 4 'independents'.

32. Rothstein, *Lenin*, p. 22.

33. Ibid.

34. Simon Sebag Montefiore, *Young Stalin* (London: Weidenfeld & Nicolson, 2004) p. 179. Curious that Montefiore should describe Morris, who was attracted to revolutionary tactics, as a 'pacifist'.

35. Rothstein, *Lenin*, p. 25.

36. Montefiore, *Young Stalin*: 'The spooks were already inside the church. [The Okhrana's] double agent Yakov Zhitomirsky, who received 2,000 francs a month, was one of two traitors inside the Congress.' p. 182.

37. Rothstein, *Lenin*, p. 24: 'Sometimes they simply sat down with the delegates in a pub and began talking to them. "I remember on one occasion we ourselves started a conversation with our guardians. We were interested to discover

whether they were working for the British or the Russian police. We treated them to a beer and began questioning them about this. The British detectives swore that they were watching both ourselves and the Russian spies, of whom quite a number had travelled in our wake. We knew this, of course, even without their testimony"' (See Martyn Liadov, *iz zhizni partii*, 2nd edn Moscow, 1956).

38. George Herbert Perris (1886–1920) was the son of a Unitarian Minister. He devoted his life to many causes including the Peace Movement, the promotion of international understanding, the encouragement of democracy at home and abroad, and particularly in Tsarist Russia, and the development of new policies to replace *laissez-faire* capitalism. In the field of publishing, he founded one of the early literary agencies and originated the Home University Library, which provided specially commissioned cheap, authoritative introductions to academic subjects for general readers. See Robert Gomme, *George Herbert Perris 1866–1920: The Life and Times of a Radical* (London: Peter Lang, 2003); TNA Kew KV2 1575: Capt. Holroyd, Precis made in H.1. for reference only from Papers filed from 25 July 1911 to 8 October 1918. ROTHSTEIN, Theodore: 'He is also said to have got on to the "Daily News" through Mr. Perris for whom he worked on the "Tribune"'.

39. *Justice*, 20 July 1907.

40. Ibid.

41. Ibid.

42. *Justice*, 20 July 1907.

43. Ibid.

44. Ibid.

45. *Justice*, 20 July 1907.

46. *Justice*, 7 September 1907.

47. Ibid.

48. Report of the Stuttgart Congress of the Second International: Militarism and International Conflicts, 1907.

49. Report Stuttgart; see also Cole, G. D. H., *Socialist Thought. The Second International 1889–1914* Part 1 (1956), p. 69.

50. Cole, *Socialist Thought*, p. 75.

51. The First International had been founded under the name of the International Working Men's Association at a mass meeting in London on 28 September 1864. Its founders were the most powerful British and French trade union leaders of the time. Though Karl Marx took no part in organising the meeting, he was elected one of the 32 members of the provisional General Council and at once took over its leadership.

52. *Justice*, 7 September 1907.

53. *Justice*, 21 September 1907.

54. *Justice*, 14 March 1908.

55. The SDF in pursuit of socialist unity became the Social-Democratic Party in 1908 and the British Socialist Party in 1912.

56. In 1908 the Dual monarchy, Austria-Hungary formally annexed the province of Bosnia-Herzegovinia claimed by Serbia. Britain supported Ottoman demand for an international conference to adjudicate on the annexation of its former province; while Russian public opinion supported Serbia. As the controversy developed Germany came quickly and decidedly to the support of its Austro-Hungarian ally.

57. *Justice*, 5 September 1908.

58. *Justice*, 3 October 1908.

59. *Justice*, 10 October 1908.

60. Ibid. See also, David Lloyd George, *War Memoirs of David Lloyd George* (London: Odhams Press Limited, 1938, Vol. 1) pp. 4–20.

61. *Justice*, 10 October 1908.

62. *Justice*, 3 April 1909.

63. David Lloyd George (DLG) announced the Liberal Party's People's Budget designed to eliminate poverty in the British Parliament on 29 April 1909. DLG: 'This is a war Budget. It is for raising money to wage implacable warfare against poverty and squalidness. I cannot help hoping and believing that before this generation has passed away, we shall have advanced a great step towards that good time, when poverty, and the wretchedness and human degradation which always follows in its camp, will be as remote to the people of this country as the wolves which once infested its forests.'

64. *Justice*, 3 April 1909.

Chapter 4   Imperialism and the Struggle of the Working Class

1. The title of a series of biographical essays on Theodore Rothstein published in Moscow under the title *Imperializm I borba rabochevo klassa* in 1961.

2. Anthony Frederick Blunt (26 September 1907 – 26 March 1983), art historian, professor, writer and spy was the grandnephew of Wilfrid Scawen Blunt.

3. Wilfrid Blunt, *Married to a Single Life* (Salisbury: Michael Russell (Publishing) Ltd, 1983), p. 2.

4. TNA Kew KV2/1575, Eastern Mediterranean, Special Intelligence Bureau, Alexandria, re Theodore Rothstein copy of a note sent to 'K' [Kell] London, 11 June 1916.

5. Egypt was to all intents and purposes a British puppet state; its army, led by British officers, was still nominally under the sovereignty of the Khedive (Egyptian monarch) and his nominal overlord the (Ottoman) Sultan of Turkey. Under the rule of Evelyn Baring, 1st Earl of Cromer, British Consul-General in Egypt (1883–1907), Egypt was governed by the so-called Granville Doctrine (named after the Foreign Secretary, Lord Granville), under which Baring and other British officials could dismiss Egyptian ministers who refused to accept British directives. Although the Liberal administration of Campbell-Bannerman

(1905–8) adopted a more lenient policy towards Egypt, replacing Lord Cromer with the Arab-speaking Eldon Gorst, in 1909 the Congress of Egyptian Youth demanded British withdrawal from Egypt.

6. TNA Kew KV2/1575. Rothstein's movements abroad were monitored by Special Branch see TNA Kew KV2/1581 79(2a): 'He [Rothstein] states that he occasionally spends his holidays abroad and in the month of August, 1907, was in Germany for a period of three weeks. On 3 April last he was seen by Special Branch officers passing through Boulogne-sur-mer, France, and Folkestone on his way back from Paris.'

7. *Justice*, 18 June 1910.

8. Wilfrid Scawen Blunt, *My Diaries: being a personal narrative of events 1888–1914* (New York: A. A. Knopf, 1921), entry for 28 October 1910.

9. Theodore Rothstein, *Egypt's Ruin. A Financial And Administrative Record*, With An Introduction By Wilfrid Scawen Blunt (London: A. C. Fifield 1910), p. viii.

10. W. S. Blunt, *Diaries*, entry for 28 October 1910. His first application was turned down in 1908 'on account of his extreme socialistic views.' TNA Kew KV2/1575, Precis of information regarding Theodore Aronovitch ROTHSTEIN. See also TNA Kew KV2/1581.

11. Keith Neild, 'Theodore Rothstein', *Dictionary of Labour Biography*, Vol. VII, edited by Joyce Bellamy & John Saville (1984).

12. The SDF had become the Social Democratic Party in 1909 following a Socialist Unity convention among British Marxist groups.

13. *Justice*, 30 July 1910.

14. *Justice*, 22 April 1911.

15. *Justice*, 11 February 1911.

16. Ibid.

17. *Justice*, 20 March 1911.

18. *Justice*, 8 April 1911.

19. *Justice*, 22 April 1911.

20. The Agadir Crisis (also called the Second Moroccan Crisis or the *Panthersprung*) was the name given to the international tension sparked by the deployment of a substantial force of French troops in the interior of Morocco in April 1911. Germany reacted by sending the gunboat SMS Panther to the Moroccan port of Agadir which arrived at Agadir on 1 July 1911.

21. *Egypt's Ruin* was written by Rothstein and is a glaring mistake by the writer of this document.

22. Rothstein was born on 26 February 1871 in Kovno, now Kaunas, in Lithuania, then part of the Russian Empire.

23. TNA Kew KV2/1575, Precis of information regarding Theodore Aronovitch ROTHSTEIN.

24. The security service MO5, the forerunner of MI5, came into being in 1909. See Chapter 5.

25. TNA Kew KV2/1575 (Torn document).

26. Ibid.

27. Ibid. Capt. Holroyd, Precis made in H.1. for reference only from Papers filed from 25 July 1911 to 8 October 1918. I. ROTHSTEIN.

28. Ibid. Eastern Mediterranean, Special Intelligence Bureau, Alexandria, re Theodore Rothstein copy of a note sent to 'K' [Kell] London, 11 June 1916.

29. Ibid: Capt. Holroyd, Precis made in H.1. for reference only from Papers filed from 25 July 1911 to 8 October 1918. I. ROTHSTEIN. (Torn document reads): '(which he knew of "eighteen [. . .] in advance")'.

30. Jean Longuet (1876–1938), French socialist and Karl Marx's grandson.

31. TNA Kew KV2 1575, Capt. Holroyd, Precis made in H.1. for reference only from Papers filed from 25 July 1911 to 8 October 1918. I. ROTHSTEIN TNA KV2 1575 (Torn document reads): 'whom he urged to [persuade] the French Cabinet to be more conciliatory'.

32. TNA Kew KV2/1575, Capt. Holroyd, Precis made in H.1. for reference only from Papers filed from 25 July 1911 to 8 October 1918. I. ROTHSTEIN.

33. In 1910 four members of the ILP's National Administrative Council (NAC) launched the 'Green Manifesto' calling for the Labour Party in Parliament to vote on the merits of each question and not on the basis of support for the Liberals. The signatories all lost their place on the NAC at the ILP conference the following year, and had to look elsewhere for their political berth.

34. Zelda Kahan, 'V borbe protiv oppoortunizma I revizionizma angliiskikh sotsial-demokratov', *Imperializm I borba rabochevo klassa* (Moskva, 1960), p. 36. 'The struggle against opportunism and revisionism in English social-democracy' (*Imperialism and the struggle of the working class*, Moscow, 1960).

35. 'The "Green Manifesto" drew support from some deterministic Socialists who supported an old ILP Socialist rallying cry, the unity of the Socialist left as an alternative to a restricting alliance with moderate trade unions.' Duncan Tanner, *Political Change and the Labour Party 1900–1918* (Cambridge: Cambridge University Press, 1990), p. 51. See also Chapter 3, note 32.

36. BSP Conference Report 1912.

37. *Justice*, 4 January 1913.

38. *Justice*, 11 January 1913.

39. *Justice*, 18 January 1913.

40. *Justice*, 11 January 1913.

41. Ibid.

42. *Justice*, 15 March 1913.

43. Ibid.

44. BSP Conference Report 1913.

45. Ibid.

46. Ibid.

47. Ibid.; see also *Justice*, 17 May 1913.

48. Walter Kendall, *The Revolutionary Movement in Britain, 1900–1921* (London: Weidenfeld & Nicolson, 1969), p. 59.

49. Ibid., p. 61.

Chapter 5   War and MI7(d). Chicherin, the Zimmerwald Manifesto and Trotsky's *Nashe Slovo*

1. MO6 ran a translation bureau for the intelligence and security services.
2. Two 'diminutive departments', MO2 and MO3, had been established within the Directorate of Military Operations at the War Office in 1903. MO3 was renamed MO5 in 1907, the Secret Service Bureau was created in 1909, Kell's section became known as the Counter-Espionage Bureau or Special Intelligence Bureau, and within the War Office as MO5(g). See Andrew, *Defence*, pp. 5–6.
3. TNA Kew WO 106/6292, 'Conclusions of the Sub-Committee requested to consider how a secret service bureau could be established in Great Britain', 28 April 1909; Andrew, *Defence*, p. 21.
4. Andrew Cook, M. *MI5's First Spymaster* (London: The History Press, 2006) p. 211.
5. See, for example, Major W. E. Evans Gordon in the House of Commons 11 and 14 June 1906: 4H, 158, cc. 701 and 1138, and on 27 Nov. 1906: 4H, 165, c.1422; Arthur Fell on 27 Feb. 1907: 4H, 170, c.39; and Charles Hay on 25 Feb. 1909: 5H, 1, c. 961.
6. Donald Rumbelow, *The Houndsditch Murders and the Siege of Sydney Street* (London: The History Press, 2009), p. 119, Colin Rogers, *The Battle of Stepney. The Sidney Street Siege: Its Causes and Consequences* (London: Robert Hale Ltd., 1981), ch. 17.
7. TNA Kew CAB 37/105, no.2.
8. Andrew, *Defence*, p. 30.
9. Apparently, Russians and presumably Russian Jews, as allies of the Triple Entente were excluded. 'The list consisted of Austro-Hungarians, Belgians, Danes, Germans, Dutch, Norwegians, Swedes and Swiss. It also included naturalized British formerly citizens of these countries. Although allied to the Central Powers, Italians were excluded, as were the small number of resident Turks'. Andrew, *Defence*, p. 48 and fn. 99, p. 882.
10. TNA Kew HO 48/10629/199699, Kell to Troup (Home Office), 11 Dec. 1913; quoted in Andrew, *Defence*, p. 48.
11. See fn. 2 above.
12. Reginal McKenna replaced Winston Churchill as Home Secretary on 23 October 1911 and remained in office until 27 May 1915.
13. Hansard, HC 5 ser vol 65 col 1986.
14. Between 1903 and 1906 a wave of pogroms had left an estimated 2,000 Jews dead and thousands more wounded.
15. *Justice*, 17 September 1914.
16. Correspondence, Andrew Rothstein to David Burke, 13 January 1981 (hereafter Rothstein to Burke).
17. Rothstein to Burke, 13 January 1981; Andrew Rothstein, '*Iz Vospominanii ob otse* ('Some Notes on My Father's Work'), *Imperializm I borba*, p. 50; David Burke, 'Theodore Rothstein, Russian Émigré and British Socialist', in John Slatter

(ed.), *From The Other Shore. Russian Political Emigrants in Britain, 1880–1917* (London: Frank Cass), pp. 90–1.

18. A future Soviet Ambassador to Britain 1932–1943.

19. TNA Kew KV2/1575 Precis of information regarding Theodore Aronovitch Rothstein.

20. Andrew, *Defence*, p. 100.

21. Fineberg had been brought to England by his parents in 1887 at the age of 18 months.

22. *Justice*, 22 October–17 December 1914; Andrew, *Defence*, p. 100.

23. *Justice*, 15 October 1914.

24. *Justice*, 22 October 1914.

25. *Justice*, 5 November 1914.

26. *Justice*, 12 November 1914.

27. *Justice*, 19 November 1914.

28. *Justice*, 26 November 1914.

29. *Justice*, 14 January 1915.

30. *Justice*, 28 January 1915.

31. See the *Labour Leader*, 25 March 1915.

32. MO5(g)A: 'Investigation of espionage and cases of suspected persons'; MO5(g) B: 'Co-ordination of general policy of Government Departments in dealing with aliens. Questions arising out of the Defence of the Realm Regulations and the Alien Restrictions Act'; MO5(g)C: 'Records, personnel and port [immigration] control'. See Andrew, *Defence*, pp. 29–31.

33. The Aliens Restriction Act, like DORA had been drafted by the Home Office in consultation with Kell and Holt-Wilson, in readiness for war. It was rushed through parliament on 5 August and gave the government carte blanche 'to impose restrictions on aliens and make such provisions as appear necessary or expedient for carrying such restrictions into effect.' See Andrew, *Defence*, p. 53.

34. TNA Kew KV2/1575.

35. TNA Kew FO371/3347/179551.

36. MO6 ran a translation bureau for the intelligence and security services.

37. 'Contemporaneously with the deliberations which resulted in the formation of this Committee, proposals had been put forward by the Admiralty and War Office for the constitution of the Press Bureau. Peace conditions, however, did not seem to demand any immediate action and the Press Bureau did not come into existence until 13 August, 1914, after the outbreak of the war.' TNA Kew WO32/10776, MI7.

38. Thomas James Macnamara (23 August 1861–3 December 1931).

39. Sir William Reginald Hall (28 June 1870–22 October 1943).

40. Harold John Tennant (18 November 1865–9 November 1935).

41. The Press Bureau was the creation of F. E. Smith [Lord Birkenhead]. It followed the foundation of the cable censorship department, created secretly on the night of Sunday 2 August 1914. It was the first time a centralised censorship organisation, such as the Press Bureau was, had been set up in Britain.

The foreign press proved a vital intelligence asset to all the belligerent nations providing 'open source' intelligence material in a number of key areas. See Frederick Second Earl of Birkenhead, *F. E. Smith first Earl of Birkenhead by his son* (London: Eyre & Spottiswoode, 1960), pp. 240–50. 'The Press, whether it liked it or not, must be strictly controlled, as the enemy sought to procure English newspapers at every possible opportunity. As late as the autumn of 1915 the Germans were all too well-informed upon miscellaneous topics relating to our internal condition, organisation, and preparations.' Ibid., p. 244.

42. TNA Kew WO32/10776, MI7.

43. Ibid. The Press Cable Censors had been transferred from MI8 to the Press Bureau on 28 August 1914.

44. TNA Kew WO32/10776, MI7.

45. Theodore Rothstein worked 'on foreign newspapers, in an office (Watergate House, on the Embankment, quite separate from the W.O.) which was run like a newspaper office.' Correspondence Rothstein to Burke, 13 August 1981. Interestingly, the codebreaker Dilly Knox's brother, Ronnie, transferred from Room 40 to MI7 at Watergate House in 1916. Room 40 itself shifting from the Admiralty Building in Whitehall to Watergate House in 1919. At that time Rothstein was still employed by MI7(d). See Chapter 9 for a discussion of MI1 (c)'s (MI6) fears that Andrew Rothstein had an agent inside the Government Code and Cypher School (GC&CS).

46. Rothstein to Burke, 13 January 1981.

47. Ibid.

48. This may have been an Irishman called Maloney. 'I was interested to hear that Maloney was in England and visited you. Has he changed politically, I wonder? He must have left Persia quite ten years ago, but he may rest assured, Persia remains exactly what she was at that time' (Fitzwilliam Museum Library (FML), Cambridge, 217–1976, Theodore Rothstein to Wilfred Scawen Blunt, 23 May 1921).

49. TNA Kew KV2/1575, 'Theodore Rothstein'.

50. FML, Cambridge, 160–1975, Theodore Rothstein to Wilfred Scawen Blunt 18 January 1916.

51. TNA Kew KV2/1575, 'Theodore Rothstein'.

52. TNA Kew KV2/1575.

53. The Rupert Murdoch of his day, Alfred Charles William Harmsworth, 1st Viscount Northcliffe (15 July 1865–14 August 1922) was owner of the *Daily Mail* and *Daily Mirror* was a pioneer of popular journalism; he exercised vast influence over British popular opinion.

54. FML Cambridge, 171–1975, Theodore Rothstein to Wilfrid Scawen Blunt 2 December 1916.

55. Ibid.

56. See Chapter 3.

57. S. Zarnitskii and A. Sergeyev, *Chicherin* (Moscow, 1966), pp. 44–58.

58. 'Trotsky had joined Martov in Paris in November 1914 and collaborated with him on *Nashe Slovo* (*Our Word*), without doubt the most brilliant pacifist organ in Europe' (Orlando Figes, *People's Tragedy* (London: Pimlico, 1997) p. 294) (Nashe Slovo was in fact a revolutionary socialist organ, not a pacifist one. Figes appreciation of it, however, is quite correct.); 'Trotsky's influence during the First World War, exercised through the medium of the paper and the group around *Nashe Slovo* was considerable, this was very apparent in Paris during the two years that he lived there, and of this his expulsion by the French Government is the best proof. *I know from him also, that the English circulation of* Nashe Slovo *was no less large than that in France.*' Alfred Rosmer, letter to Walter Kendall, 20 March 1960 (Kendall's emphasis). Kendall, *Revolutionary Movement*, pp. 376−7.

59. 'Trotsky's paper circulated widely, the articles [...] being translated into German and republished in Robert Grimm's *Berner Tagwacht*, copies of which crossed the Swiss border and were sent to leaders such as Liebknecht.' Kendall, *Revolutionary Movement*, p. 112.

60. See Simon Sebag Montefiore, *Young Stalin*, pp. 176−86.

61. 'Both Stalin and Litvinov have been blamed or credited, according to the point of view, with participation in the Tiflis exploit, but while Stalin as Chairman of the Tiflis Committee must have known the plan in advance [...] there is no reason to suppose that he himself was actively engaged, while Litvinov, despite the oft-repeated legend depicting him as a gun-man storming through the streets of Tiflis, was really several thousand miles away in Paris.' Arthur Upham Pope, *Maxim Litvinov* (London: Martin Secker & Warburg Ltd., 1943) p. 92.

62. TNA Kew KV3/39, 'The Political background to the Houndsditch Murders and The Siege of Sydney Street.'

63. Passed in July 1915 the Munitions Act suspended trade union rights in the munitions industries and declared strikes in factories engaged on 'war work' illegal. All future labour disputes were to be submitted to compulsory arbitration. TNA Kew MUN 5/19/221.1/2 (July 1915).

64. TNA Kew MUN 5/19/221.1/2 (July 1915).

65. *Kommunist*, September 1915.

66. The Second International had effectively collapsed on the 3 August 1914, two days after Germany declared war on Russia, when the SPD parliamentary group in the Reichstag voted overwhelmingly for the war credits. The Socialist and Labour parliamentary groups in Austria, France and Great Britain quickly followed suit. Only the Serbians and the Russians, both Bolshevik and Menshevik factions of the RSDLP, along with Kerensky's Labour Party walked out of the Duma refusing to vote the credits through.

67. Quoted in Figes, *People's Tragedy*; see pp. 294−5 for a good discussion on the impact of the Zimmerwald Manifesto on labour movements.

68. Emile Vandervelde, leader of the Belgian socialists, the *Parti Ouvrier Belge* and Chairman of the International Socialist Bureau 1910−18.

69. *Vanguard*, December 1915.

70. *Nashe Slovo*, 7 December 1915.

71. The BSP had affiliated to the Labour Party in 1911.
72. *Nashe Slovo*, 7 December 1915.
73. Johnson, 'Zagranichnaya Agenture', p. 225.
74. *Nashe Slovo*, 8 October 1915.

Chapter 6   War, the Clyde Workers' Committee and Peter Petrov

1. *Labour Leader*, 4 November 1915.
2. Ron Grant, 'G. V. Chicherin and the Russian Revolutionary Cause in Great Britain', in Slatter (ed.), *Other Shore*, pp. 123–4.
3. See Grant, 'Chicherin', p. 124.
4. Established in February 1915 to protest against profiteering among companies producing war materials the CWC was neither revolutionary nor opposed to the war itself.
5. *Justice*, 23 December 1915.
6. Irma Gellrich.
7. Tom Bell, *John Maclean* (Glasgow: 1944), pp. 43–8.
8. Kendal, *Revolutionary Movement*: 'An independent authority considers that between July 1914 and February 1915 the purchasing power of an engineer's sovereign had been reduced by about twenty per cent. In the same period rents in some areas had risen by as much as ten per cent. The level of profits was running high,' p. 113.
9. Kendall, *Revolutionary Movement*, p. 116.
10. See Kendall, *Revolutionary Movement*, pp. 116–17.
11. The introduction of unskilled workers to skilled work.
12. 'William Gallacher. Born Paisley, Scotland, 25 December 1881. Died 12 August 1965. Trade unionist, socialist leader and agitator. Originally a member of ILP, joined SDF in 1905. Seaman and later engineer. Visited Chicago in 1913. Influenced by syndicalist ideas. A leader of the Clyde Workers' Committee 1915–16, and a prominent member of the shop stewards' movement on the Clyde. Attended Second World Congress of the Communist International in August 1920, joined Communist Party of Great Britain, January 1921. Most prominent Scots member of the Communist Party for the rest of his life. Communist MP for West Fife from 1935 till 1950.' See Kendall, *Revolutionary Movement*, p. 331.
13. John Muir. Born Glasgow 15 December 1879. Died 11 January 1931. A leader of the Clyde Workers' Committee 1915–16, and a prominent member of the shop stewards' movement.
14. *Justice*, 6 January 1916.
15. Ibid.
16. *Justice*, 13 January 1916.
17. *Justice*, 20 January 1916.
18. Petrov to Chicherin, letter post-marked 24 January 1916 (Bridges Adams Papers) cited Grant in Slatter (ed.), *Other Shore*, p. 123.

19. Correspondence: Rothstein to Burke 15 August 1982.
20. Headingley, a spiritualist, may well have been working with the authorities since 1898. An interesting article in *The Social-Democrat* entitled 'Spiritualism and Socialism' would suggest that Melville's Special Branch had their agents in the most unlikely of places: 'For instance, some socialists hold a séance. They have a good sensitive, who goes off into a condition of hypnosis, or trance. There is a traitor in their midst, and by sheer force of thought transference, without uttering a word aloud, the traitor makes the sensitive declare that he is controlled by a spirit, that this is the spirit of a good Socialist, who has come to inform his friends that one of their best and most trusted leaders is at heart only a self-seeker, ready to sell out at the first profitable occasion.' A. S. Headingley, 'Spiritualism and Socialism', *The Social Democrat*, II, No. 8 (August 1898).
21. *Nashe Slovo*, 19 January 1916.
22. *Forward, Labour Leader, Vanguard* and *The Worker*. On Christmas Day the platform had to be barricaded and protected by police; the chairman, Arthur Henderson, was repeatedly shouted down, and Lloyd George was met with 'loud and continued booing and hissing [. . .] two verses of the Red Flag were sung before the Minister could utter a word.' *Forward*, 1 January 1916.
23. Raymond Challinor, *The Origins of British Bolshevism* (London: Croom Helm Ltd., 1977) p. 140. The Socialist Labour Party had been formed in 1903 when a section of the BSP, based predominantly in Scotland, broke away to form a party more in tune with the aspirations of industrial unionism.
24. Challinor, *Origins*, p. 140.
25. Andrew, *Defence*, p. 96.
26. Ibid.
27. Ibid.
28. Challinor, *Origins*, pp. 141–2.
29. Ibid.
30. V. I. Lenin, 'Split or Decay.' Written between Feb/April 1916 but not published until 1931. Lenin, *Collected Works*, 4th edn. Vol. xxii (Moscow: 1964).
31. 'On 11 April 1916, John Maclean faced indictment on six charges, which ranged from inciting soldiers to lay down their arms, sleeping in in the morning and not to go to work.' He received a three-year sentence. Those associated with *The Worker's* production, Muir and Gallacher, each got 12 months while Walter Bell got three; other leading militants were deported from Glasgow. Challinor, *Origins*, p. 140.
32. *Nashe Slovo*, 11 February 1916.
33. *Justice*, 9 March 1916.
34. The Berne International Committee, also known as the International Socialist Committee and the Internationalist Socialist Commission, was a co-ordinating committee of socialist parties adhering to the Manifesto of the Zimmerwald Conference of 1915.
35. *Justice*, 24 February 1916; see also *The Call*, 23 March 1916.
36. *Justice*, 20 April 1916.

37. A. S. Headingley a.k.a. Adolphe (Adolf) Smith a supporter of Hyndman had volunteered as a stretcher-bearer during the Paris Commune and was by this time working covertly for British intelligence.

38. *The Call*, 20 April 1916.

39. TNA Kew KV2/1575, 'Precis of information regarding Theodore Aronovitch ROTHSTEIN.'

40. TNA Kew KV2/1575, 'Precis made in H.1. for reference only from Papers filed from 25 July 2011 to 8 October 2018. ROTHSTEIN, Theodore.

41. Now the Marx Memorial Library.

42. Andrew, *Defence*, p. 99; TNA Kew KV 1/1532 G1, 'The British Socialist Party', 4 October 1916; TNA Kew KV2/1575/.

43. Andrew, *Defence*, p. 99; TNA Kew KV 2/1532, Undated note by Major Ferguson on information from Victor Fisher [*sic*].

44. Andrew, *Defence*, p. 94.

45. See *Labour Leader*, 1 June 1916.

46. See the discussion in *The Call*, 7 September 1916.

47. *The Call*, 5 October 1916.

48. 'Memorandum regarding the Russian section of the Communist Club', enclosed with recommendation by Kell for Chicherin's internment, dated 26 January 1917, TNA Kew HO 144/2158; Andrew, *Defence*, p. 95.

49. See Andrew, *Defence*, p. 96 and fn.66, p. 893: 'Two other gang members perished in the celebrated "Siege of Sydney Street" in January 1911. Winston Churchill, then home secretary, could not resist visiting the scene and advising on operations from the front line'. Leggett, George, *Cheka: Lenin's Political Police* (Oxford: Oxford University Press, 1986) pp. 266–7. Cook, *M: MI5's First Spymaster*, pp. 266–7. Rogers, Colin, *The Battle of Stepney. The Sidney Street Siege: Its Causes and Consequences* (London, 1981), Ch. 17.

50. Andrew, *Defence*, p. 97; TNA Kew KV1/43, 'Revolutionary Agencies at Work'.

51. Andrew, *Defence*, pp. 96–7. The Petrov affair had made it unlikely that the Minister of Munitions would have welcomed any MI5 involvement in the Munitions factories on the Clyde after 1916, and Thomson was the safer pair of hands.

52. Andrew, *Defence*, p. 95.

53. Gordon, a disreputable character, later achieved celebrity status in the Wheeldon case of March 1917 where he was 'the *agent provocateur* used to convict Mrs Alice Wheeldon, a socialist of Derby and her family, in an alleged assassination plot against Lloyd George and Arthur Henderson. The story was headline news. Mrs Wheeldon was sentenced to ten years, while the chief witness, Gordon, was spirited away to South Africa. The trial was reputedly the outcome of a "frame-up" by the Secret Service.' See Challinor, *Origins*, Chapter 6, pp. 37, 43.

54. Andrew, *Defence*, p. 97; TNA Kew KV1/43, 'Revolutionary Agencies at Work.'

55. Andrew, *Defence*, p. 97; TNA Kew HO 144/2158, (322428/2) 'Memorandum regarding the Russian section of the Communist Club' and 'The Russian

Political Prisoners and Exiles Relief Committee in London.' See also, Andrew, *Defence*, fn.77 pp. 97, 893–4, 'recommendation for Chicherin's internment, dated 26 January 1917' TNA Kew HO 144/2158 (322428/2). In November 1916 Chicherin had publicly announced that his Committee's campaign to persuade Russian exiles not to enlist had been largely successful. Richard Kent Debo, 'The Making of a Bolshevik: Georgii Chicherin in England, 1914–1918', *Slavic Review* 25 (1966), pp. 656–7.

56. Andrew, *Defence*, p. 97; 'Recommendation by Kell for Chicherin's internment, 26 January 1917, TNA Kew HO/144/2158.

57. TNA Kew F.O.371/3004/28533, 6 February 1916. The Alice Wheeldon case was nothing if not timely.

58. Sirnis's daughter, Melita Norwood would become one of the most effective atom bomb spies working for the Soviets in Britain during World War II and early Cold War periods. See David Burke, *The Spy Who Came In From The Co-op* (Suffolk: Boydell & Brewer, 2008).

59. The Doukhobors were a persecuted Russian sect who shared many of Tolstoy's precepts – chastity, vegetarianism, abstinence from alcohol and tobacco, the pooling of all goods and property, cooperation and non-resistance to evil. Tolstoy had defended their refusal to bear arms in the Russian Army and had written a tract in their defence for which he was banished to his estates at Yasnaya Polyana and Count Chertkov exiled, initially to the Baltic Provinces. Chertkov was later allowed to settle in Bournemouth with Tolstoy's manuscripts where he engaged Rothstein as a translator of Tolstoy from Russian to French; while Sirnis translated Tolstoy into English for the Free Age Press. See Burke, *Spy*, pp. 25–38.

60. William Paul the editor of the SLP's newspaper *The Socialist*.

61. FML, Cambridge, 820–1975 Theodore Rothstein to Wilfred Scawen Blunt, 7 January 1917.

62. Ibid.

63. Alexander Sirnis's Diary. Melita Norwood Papers, Hoover Institute, University of Stanford.

Chapter 7   Revolution

1. TNA Kew F.O. 371/2995/57146, 17 March 1917.

2. *The Call*, 22 March 1917.

3. TNA Kew F.O. 371/2995/57146, 17 March 1917.

4. *The Call*, 22 March 1917; 'Harold Williams of the *Daily Chronicle* thought the crowds on the 24th were "mostly women and boys" with only a 'sprinkling of workmen'. Robert Wilton of *The Times* reported that on the 26th the fine weather had 'brought everybody out of doors' and that 'crowds of all ages and conditions had made their way to the Nevsky Prospekt.' Figes, *People's Tragedy*, p. 319; *The Times*, 16 March 1917.

5. *The Call*, 22 March 1917.
6. Ibid.
7. *Labour Leader*, 22 March 1917.
8. Leader of the *Trudoviki* (the Parliamentary breakaway group of the SRs).
9. TNA Kew F.O. 371/2995/56485, 16 March 1917.
10. Nikolai Chkeidze Chairman of the Petrograd Soviet.
11. TNA Kew F.O. 371/2995/56485, 16 March 1917.
12. Ibid.
13. *Labour Leader*, 22 March 1917.
14. *Labour Leader*, 12 April 1917.
15. TNA Kew F.O. 371/2996/96045, 12 May 1917.
16. *Soldat-Grazhdanin*, 3 May 1917; TNA Kew F.O. 371/2996/105142, 26 May 1917.
17. Kendall, *Revolutionary*, p. 174 and fn.29 p. 378.
18. Service, *Russia*, p. 47.
19. G. H. Mair (1887–1926) former assistant editor of the *Daily Chronicle*.
20. TNA Kew KV2/1575.
21. TNA Kew KV2/1575.
22. It says something about Rothstein's influence and importance within MI7(d) that he was being considered for employment in John Buchan's Ministry of Information, then in the process of being set up.
23. TNA Kew KV2/1575.
24. Gleichen was director of the Political Intelligence Bureau. See Major-General Lord Edward Gleichen, *A Guardsman's Memories* (Edinburgh and London: William Blackwood & Sons Ltd, 1932) p. 396.
25. TNA Kew KV2/1575 'Theodore Rothstein'.
26. TNA Kew KV2/1575, 'COPY of B. M. received from M.I.7 on 21.5.17 and returned on 9.6.17.'
27. Strange, since both MI7 and MI5 were then, according to independent reports from Christopher Andrew and Andrew Rothstein, based at Watergate House. See chapter 4 fn. 36 and Andrew, *Defence*, p. 50.
28. TNA Kew KV2/1575.
29. Ibid.
30. Ibid.
31. Ibid.
32. Ibid.
33. Ibid.
34. FML, Cambridge, 186–1975, Theodore Rothstein to Wilfred Scawen Blunt 26 June 1917. See also TNA Kew KV2/1575, '3 May 1917. MI5 E2 Secret. The following have been granted Special No Return permits to leave the UK and should not therefore obtain further visas. They are Russian Political Refugees, and separate reports have been sent to Petrograd about some of them. *Name.* Rothstein. *Nationality.* Russian. *Age.* 50. *Destination.* Russia. OR. *Name.* Samuel Ivanovitch Rotstein. *Nationality.* Russian. *Age.* 43. *Destination.* Russia.'

35. Ibid.
36. Figes, *People's Tragedy*, p. 441.
37. Service, *Russia*, pp. 54–5.
38. *Plebs Magazine*, August 1917.
39. Ibid.
40. Service, *Russia*, p. 56.
41. Ibid., pp. 58–9.
42. Ibid., p. 62.
43. Ibid., pp. 62–3.
44. *The Call*, 15 November 1917.
45. *Workers Dreadnought*, 17 November 1917.
46. *Labour Leader*, 29 November 1917.
47. *The Socialist*, December 1917.
48. Correspondence: Socialist Labour Party to Sirnis, December 1917, Jurgen Kuczynski Papers, Berlin, hereafter JK Papers, Berlin (The JK Papers are in the possession of Jurgen's son Thomas Kuczynski, Weisensee, Berlin).
49. Correspondence: Socialist Labour Party to Sirnis, January 1918, JK Papers, Berlin.
50. Correspondence: W. R. Stoker to Sirnis, n.d., JK Papers, Berlin.
51. Ibid.
52. Correspondence: W. R. Stoker to Sirnis, 7 February 1918 (JK Papers, Berlin).
53. Sir Robert Bruce Lockhart, *Memoirs Of A British Agent. Being An Account Of The Author's Early Life In Many Lands And Of His Official Mission To Moscow in 1918.* (Middlesex: Harmondswoth, 1932), p. 197.
54. Lockhart, *Memoirs*, p. 200.
55. See Vladimir Nabokov, *Ordeal of a Diplomat* (London: Duckworth And Company, 1921).
56. 'In his unsuccessful appeal against internment, Chicherin made one potentially embarrassing charge: Claiming that he had been mandated by the Russian Provisional Government to investigate relations between the Tsarist Okhrana and Scotland Yard, he accused the British government of preventing his inquiry in order to conceal "dark doings" of the Okhrana. There were indeed potential embarrassments to be uncovered – not least the past dealings between MI5's chief detective William Melville [. . .] and the unscrupulous Okhrana chief, Pyotr Rachkovsky.' Andrew, *Defence*, pp. 100–1.
57. Lockhart, *Memoirs*, p. 201.
58. Ibid., p. 198. Rothstein, Lockhart points out, was only six weeks out in his prediction of the end of the war.
59. Now a Pizza Express (but no plaque).
60. Lockhart, *Memoirs*, p. 198.
61. Ibid.
62. Ibid., pp. 199–200.
63. Ibid., p. 200.

Chapter 8   The 'Dual Policy'

1. A. U. Pope, *Maxim Litvinov* (New York: L. B. Fischer Publishing Corp., 1943) pp. 110–12.
2. Leslie Haden-Guest divorced Edith Low in 1909. He converted to Judaism before his marriage to Muriel Carmel in 1910. A member of the London County Council for Woolwich East between 1919–22 he was the first Jew to stand for Parliament as a Labour candidate. He renounced Judaism in 1924.
3. Sharman Kadish, *Bolsheviks and British Jews*, (London: Frank Cass, 1992) pp. 230–1.
4. Captain Hicks had recently returned from Russia where he had done useful work as a poison gas expert. See Lockhart, *Memoirs*, p. 200.
5. Kendall, *Revolutionary*, p. 240.
6. Published in *The Call*, 10 January 1918.
7. *The Call*, 17 January 1918.
8. E. H. Carr, *The Bolshevik Revolution 1917–1923* Vol. 3, London, 1953 (p. 31); *Labour Leader*, 24 January 1918.
9. Service, *History Twentieth-Century Russia*, p. 75.
10. Tony Barber, 'Only Greek PM knows what price he will pay for leftwing ambitions', *Financial Times*, 13/14 June 2015.
11. Service, *History* pp. 76–7.
12. Ibid., p. 77.
13. *The Call*, 28 February 1918.
14. TNA Kew KV2/1575/1; KV2/1575: Text of the telegram: 'Petrograd telegraph Agency cabled Rothstein requesting contribute by cabling dialling no answer please arrange for Jszvestia [*Izvestia*] to receive cable regularly economic political life from London Petroff. Stop.'
15. *The Call*, 9 May 1918.
16. *The Call*, 4 July 1918.
17. TNA Kew KV2/1575/1.
18. On the 17 November 1918 Rothstein sent the MS. of Trotsky's *History of the Russian Revolution* to the publisher George Allen & Unwin, Limited. See TNA Kew KV2/1575/27,
19. Correspondence: Thomas Bell to Sirnis, 23 August 1918. JK Papers, Berlin.
20. Correspondence: W. R. Stoker to Sirnis, 17 July 1918, JK Papers, Berlin.
21. TNA Kew KV2/1575, 'The brothers Theodore, Albert and Samuel Rothstein.'
22. Ibid.
23. Ibid.
24. TNA Kew KV2/1575, 'The brothers Theodore, Albert and Samuel Rothstein.'
25. Articles from Rothstein published in the *Manchester Guardian* included 'The Ukraine and its People'; 'The Disputed Baltic States'; 'The Turk Homeland'; 'The Bolshevik Proposals'; 'Adriatic Turkey. Allies Agreement with Ex-Tsar'; 'Bolsheviks and Class Struggle' (2, 5, 9, 11, 18 and 23 January 1918 respectively), TNA Kew KV2/1575.

26. Arnold pseudonym of William Paul then on the 'dodge' from conscription and hiding in Sirnis's house.
27. Correspondence: Stoker to Sirnis, 31 August 1918. JK Papers, Berlin.
28. TNA Kew KV2/1575/1c.
29. TNA Kew KV2/1575/5, 'The letter does not appear to be written by a Russian, unless by a very uneducated one. The hard signs are left out in all the words, and there are mistakes in spelling.'
30. TNA Kew KV2/1575, 'The brothers Theodore, Albert and Samuel Rothstein.'
31. TNA Kew KV2/1575/7, Letter addressed to the Mission Anglaise, Ministere de la Guerre, Paris, dated 1 October 1918: 'I am forwarding you herewith an intercepted letter to a Bolshevik here whom we expect to deport shortly. He is asking for subscriptions to enable a new paper or pamphlet to be brought out. Perhaps you might hand it to the Sûreté for their information and possibly they might be able to trace the author.'
32. TNA Kew KV2/1575, 'The brothers Theodore, Albert and Samuel Rothstein'; see also TNA Kew KV2/1575/9.
33. TNA Kew KV2/1575, 'The brothers Theodore, Albert and Samuel Rothstein.'
34. TNA Kew KV2/1575/9a.
35. The British had a bad track record. Kornilov had been backed by the British military attache, Brigadier-General Alfred Knox, whom Kerensky accused of producing pro-Kornilov propaganda. Kerensky also claimed that Lord Milner wrote him a letter expressing support for Kornilov. A British armoured car squadron commanded by Oliver Locker-Lampson, all occupants dressed in Russian uniforms, participated in the failed coup. See Richard Ullman, *Intervention and the War* (Princeton University Press, 1961) pp. 11–13.
36. Lockhart, *Memoirs*, p. 313.
37. Ibid.
38. 'Doubtless, it has its uses and its functions, but political work is not its strong point. The buying of information puts a premium on manufactured news. But even manufactured news is less dangerous than the honest reports of men who, however brave and however gifted as linguists, are frequently incapable of forming a reliable political judgement.' *Memoirs*, p. 274.
39. Lockhart had been arrested along with Captain Hicks, a MI6 agent who had been responsible for introducing Lockhart to anti-Bolshevik elements in Moscow.
40. Lockhart, *Memoirs*, pp. 318–19.
41. The Bolshevik Party had adopted the name Communist Party in March 1918 following the signing of the Brest-Litovsk Treaty.
42. E. H. Carr, *The Bolshevik Revolution 1917–1923* Vol. 3 (London and Middlesex: Harmondsworth, 1953), p. 32.
43. *The Call*, 11 July 1918.
44. *The Call*, 29 August and 24 October 1918.
45. *The Call*, 25 July 1918.

46. *The Call*, 8 August 1918.
47. Ibid.
48. *The Call*, 29 August 1918.
49. Leonard Woolf, *Downhill All The Way: An Autobiography of the Years 1919 – 1939* (London: Harcourt Brace Jovanovich, 1960), p. 27.
50. Rothstein sat on the Labour Party's Advisory Committee on Foreign Affairs from 4 June – 7 September 1918.
51. TNA Kew KV2/1575, 'Precis of information regarding Theodore Aronovitch Rothstein.'
52. TNA Kew FO371/3347/179551, 29 October 1918; KV2/1575/18, 'On November 19th 1918 Sir Basil THOMSON reports an interview with Theodore ROTHSTEIN, who replied that he had always been a Socialist and had never concealed his opinions, that he was a personal friend of Litvinoff, but that he strongly disagreed with him on Bolshevik principles and that he was not in favour of the proceedings of the Bolshevists in Russia. Sir Basil THOMSON adds: "I think that the decision to allow him to continue his work at the War Office is a wise one"'. See also TNA KV2/1575/52, 28 May 1920, Thomson's interview with Klishko of the Soviet Trade Delegation: 'I had a personal interview with him about two years ago and he specifically denied that he was carrying on anything of this kind. Of course, I knew it wasn't true.' (Thomson had told Klishko that Rothstein was an agent of the Soviet Government).
53. TNA Kew FO371/3347/179551, 29 October 1918.
54. TNA Kew KV2/1575/45, Letter from Lt. Col Wake to Rothstein.
55. TNA Kew FO371/3347/179551, 29 October 1918.
56. TNA Kew/1575/19/20, and 25.
57. Labour Party, Annual Conference Report, 1919, Appendix V; Stephen White, *Britain And The Bolshevik Revolution. A Study in the Politics of Diplomacy 1920 – 1924* (London and Basingstoke, The Macmillan Press: 1979), p. 30.
58. White, *Britain*, p. 30; Labour Party, Annual Conference Report, 1919, pp. 25 and 26; Labour Party, National Executive Committee minutes, 18 December 1918, vol. 14, and 3 January 1919, vol. 6.
59. White, *Britain*, p. 31; *Labour Leader*, 9 January 1919; see also Glasgow Trades Council minutes, 19 March 1919; East Ham ILP minutes, 1 December 1918; Glasgow ILP executive committee minutes, 15 November 1918.
60. *Labour Leader*, 3 April 1919; White, *Britain*, p. 31.
61. *The Call*, 26 December 1918.
62. *The Call*, 23 January 1919.
63. 30 April 1919, Cabinet Paper GT 7196, Cab 24/76; White, *Britain*, p. 31.
64. Henry, Pelling, *The British Communist Party: A Historical Profile* (Black, 1958), p. 191.
65. Churchill had become Minister of War in 1918.
66. Jonathan Haslam, *The Vices of Integrity. E. H. Carr, 1892 – 1982.* (London: Verso, 1999), p. 30.
67. Lloyd George to Churchill, 16 February 1919; Haslam, *Vices*, p. 31.

68. *The Call*, 17 April 1919.
69. Thomson's first report was submitted on 30 April 1919.
70. Andrew, *Defence*, p. 108.
71. Ibid.
72. Ibid., p. 109.
73. Ibid.
74. The armed opposition to the Soviets.
75. TNA Kew KV2/1575/38.
76. TNA Kew KV2/1575/32a/ 32b and 31a.
77. TNA Kew CAB/24/79/18, Report On Revolutionary Organisations In The United Kingdom. No. 2.
78. Kadish, *Bolshevism*, p. 80.
79. TNA Kew CAB24/81/63. Report On Revolutionary Organisations In The United Kingdom, 12 June 1919.
80. TNA Kew CAB24/82/66, Report On Revolutionary Organisations In The United Kingdom, 26 June 1919.
81. Ibid.
82. TNA Kew CAB24/83/16. Report On Revolutionary Organisations In The United Kingdom, 3 July 1919.
83. Born Boris Konstantinovich Lifschits in Kiev to a Jewish family Souvarine's family moved to Paris in 1897 where he became a leading socialist and founder member of the French communist party.
84. Kendall, *Revolutionary*, p. 248: 'Nosovitsky was already employed by the US government when he was hired by Scotland Yard in 1919. The Britain-USA run was the connecting link.'
85. TNA Kew CAB 24/96/91.
86. Woolf, *Downhill All The Way*, p. 20; See also TNA Kew KV2/1575/33.
87. Basil Thomson, *Queer People* (1922) (London: Classic Reprint, Forgotten Books, 2012), p. 290.
88. *The Call*, 12 June 1919.

Chapter 9   The CPGB and 'Hands Off Russia'; 'Zionism versus Bolshevism'; Enter Zinoviev

1. Haslam, *Vices of Integrity*, p. 32.
2. Fineberg had returned to Russia in June 1918. He was employed in the Department of Revolutionary Propaganda, producing 'British newspapers, flysheets and so on [...] for distribution amongst 'Anglo-American soldiers in the Armies of intervention.' See Boris Reinstein, *Communist International*, April 1929, p. 431; Kendall, *Revolutionary*, p. 396. In the run-up to the BSP's Annual Conference in 1918 Fineberg had written three articles in *The Call* between 7 and 21 March in favour of continued affiliation; 86 delegates voted in favour while 32 voted against.

3. Tom Quelch (1886–1954) was the son of veteran Marxist Harry Quelch and a member of the BSP.

4. The full text of this letter written by Sylvia Pankhurst on 16 July 1919 was not published in English until 2 April 1920 in *The Call*.

5. *Kommunisticheskii Internatsional* March 1920.

6. *The Call* 22 April 1920.

7. Winston Churchill, 'Zionism versus Bolshevism. A Struggle For The Soul Of The Jewish People,' *Illustrated Sunday Herald*, 8 June 1920; see Kadish, *Bolsheviks*, p. 135.

8. Kadish, *Bolsheviks*, p. 136.

9. Churchill, 'Zionism'; Kadish, *Bolsheviks*, p. 137.

10. Kadish, *Bolshevism*, p. 137.

11. *The Call*, 22 April 1920.

12. Although united under communist leadership, Soviet Russia and Soviet Ukraine were two separate entities since the Soviet republics did not unite into the Soviet Union until 1922.

13. Kadish, *Bolshevism*, p. 7. In 1903 Woolf had been co-opted onto the Conjoint Committee of the Board of Deputies and the Anglo-Jewish Association, set up in 1878 as 'a clearing house for information which reached the community about the situation of Jews abroad'. The Conjoint Committee 'compiled reports and memoranda and cultivated channels of communication with the real Foreign Office, in the hope that the latter could be prevailed upon to intercede on behalf of Jews overseas should the need arise.' Kadish, *Bolshevism*, p. 60.

14. Entry for 12 August 1919, cited in Kadish, *Bolsheviks*, p. 84.

15. *Jewish World* 12 November 1919; Kadish, *Bolsheviks*, pp. 84–5.

16. R. F. Andrews (Andrew Rothstein), 'What Lenin said about the Jews', Marxist Internet Archive, 2008.

17. TNA Kew CAB24/105/56.

18. White, *Britain*, p. 16; see *The Times*, 29 September 1920 cited in White, *Britain*, p. 117.

19. Lloyd George Papers, House of Lords Library, F202.3.19, cited in Richard Uhlmann, *Anglo-Soviet vol. 3*, p. 105.

20. The decision to accept the German peace terms produced an open opposition to Lenin, led by Bukharin, which became known as 'Left Communism'. See Leonard Schapiro, *The Communist Party of the Soviet Union* (London: Eyre & Spottiswoode, 1980), pp. 186–7.

21. Lloyd George Papers, House of Lords Library, F202.3.19.

22. Leon Trotsky's brother-in-law, Kamenev (Kamenev had been appointed to the Trade Delegation

23. TNA Kew CAB24/111/30, Report On Revolutionary Organisations In The United Kingdom, 2 September 1920.

24. TNA Kew KV2/1576/68. The trade delegation now comprised Krasin, Kamenev, Miliutin and Rothstein. See Louis Fischer, *The Soviets in World*

Affairs, Vol. 1, Princeton University Press, pp. 261–2 (1951). The secretary of the delegation, Klishko, had formerly lived in England and spoke English perfectly. *The Times*, 7 February 1921.

25. *The Times*, 7 February 1921; Thomson, *Queer People*, p. 290; Kendall, *Revolutionary*, p. 238.

26. TNA Kew CAB24/111/88, Report On Revolutionary Organisations in The United Kingdom, 23 September 1920; Andrew Rothstein, 'The Revolutionary Movement in Britain 1900–1921' (review), *Labour Monthly*, December 1969: A 'handful of organisers and staff got some £5 a week – less than such skilled workmen as Tom Bell, Arthur McManus, William Gallacher or Harry Pollitt could and did earn in their own trade with far smaller discomfort'. 'The War of Intervention, on the other hand, according to Lloyd George's own estimation in a speech delivered at the Guildhall on 8 November 1919, cost Britain £100 millions.' Rothstein, *Labour Monthly*.

27. Chicherin to Litvinov, 11 February 1920, quoted in *The Times*, 19 August 1920.

28. Francis Meynell, *My Lives* (London: The Bodley Head) 1971, p. 119.

29. See David Burke, *The Lawn Road Flats. Spies, Writers and Artists* (Suffolk: The Boydell Press, 2014), pp. 75–8.

30. Meynell, *Lives*, p. 121.

31. Ibid.

32. TNA Kew KV2/1576/68.

33. Kendall, *Revolutionary*, p. 254.

34. TNA Kew Cab 24/97, 'Revolutionaries And The Need For Legislation 2nd February 1920', p. 6.

35. TNA Kew Cab 24/111/1804, 'A Monthly Review of Revolutionary Movements in British Dominions, Overseas and Foreign Countries', 21 July 1920.

36. TNA Kew KV2/573/64.

37. Meynell, *Lives*, p. 125.

38. 'When in London he resides at his mother's house at 53 Whitehall Park, Highgate, but he also occupies a converted Pullman car at Tophill, Windermere. His son, a Brackenbury scholar at Balliol College, Oxford, assists him.' TNA Kew CAB24/97/544.

39. Pelling, *Communist Party*, pp. 8–9.

40. TNA Kew KV2/1575, 'Precis of information regarding Theodore Aronovitch ROTHSTEIN'.

41. TNA Kew CAB24/111.

42. Correspondence: Rothstein to Burke, 13 August 1981.

43. Lenin, V.I.: *Collected Works*, 4th edition Vol. 44, p. 403.

44. TNA Kew KV2/1576/68.

45. TNA Kew KV2/1576, Extract from 'Plain English' 31 December 1921. 'It will be remembered that a destroyer was placed at the Bolshevik envoy's disposal. Rothstein took advantage to begin propaganda of a violent nature among the sailors.'

46. TNA Kew KV2/1575/56.

47. TNA Kew KV2/1575/62.
48. TNA Kew KV2/1575/62.
49. Ibid.
50. TNA Kew KV2/1575/65.
51. Albert Rothstein had become a naturalized British citizen on 28 December 1899.

Chapter 10   Prising Open the Lion's Jaws

1. FML, Cambridge, 201–1975, Andrew Rothstein to Wifred Scawen Blunt, 19 November 1921.
2. One of Rothstein's first engagements in Moscow was to accompany the British writer H. G. Wells on a visit to Lenin at the Kremlin, where he acted as interpreter. According to Wells he chastised Lenin for his lack of 'diplomatic reserve' during this visit. 'Wells argued [. . .] that capitalism could be "civilised" through reforms "into a Collectivist world system." Lenin laughed briefly. To him capitalism "is a scramble, and it will inevitably make wars." Wars, Wells objected, "sprang from nationalist imperialism and not from a Capitalist organisation of society." "But what do you think of this new Republican Imperialism that comes from America?" Lenin suddenly asked. "Here [. . .] "Mr. Rothstein intervened in Russian with an objection that Lenin swept aside." Disregarding Rothstein's plea for diplomatic reserve,"' (Fischer, Louis, *The Life of Lenin* (London: Phoenix Press, 1964), pp. 46–7.
3. TNA Kew KV2/1576.
4. The reputation owed much to the reforming zeal of Benjamin Jowett, Master of Balliol in 1870. Jowett had offended traditional churchmen by his contribution to the notorious *Essays and Reviews*, published in 1860, a book which tried to reconcile Anglicanism with both the theories of Darwin and the largely German school of biblical criticism; in his own essay he had emphasised the use of reason in the interpretation of scripture. Balliol attracted a number of poorer students across Britain, as well as a number from Asia. Many were funded by the foundation of a number of scholarships and exhibitions set up by Jowett during his time as Master.
5. TNA Kew KV2/1576/298A.
6. Formed on the 9 August 1920 to oppose intervention in Russia by industrial means and dubbed the 'Councils of Inaction' by the Communist Party of Great Britain.
7. TNA Kew F.O. 371/6399, 12 January 1921.
8. Poale Zion a movement of Marxist-Zionist Jewish workers founded in 1901 in Central Europe and the Pale of Russia followed the Bund's rejection of Zionism. Branches of Poale Zion had been established in London and Leeds, 1903 and 1905 respectively, and in Palestine in November 1905. During World War I Poale Zion had been influential in the British Labour

Party and, unlike the BSP, supported the British war effort in the Middle East and called on Jews to join the Jewish Legion to fight against the Ottoman Empire in Palestine. See also 'To The Communists Of All Countries To The Jewish Proletariat Statement On The Decision Of The Poale Zion Not To Affiliate To The Third International', *Communist International*, July 1922.

9. TNA Kew KV2/1576, 'B2 Mr Selwyn Jackson. In August 1920 A. Rothstein applied for facilities for the journey to Russia. His case was referred to S.Y. who stated that they considered it would be unwise to withhold a passport and in view of this M.I.5. raised no military objection. P.P. No. 242860 was accordingly issued.'

10. TNA Kew KV2/1578.

11. TNA Kew KV2/1578/409a.

12. Born on Mill Road, Cambridge to Upendra Dutt, an Indian surgeon, and Anna Palme the great aunt of the future Prime Minister of Sweden, Olof Palme, the Dutts remained active communists throughout their lives.

13. TNA Kew KV2/1415.

14. Ibid.

15. TNA Kew KV2/1415.

16. Ibid.

17. Ibid.

18. Ibid.

19. Known as TASS since 1925.

20. TNA Kew KV2/1582/820b.

21. G. D. H. Cole and Raymond Postgate, *The Common People 1746–1946* (London: Metheun & Co. Ltd., 1946) p. 559; 'The *Herald*, which had been restored as a daily in 1919 and had continued to be a journal of the left, in 1922 for financial reasons fell under the control of the Labour Party and the TUC, and the left-wing George Lansbury ceased to be editor.' Henry Pelling, *A Short History of the Labour Party* (London: Macmillan, 1968), p. 53.

22. MI5 had a handful of officers and two Branches (also known as Divisions): A, which was responsible for administration, personnel, records and 'precautionary measures' (later known as protective security); and B, which conducted 'investigations and inquiries'. B Division lacked an agent-running section but had a three-man Observation section (B4), responsible for shadowing suspects and making 'confidential' inquiries. Andrew, *Defence*, pp. 127–8.

23. TNA Kew KV2/1576, 'B2 Mr Selwyn Jackson'.

24. Following his visit to Russia in 1920 his British passport was retained and he was informed by the F.O. that it was preferable he should travel on a Russian passport. See TNA Kew KV2.1576/298A.

25. Minnie Lansbury, a founder member of the CPGB and Poplar Alderman, 1919–22, had been a schoolteacher before her marriage to Edgar Lansbury in 1914. During the war she had been assistant secretary to Sylvia Pankhurst. She was well known among the war disabled and for her work in Poplar for the local

War Pensions Committee which, among other matters, had responsibility for some 500 war orphans in the borough (see Noreen Branson, *Poplarism 1919–1925. George Lansbury and the Councillors' Revolt* (London: Lawrence & Wishart, 1979)).

26. A phrase for what Desmond Morton's biographer, Gill Bennett, rightly suggested 'might today be called global capitalism.' See: Gill Bennett, *Churchill's Man of Mystery. Desmond Morton and the World of intelligence* (Abingdon, Oxon: Routledge 2007) p. 61.

27. See Bennett, *Churchill's Man*.

28. Bennett, *Churchill's Man*, pp. 71–2.

29. TNA Kew KV2/1576 B.2. Mr Selwyn Jackson.

30. Fourth Congress of the Communist International. Theses on Comintern Tactics, 5 December 1922; http://www.marxists.org/history/international/comintern/4th-congress/tactics.htm.

31. Ibid.

32. Victor Madeira, *Britannia and the Bear* (Suffolk: Boydell & Brewer, 2014), p. 70.

33. Andrew, *Defence*, p. 145.

34. Curzon, who in his last year at Eton failed the scholarship examination to Balliol, was admitted as a commoner to read for a classical degree and studied at Oxford between 1878 and 1883, see David Gilmour, *Curzon* (London: John Murray, 1994). Communism at Balliol would become a preoccupation of MI5 and the college authorities; a H.O.W was taken out by Scotland Yard on HIGGINS, Esmonde M. on 24 February 1921, Balliol College: 'HIGGINS has been in Russia and is more or less the centre of Young Oxford Bolshevism now that Andrew Rothstein has left. He is acting as an intermediary between Theodore Rothstein and his wife.'

35. TNA Kew Cab 24/106, 'Negotiations with M. Krassin', 27 May 1920, Cabinet Paper CP 1350 cited in White, *Britain*, p. 85.

36. Jonathan Haslam, *Russia's Cold War: From The October Revolution to the Fall of the Wall* (Yale University Press, 2012), p. 4.

37. Persia, the historic region of southwestern Asia did not officially adopt the name Iran until 1934.

38. At Brest-Litovsk Trotsky had promised to evacuate all Russian forces stationed in Persia by the Tsarist Government. On 14 January 1918 he declared that the Bolsheviks no longer considered the treaty of 1907 as binding and annulled all special privileges granted to previous Russian Governments by Persia. Persian statesmen demanded similar concessions from the British Government who responded by occupying North Persia with Balfour appearing on the scene to take charge of Persian fiscal affairs. During the civil war British and Indian troops operated against the Bolsheviks in Turkestan and Baku using Persia as their base; while Denikin's naval forces operated without hindrance in the Caspian Sea. By June 1919 Britain's occupation of Persia was complete. In July 1920 British troops were driven out of northern Persia by the Red Army and Rothstein was appointed Soviet Ambassador in Teheran on 28 November 1920.

39. FML, Cambridge, 167–1976, Theodore Rothstein to Wilfred Scawen Blunt, 24 January 1921.
40. Madeira, *Britannia*, pp. 50–1.
41. TNA Kew HW/12/6, Chicherin, Moscow – Litvinov, Copenhagen; 12 March 1920-001607; 20 February cited Madeira, *Britannia*, p. 51.
42. Fisher, *Soviets in World Affairs*, p. 316.
43. Semyon Mikhailovich Budyonny's cavalry force was credited with having been a major factor in the Bolsheviks' victory during the civil war.
44. Fisher, *Soviets in World Affairs*, p. 316.
45. TNA Kew KV2/1576/81B.
46. FML, Cambridge, 217–1976, Theodore Rothstein to Wilfred Scawen Blunt.
47. In Central Asia and the Caucasus the Red Army continued to face resistance until 1923 where armed bands of Islamic guerrillas continued to fight the communist takeover.
48. TNA Kew KV2/1576: 'In the leading article of "The Times" of recent date under the heading "England in Persia" there appears the following extract:- "Persia is now at the mercy of the Bolshevists, who, entrenched in Transcaucasia and Turkestan, are extending their influence at our expense throughout the Middle East. They have in Tehran as their envoy Mr T. Rothstein, who spent many years in England as a political refugee, practiced journalism here, published a book attacking our policy in Egypt, was employed by the British War Office during the war, and acted as right-hand man to the first Bolshevist envoy to this country, M. Litvinoff. He thus has exceptional qualifications for the task assigned him of destroying our influence in Persia, for this, rather than any hopeless effort to convert the Persians to communism, would appear to be the main object of his mission".'
49. FML, Cambridge, 217–1976, Theodore Rothstein to Wilfred Scawen Blunt.
50. TNA Kew KV2/1575/728, 26 January 1923. Among Theodore Rothstein's collaborators in Persia was Sultanzade, a member of the executive committee of the Communist International. Sultanzade, an Armenian, was not a Muslim, had joined the RSDLP(B) in the Caucasus before the October Revolution and opposed Stalin's protege Kuchek Khan in the Soviet province of Gilan.
51. See also A. Sultanzade's report for the Committee on the National and Colonial Questions on the prospects of a social revolution in the East delivered at a plenary meeting of the Second Congress of the Communist International on 28 July 1920 in which Sultanzade described the larger part of the population of the East as peasants under medieval exploitation.
52. Fischer, *Lenin*, p. 421.
53. TNA Kew KV2/1576, Relating to Rothstein. S.F.400/20/Persia. Author of original B.M.A. Teheran. Date of origin 29 August 1921 Extract made by DCOH on 9 September 1921. 127 cipher. 29 August 1921.
54. TNA Kew KV2/1576/89, Relating to Rothstein. Extracted from P.F.R. EPSTEIN, Samuel. Author of original G.O.C. Mesopotamia. Date of origin 17 August 1921 Extract made by DCOH on 31 August 1921 X2682 cipher, 17 August.

55. This was reminiscent of 1916 when Scotland Yard and MI5 had a H.O.W. in place on Rothstein's correspondence while he was being investigated for suspected Ottoman and German secret service connections while working for MI7(d).

56. FML, Cambridge, 216–1976, Andrew Rothstein to Wifred Scawen Blunt, 27 July 1921.

57. FML, Cambridge, 201–1975, Andrew Rothstein to Wifred Scawen Blunt, 19 November 1921.

58. Feodor Rotshtein, '*Pamyati odnovo pechal'nika Vostoka. Nekrolog o Wilfrid Scawen Blunt*' in *Novii Vostok*, 1922, No. 2, pp. 713–14.

59. See Miranda Carter, *Anthony Blunt, His Lives* (London: Pan, 2002).

60. TNA Kew KV2/1578.

61. The Japanese Communist Party was immediately suppressed. Following clashes at Waseda University over the issue of military training in May 1923 a roster of the Japanese Communist Party was discovered in the quarters of Sano Manabu, a Waseda lecturer. Early on the morning of 5 June ten police cars spread out over Tokyo and arrested almost every party member of the city; similar raids were conducted elsewhere and all official party members rounded up. The first Japanese Communist Party was wiped out. See Robert A. Scalapino, *The Japanese Communist Movement, 1920–1966* (Berkeley and Los Angeles: University of California Press, 1967) pp. 18–19.

62. TNA Kew KV2/1576, 'B.2. Mr. Selwyn Jackson: 'Theodore Rothstein is in very close association with the directing hands of the Soviet regime. He is one of the most important directors of IIIrd International propaganda and agitation in the East.'

63. Fischer, *Lenin* p. 629.

64. The Weinstein Notes and the Curzon Memorandum are in *Parliamentary Papers* 1869 of 1923 (Russia No.2) cited in R. B. Mowat, *A History of European Diplomacy 1914–1925* (London: Edward Arnold & Co., 1927), pp. 282–3.

65. Acronym of the *Sovet Narodnykh Komissarov* (Council of People's Commissars), the government of the early Soviet Union.

66. *PP* 1869 of 1923, Russia No. 2; Mowat pp. 282–3.

67. TNA Kew KV2/1576/295a/296a/294a.

68. Soviet Russia at this time was nominally in a state of war with Britain, France and Italy: that is to say, no definite treaty of peace had been made between these Powers and Russia.

69. *The Times*, 25 May 1923; TNA Kew KV2/1576/112.

70. Gilmour, *Curzon* p. 187; Madeira, *Britannia* p. 113.

71. 'Berzin to Litvinov', 29 May, f. 04, op. 4, p. 24, d. 332., II. 37–8, AVP RF cited Madeira, *Britannia*, p. 117.

72. TNA Kew KV2/1576 B.2. 10.10.22.

73. MI3c was a division of the British Directorate of Military Intelligence and was part of the War Office. It was originally set up to handle geographical information and during the war had dealt with Germany. After WWI its role was changed to intelligence in Europe.

74. TNA Kew KV2/1576 B.2. 20 October 1922.
75. Ibid.
76. TNA Kew KV2/1576 B.2. 17 November 1922.
77. TNA Kew KV2/1576 B.2. 21 November 1922.
78. TNA Kew KV2/1576 B.2. 22 November 1922 signature ineligible.
79. TNA Kew KV2/1576/11A; TNA Kew KV2/2317/21A.
80. TNA Kew KV2/2317/1c.
81. TNA Kew KV2/2317/21A.
82. TNA Kew KV2/2317/1d.
83. TNA Kew KV2/2317/1A.
84. TNA Kew KV2/2317/T.42.
85. The father reportedly 'threw out' Edith 'by reason of her Bolshevik sympathies' in 1925. TNA Kew KV2/2317/3A.
86. Mrs Zicha Mitroff. Edith Lunn had a miscarriage four months into her pregnancy at lodgings in Salcombe, Devon.
87. TNA Kew KV2/2317/35A.
88. TNA Kew KV2/2317/11A.
89. TNA Kew KV2/2317/21A.
90. TNA Kew KV2/2317 Minute Sheet No. 32.
91. TNA Kew KV2/2317.
92. Madeira, *Britannia*, p. 113.
93. TNA Kew KV2/1576/114, 22 May 1923.
94. Petrovsky, a Russian-Jewish Bolshevik, had been a political prisoner in Siberia before escaping to the United States in 1913 where he went by his real name Max Goldfarb. He had returned to Russia in 1917 and had organised the first officers' training school in the new Red Army under Trotsky.
95. Petrovsky filled the vacuum left by Klishko, as well as that left by the Comintern's special representative in Britain, Michael Borodin who used the alias 'George Brown'. Borodin had been arrested in 1922 and after serving a short sentence was deported.

Chapter 11 The Anglo-Russian Committee and the Zinoviev Letter

1. Fourth Congress of the Communist International. Theses on Comintern Tactics, 5 December 1922; http://www.marxists.org/history/international/comintern/4th-congress/tactics.htm.
2. Daniel F. Calhoun, *The United Front: The TUC and the Russians 1923–1928* (Cambridge: Cambridge University Press, 2009), p. 12.
3. See ch. xiv of RILU, 'International Labour Movement 1923–4', typescript report of executive bureau to Third Congress delegates. Copy in T.U.C. Library, quoted in Pelling, *British Communist*, p. 26.
4. Brian Pearce and Michael Woodehouse, *A History of Communism in Britain* (London: Bookmarks, 1969). Introduction by Chris Bambery, pp. v-vi. At the

time the Anglo-Russian Unity Committee claimed to represent 11,000,000 trade unionists in Britain and Russia.

5. Calhoun, *United Front*, p. 86.

6. Ibid., pp. 86–7.

7. Ibid.

8. White, *Britain*, p. 199.

9. The legislative programme with which the Conservatives had met the House of Commons in January 1924, following their electoral defeat, made no mention of relations with Russia; while the Liberal Party's general election manifesto had similarly advocated *de jure* recognition of the Soviet Union.

10. *The Times* 5 December 1923; *Herald* 9 January 1924 cited White, *Britain*, p. 199.

11. White, *Britain*, p. 197.

12. Minute, 19 December 1923, F.O. 371/9353/N9988; White, *Britain*, p. 197.

13. White, *Britain*, p. 224.

14. See Ibid., p. 237n.14

15. Lewis Chester, Stephen Fay and Hugo Young, *The Zinoviev Letter* (London: Heinemann, 1967), p. 27.

16. While the Labour Party consistently rejected applications from the CPGB for affiliation to the 'official' labour movement, individual members of the Communist Party were free to join the party and, if they could secure adoption, become Labour Party candidates. In the first 1923 election, two were returned to Parliament. Shapurji Saklatvala, a wealthy Parsee, was elected as official Labour candidate for Battersea North, and Walton Newbold, a former Quaker, was returned for Motherwell without Labour opposition. Both lost their seats in the election later in the year. Thus there were no communists in the House of Commons during MacDonald's administration. See Chester, Fay and Young, *Zinoviev*, p. 17; White, *Britain*, p. 237.

17. White, *Britain*, p. 237 fn15.

18. Aristocrats and members of the landed gentry accounted for some 33 members of the Conservative government of 1902 (62.3 per cent); but for only 28 (41.1 per cent) in 1924. Within the Cabinet itself the relative decline of the more traditional sections of the party was even more pronounced, aristocrats and the landed gentry accounting for 61.1 per cent of the Conservative Cabinet of 1902; but for only 28.5 per cent in 1924. Landowning was the occupation of half of the members of the 1902 Conservative Cabinet; but only of 14.5 per cent in 1924; while members with a background in industry and commerce had increased from about a quarter to a third of the total. Curzon himself, Lord Davidson remarked, was an 'ancient monument and constructed like one'. White, *Britain*, p. 237.

19. Andrew, *Defence*, p. 122.

20. Renamed the British Fascists later in the year.

21. Andrew, *Defence*, p. 124.

22. There were three sub-branches within Scotland Yard's Special Branch under the overall control of Sir Wyndham Childs: SS1 (formerly 'F' branch), the liaison section with SIS; SS2 (formerly 'L' branch), liaising with Chief Constables and

dealing with matters relating to revolutionary organisations in the UK other than of alien or Irish origin; and a branch under the Deputy Assistant Commissioner, whose task was to take action on information received, liaising with Passport Control and the Aliens Branch of the Home Office. See Bennett, *Morton*, p. 77.

23. See Bennett, *Morton*, p. 71.
24. Andrew, *Defence*, p. 147.
25. The dispute was settled within three days.
26. See Andrew, *Defence*, pp. 147–8.
27. White, *Britain*, p. 208n.22
28. TNA Kew KV2/1576.
29. TNA Kew KV2/1576/291a. Jane Archer went on to become MI5's recognised Soviet expert.
30. TNA Kew KV2/1576.
31. TNA Kew KV2/1576/292A.
32. Berlin hosted the publishing headquarters of *Ost Information*, 'an uninhibited anti-Bolshevik journal given to the revelation of "Secrets of the Kremlin" for private circulation. Curzon's [...] diplomatic note of 1921 seems to have borrowed generously from the lucubrations of this little publication.' Chester et al., *Zinoviev*, p. 49.
33. TNA Kew KV2/1576/293a.
34. Ibid.
35. TNA Kew KV2/1576.
36. Ibid.
37. TNA Kew KV2/1576/294A, 13 September 1924; YCL – Young Communist League.
38. Rothstein's second son Eugene was also an active British communist.
39. William Paul a former member of the British SLP had been instrumental in bringing the predominantly industrial unionist SLP into the Communist Party in 1920. During World War I, when he was on the dodge from the military authorities he stayed with the Sirnis's at their cottage in Pokesdown, close to Tuckton House. He visited Russia in mid-September 1920.
40. Chester et al., *Zinoviev*, p. 31.
41. See ibid., p. 33.
42. The Conservatives were the largest party in Parliament following the December 1923 general election with 258 seats, the Labour Party secured 191 seats while the Liberals slumped to 158. The Labour Party, therefore, had no parliamentary majority, and the government survived only on the goodwill of the Liberals.
43. Pelling, *Communist Party*, p. 29; *Workers' Weekly*, 25 July 1924; Patrick Hastings, *Autobiography* (London: Heinemann, 1948), pp. 238–40.
44. Pelling, *Communist Party*, p. 30.
45. TNA Kew FO371/10478, SIS to Gregory (F.O.), 9 October 1924 cited in Keith Jeffrey, *MI6. The History Of The Secret Intelligence Service 1909–1949* (London: Bloomsbury, 2010) p. 218.

46. See FO 371/10478 N7838/108/38: 'Special Intelligence Service to the Foreign Office', 9 October 1924; ibid. N8 105/108/38, Crowe to MacDonald, 26 October 1924.

47. Chester et al., *Zinoviev*, p. 67.

48. Bennett, Gill, '*A most extraordinary and mysterious business': The Zinoviev Letter of 1924* (Foreign & Commonwealth Office, *Historians, LRD* No. 14 February 1999).

49. Bennett, *Morton*, p. 80; Bennett, *A most extraordinary*, p. 35; Andrew, *Defence*, pp. 148–52.

50. Bennett, *Morton*, p. 81.

51. Minute by Morton of 11 October, SIS records, cited in Bennett, *A most extraordinary*, p. 37.

52. Ibid.

53. Gabriel Gorodetsky, 'The Other "Zinoviev Letters" New Light on The Mismanagement Of The Affair', p. 7. Both Gregory, head of the Northern Dept., and Strang 'doubted the wisdom of publication'. Crowe, however, was adamant that the 'Russian machinations' should for once be exposed.

54. Chester et al., *Zinoviev*, p. 107.

55. Ibid., p. 72.

56. Ibid., Appendix A. 'The complete diary of Donald im Thurn, discovered among Major Guy Kindersley's papers', p. 198.

57. Ibid.

58. See MacDonald's account of the events in *The Times*, 27 October 1924 and in *Parl. Deb. H. C.*, vol. 215, cols. 47–51, 19 March 1928; Gorodetsky, 'The Other 'Zinoviev Letters', p. 7.

59. Gorodestky, 'The Other "Zinoviev Letters"' p. 7; Strang's *Home and Abroad* (London: Andre Deutsch, 1956) claims that MacDonald's corrected draft was 'in some respects stronger than Crowe's'; MacDonald's final draft was removed from the FO's files, apparently unintentionally by 'weeders' in the early 1950s. Austen Chamberlain admitted in December 1924 that MacDonald had not sanctioned the dispatch of the Note: *Parl. Deb. H. C.*, vol. 179, col. 673, 145, December 1924.

60. Chester et al., *Zinoviev*, p. 107.

61. A decoded intercept from the German Foreign Office to its Mexican ambassador suggesting that plans be laid for a joint German-Mexican invasion of the US was released at exactly the right moment to make it a vital influence on America's decision to enter the war on the side of the Allies.

62. Arthur McIvor, '"A Crusade for Capitalism": The Economic League, 1919–1939', *Journal of Contemporary History* 23 (1988), pp. 631–55; Thomas Lineham, *British Fascism, 1918–1939: Parties, Ideology and Culture.* (Manchester: Manchester University Press, 2000).

63. Chester et al., *Zinoviev*, p. 107; Appendix A, p. 199.

64. Andrew, Christopher, *Security Service* (London: Heinemann, 1985) p. 99.

65. Both boys often visited the Browning family home.

66. Kommersant vlast', 'Zdes' lezhit Chicherin, zhertva sokrashchenii I chistok', 1 February 2010; NA Kew KV2/3331.3/CX/1174/Ib, 17 November 1924.

Chapter 12   The 1926 General Strike and the Anglo-Russian Committee

1. MacDonald's Labour government 'was plagued by what seemed unusually virulent labour troubles in the first half of 1924'. British Communists participated 'fiercely and tirelessly in a number of disputes'. 'The locomotive engineers and firemen struck the railways in January, the dockers went out in February, municipal transport was hit in March, the shipyards in April, and a mass walkout of miners was only narrowly averted in May. The troubles persisted right into the summer months: the London Underground system was struck in June and the builders downed tools in July' (Calhoun, *United Front*, p. 43).

2. A copy of which, classified as 'Most Secret', made its way to MI6 and MI5 on 17 November 1924.

3. Arthur MacManus, chairman of the CPGB counter-signed the Zinoviev Letter.

4. TNA Kew KV2/3331.3/CX/1174/Ib, 17 November 1924.

5. Ibid.

6. Ibid.

7. TNA Kew KV2/3331.2/CX/1174, dated 2 December 1924.

8. Ibid.

9. Not to be confused with the All-Russian Central Council of Trades Unions.

10. *Daily Herald*, 28 October 1924.

11. *Russia Today*, p. 262.

12. The IFTU was founded in Amsterdam in July and August 1919.

13. See Calhoun, *United Front*, fn2. P.135. 'The theory was first proposed in an essay of Dec. 1924 (*Sochineniia*, vi, 358−401). Although published in the daily press, the theory was hardly noticed at the time. His colleagues did not yet take Stalin seriously as a Marxist theorist.'

14. Swales, Purcell and Bramley for the TUC and Tomsky and Melnitchanski for the All-Russian Central Union of Trades Unions.

15. TNA Kew KV2/3331.2/Zinoviev.

16. TNA Kew KV2/331.2/Zinoviev.

17. Calhoun, *United Front*, p. 147.

18. TNA Kew KV2/1576.

19. TNA Kew KV2/1109/4, Walter Citrine to Andrew Rothstein, 17 July 1925.

20. Calhoun, *United Front*, p. 151.

21. See *The Times*, 8 and 14 May 1925; Calhoun, *United Front*, p. 151.

22. Calhoun, *United Front*, p. 154.

23. Ibid.

24. Ibid., p. 155.

25. Stalin, *Sochineniia*, vii, 90−106.

26. Calhoun, *United Front*, p. 160.

27. *Daily Herald*, 18 May 1925.

28. Ibid.

29. TNA Kew KV2/1576/299B.
30. TNA Kew KV2/1109/1A.
31. TNA Kew KV2/1109/3A. GPO Special Section.
32. Editor of the *Daily Herald*.
33. Given the Russian background and employment history of the Lunn sisters it is unlikely that they would have been overlooked by Ewer's outfit.
34. Beatrice Webb, *Diaries, 1924–1932* (London:Virago; new edition, 2002), p. 68.
35. Margaret Cole, *Beatrice Webb* (London: Longmans, 1945), p. 157.
36. Quoted in Arnold Wesker, 'The Secret Reins "Centre 42"', *Encounter*, March 1962.
37. While the miners got their seven-hour day, and some wage increases, the Prime Minister, Lloyd George, flatly rejected the idea of nationalisation as impractical (see Julian Symons, *The General Strike* (London: The Cresset Press, London, 1959), pp. 14–15.
38. See TNA Kew KV4/246, 'Summary of Military Security Intelligence action in connection with the Civil Emergency, 1st to 18th April 1921.'
39. G. D. H Cole, *The Common People 1746–1938* (London: Meuthen & Co., Ltd, 1938), p. 363. Lord Birkenhead said 'that he thought the miners' leaders the most stupid men he had ever met, until he met the owners.' See Symons, *General Strike*, p. 47.
40. Quoted in Symons, *General Strike*, p. 19.
41. *Workers Weekly*, 7 August 1925 quoted in Calhoun, *United Front*, p. 174.
42. See, for example, the manifesto in *Inprecorr*, v, 64 (13 August, 1925), 915–16 cited in Calhoun, *United Front*, fn.3, p. 174.
43. Among them the hero of the Battle of Jutland, Lord Jellicoe and the ex-Viceroy of India, Lord Hardinge of Penshurst,
44. 'It has been estimated that on the eve of the First World War 87 per cent of aggregate personal wealth [...] was owned by the richest five per cent of the population. In the period 1924–30 this proportion fell slightly to 84 per cent, but even then 90 per cent of the total population owned less than 10 per cent of aggregate personal wealth ... these economic divisions in British society were reinforced by a complex set of non-economic factors such as education, dress, residence, accent, recreation, and so on – which made both the owner and the worker fairly readily identifiable. (Macintyre, *Proletarian Science*, p. 173).
45. Suitable people were to be recommended for work as transport drivers. An earlier 1919 scheme had seen volunteers drive away trucks and vans never to be seen again.
46. Cole, *Common People*, p. 564.
47. MI(B) opened at the War Office on 1 May at 1200 hrs. and on 3 May liaison was established between MI(B) and New Scotland Yard under Sir Wyndham Childs. See TNA Kew KV4/246, 'Extracts from Diary kept by M.I.(B)': 'Close touch

was maintained with Scotland Yard throughout the period of the General Strike, and all information of interest was exchanged. [. . .] An Officer from M.I. (B) called at Scotland Yard each morning to see Sir W. Childs and to obtain a copy of the Police Summary.'

48. Andrew, *Defence*, p. 125.
49. When A. B. Swales, one of the Trade Union Delegation to have visited the Soviet Union in 1924, resigned as chairman of the General Council in 1926 his place was taken by Arthur Pugh, a man 'further to the right of the movement than Swales had been to the left.' This trend continued with the return of the railwaymen's leader, J. H. Thomas, to the General Council following the fall of the Labour Government in 1925, and the election to the Council at Scarborough of Ernest Bevin. Bevin did not share the left trade unionists appreciation of the Soviet Union and could see no point in the Anglo-Russian trade union negotiations. See Calhoun, *United Front*, p. 177.
50. Cole, *Common People*, p. 566.
51. The word 'general' was never used by the unions in reference to the strike.
52. Quoted in Symons, *General Strike*, p. 57.
53. The General Council had drawn up a plan for calling out industries in sections. The first and most powerful battalions were to come out on the Monday: all transport workers of every kind, sea, land or air. The whole printing trade, iron and steel workers, metal workers, chemical workers, building workers, except for hospital and housing work, and electrical and gas workers. See Cole, *Common People*, p. 566.
54. Cole, *Common People*, p. 567.
55. TNA Kew KV4/282, 'Publication Entitled "Aspects of The General Strike Of 1926" Issued By New Scotland Yard', June 1926.
56. Telegraph Agency of the Soviet Union.
57. TNA Kew KV4/282, 'Publication Entitled "Aspects of The General Strike Of 1926" Issued By New Scotland Yard', June 1926. Foreign Influences on The Strike.'
58. Ibid.
59. Ibid.
60. Ibid.
61. Most probably the Moscow Narodny Bank.
62. Cole, *Common People*, p. 571.
63. The IFTU also contributed funds to the striking miners, a total of £80,000 or less than 2d per IFTU member. British trade unionists raised about £450,000 equivalent to 1/-3d from each TUC member. Russian donations totalled £1,233,788 averaging out at almost 3/- from every Soviet trade unionist. See Calhoun, *United Front*, p. 250.
64. Cole, *Common People*, p. 572.
65. Calhoun, *United Front*, p. 233.

Chapter 13   The ARCOS Raid and 'Class Against Class'

1. TNA Kew KV4/246, Summary of General Strike, Appendix 4.
2. TNA Kew KV4/246.
3. On the 8 May; report sent to MI(B) on 10 May.
4. Maisky, an atheist of Jewish Polish descent, had first arrived in Britain to study the British labour movement in November 1912.
5. TNA Kew KV4/246, 'Interview with Maisky 8 May 1926'. See also note 117.
6. TNA Kew KV4/246, 'Interview with Maisky 8 May 1926'.
7. Gavrilov was strongly linked with Gertrude Sirnis, the mother of the 'atomic power' spy Melita Norwood, in 1925 and 1926. See Burke, *The Spy Who Came In From The Co-op*, p. 60; also TNA Kew KV2/111/146a.
8. TNA Kew KV4/246, 'Interview with Maisky 8 May 1926'.
9. TNA Kew KV2/2904, Maisky, Ivan Mikhailovich.
10. TNA Kew KV4/246, 'Report sent to M.I.(B) 10th May, 1926.'
11. The five lines have a different type face and presumably were added on a different typewriter to the one that the main report was written on.
12. TNA Kew KV2/1576/298a. In 1925 SCR could call on a number of prominent academics as lecturers some of whom would later be involved in agent recruitment in the universities including Maurice Dobb, Kim Philby's future tutor at Cambridge. See TNA Kew KV2/1109 ROSTA. Letter from Maurice Dobb to A. F. Rothstein 22 June 1925.
13. TNA Kew KV2/1577/'315B, 'Another field of communist activity is the S.C.R. upon the Executive of which is Rothstein. This Organisation is concerned with getting as many professors and intellectuals as possible into its ranks, as it is hoped that when the need arises these people will be a strong propagandist weapon wisely directed.' The S.C.R's Vice Presidents certainly included an impressive array of literary and academic talent including E. M. Forster, Julian Huxley, J. M. Keynes, H. G. Wells and Virginia Woolf.

    Rothstein, who would later have a role in the collection of Science & Technical Intelligence (S & T), recruited the spy Melita Norwood through the Friends of the Soviet Union, an associate body of the S.C.R.
14. January 26, Theodore Rothstein frequently commented on British affairs and appeared to follow the Great Game closely: 'At a session of the Collegia of the NKID, held on 5 December 1925, a report was made by '[Theodore] ROTHSTEIN on the re-inforcement of British Aviation in Wazi-Ristan, and the agreement concluded between the British Government and the "Imperial Air Ways" to ensure the Indian-Egyptian air routes.'
15. TNA Kew KV2/1576/305, 2 'CX/1174 to Captain Miller, Scotland Yard.'
16. Andrew Rothstein was head of the Rosta office from January 1921 to mid-1925, then of TASS (as Rosta was renamed following its amalgamation with the press agencies of the other Soviet Republics) until 1926.
17. TNA Kew KV2/1582/820b.

18. Theirs was a natural alliance: all three were Jewish internationalists and as such naturally claimed priority for the message of world revolution and opposed 'socialism in one country'. '"When we read that in Odessa, under Skoropadsky, the rabbis assembled in special council, and there these representatives of the rich Jews, officially, before the entire world, excommunicated from the Jewish community such Jews as Trotsky and me, your obedient servant and others − no single hair of any of us has turned gray because of grief"; Zinoviev, *Sochineniia*, 16:224, quoted in *Bezbozhnik* (*The Godless*), no. 20 (12 September 1938). Sometime in 1918, while Ukraine was under German occupation, the rabbis of Odessa ceremonially anathematized Trotsky, Zinoviev and other Jewish Bolshevik leaders in the synagogue.
19. Calhoun, *United Front*, p. 242.
20. Stalin, Bukharin, Tomsky.
21. See Calhoun, *United Front*, p. 263.
22. 'Workers' Bulletin' (CPGB), Strike Special No. 9, 13 May 1926, cited in Calhoun, *United Front*, p. 244.
23. See Calhoun, *United Front*, p. 272.
24. Ibid., p. 254.
25. TNA Kew CAB24/180/CP.236(26), 'Russian Money', 11 June 1926; see Calhoun, *United Front*, p. 254.
26. TNA Kew KV2/1576/307A, 'Secret Communist Organisation'.
27. Ibid.
28. See Calhoun, *United Front*, pp. 254−5.
29. Ibid.
30. Calhoun, *United Front*, p. 257; TNA Kew CAB24/180/CP.236(26), 'Russian Money', 11 June 1926.
31. Calhoun, *United Front*, p. 257.
32. Ibid., p. 259.
33. Degras, *Communist International*, p. 302.
34. Ibid.
35. These events took place on 22 November 1926.
36. TNA Kew KV2/1576.
37. Calhoun, *United Front*, p. 274.
38. The influence of the British Russian political emigration on Soviet foreign policy is interesting and, surprisingly, often overlooked. Maisky, who had known and worked with Andrew Rothstein's father in London, had also been closely associated with both Chicherin and Litvinov in exile (See Gorodetsky, Gabriel (ed.)), *The Maisky Diaries. The Wartime Revelations Of Stalin's Ambassador In London* (London: Yale University Press, 2016), pp. xxxviii−xxxix.
39. TNA Kew KV2/1576/307B.
40. TNA Kew KV2/2318.
41. TNA Kew KV2/1577/348.
42. See TNA Kew KV2/2318, Edith Lunn.
43. TNA Kew KV2/1577/348.

44. Degras, *Communist International*, p. 314.
45. Cited Degras, *Communist International*, p. 314.
46. The United Front 'from above' as opposed to the United Front 'from below'.
47. Despite the Communist Party's low membership figures – at the end of 1926 they had no more than 7,900 members – there were approximately 1,500 communists known to be active in the Labour Party itself. Until 1926 there had been nothing to stop individuals from becoming members of both the Labour Party and the CPGB, while trade unions could elect Communists as delegates to Labour organizations and meetings. At the end of 1926 as many as 1,544 Communists still belonged to the Labour Party as individuals, and another 242 were trade union delegates to Labour organisations. The leaders of the Labour Party, in accordance with a decision first adopted at the 1924 Labour Party Annual Conference, began to purge the Communists from its ranks in 1926. Local Labour parties who refused to expel their communists were simply disbanded and 'official' parties set up in their place. This purge of communists was made easier in 1927 by changes taking place inside the CPGB itself in response to directives coming from the Communist International.
48. TNA Kew KV2/1582/820b.
49. TNA Kew KV2/1577/315, extract dated 25 February 1927.
50. TNA Kew KV2/1576/309a, The Belgians agreeing to the congress despite strong protests from the USA and Dutch authorities.
51. Fredrik Petersson, '"We Are neither Visionaries". Willi Munzenberg, the League Against Imperialism, and the Comintern, 1925–1933'. Unpublished PhD thesis, Abo Akademi University (2013), p. 130.
52. TNA Kew KV2/1577/310b.
53. A subsidiary but ostensibly an independent company of ARCOS.
54. TNA Kew KV3/17, 'Copy of a letter addressed to Mr. P. Miller' 1925. Letter No. 47.
55. TNA Kew KV3/35 Note 19.
56. TNA Kew MEPO38/72.
57. TNA Kew KV3/35/7A, 'Documents Obtained From ARCOS Ltd.'
58. All-Russian Communist Party (Bolshevik).
59. TNA Kew KV3/35/7A, 'Documents Obtained From ARCOS Ltd.'
60. TNA Kew HO144/8403, 'S.S.1 Report On Documentary Evidence Implicating Officials Of The Russian Trade Delegation And ARCOS In Revolutionary Propaganda And Espionage', 1927.
61. Ibid.
62. TNA Kew KV3/17, 'Letter No. 48. Copy of a letter addressed to J. Kirchenstein 29 September 1925, translated from the Lettish'; TNA Kew KV2/1576/308, 'Correspondence of Jacob KIRCHENSTEIN and his associates'. Charles's identity was unknown to MI5. It was probably Charles Ashleigh.
63. TNA Kew HO144/8403, 'Report On Documentary Evidence Implicating Officials Of The Russian Trade Delegation And ARCOS In Revolutionary Propaganda and Espionage.'

64. TNA Kew HO144/8403.

65. Ibid.

66. Maisky, along with the entire Soviet Embassy, left Dover on 3 June 1927.

67. TNA Kew KV2/1577/328.

68. TNA Kew KV2/1576/298A.

69. His proper title was Director of the Press Department of the Commissariat for Foreign Affairs. He also wrote regularly for the Comintern press under the name Iranski.

Bibliography

Primary Sources

Alexander Sirnis's Diary. Melita Norwood Papers, Hoover Institute, University of Stanford.

BSP Conference Reports (Marx Memorial Library).

Correspondence: Andrew Rothstein to David Burke, 1980–91.

Correspondence: Socialist Labour Party to Sirnis, December 1917, Jurgen Kuczynski Papers, Berlin.

Correspondence: W. R. Stoker to Sirnis, n.d., Jurgen Kuczynski Papers, Berlin.

Fourth Congress of the Communist International. Theses on Comintern Tactics, 5 December 1922; http://www.marxists.org/history/international/comintern/4th-congress/tactics.htm.

Hansard, Parliamentary Debates.

Kell, Vernon, private papers, Imperial War Museum (IWM); Lady Kell, 'Secret Well Kept', IWM.

Kuczynski, Jurgen, private papers, Berlin, in the possession of Jurgens Kuczynski' son Thomas Kuczynski, Weisensee, Berlin.

Lloyd George Papers, House of Lords Library, F202.3.19.

Okhrana. Archive of the Imperial Russian Secret Police (Okhrana), Box #35 Index#Vc Folder 1, 'Relations with Scotland Yard', Hoover Institution, Stanford, CA.

Report of the Stuttgart Congress of the Second International: Militarism and International Conflicts, 1907.

SDF/SDP Conference Reports (Marx Memorial Library).

TNA Kew CAB24, 'Report on Revolutionary Organisations In The United Kingdom, 1919–20'.

TNA Kew Cab 24/97, 'Revolutionaries and The Need For Legislation 2nd February 1920'.

TNA Kew CAB24/180/CP.236(26), 'Russian Money', 11 June 1926.

TNA Kew CAB 24/1106, 'Negotiations with M. Krassin – Note by Lord Curzon', CP 1350, 27 May 1920.

TNA Kew CAB 37/105/2, Criminal aliens (Aliens Prevention of Crime) Bill.

TNA Kew F.O. 371/2995/56485, 16 March 1917.

TNA Kew F.O. 371/2995/57146, 17 March 1917.

TNA Kew F.O. 371/2996/96045, 12 May 1917.

TNA Kew F.O. 371/2996/105142, 26 May 1917.

TNA Kew F.O. 371/3004/28533, 6 February 1916.

TNA Kew F.O. 371/3347/179551, Russia, 1918.

TNA Kew F.O. 371/6399, 12 January 1921.

TNA Kew F.O. 371/9353/N9988, Russia, 1923.

TNA Kew HO 48/10629/199699.

TNA Kew HO 144/545/A55176 item 44, 'Memorandum by E. R. Bradford', 24 May 1902.

TNA Kew HO 144/2158 (322428/2), 'Memorandum regarding the Russian section of the Communist Club' and 'The Russian Political Prisoners and Exiles Relief Committee in London'.

TNA Kew HO144/8403, 'S.S.1 Report On Documentary Evidence Implicating Officials Of The Russian Trade Delegation And ARCOS In Revolutionary Propaganda And Espionage', 1927.

TNA KV1/8, Memoir of William Melville MVO MBE, 31 December 1917.

TNA KV1/43, 'Revolutionary Agencies at Work'.

TNA Kew KV 1/1532 G1, 'The British Socialist Party', 4 October 1916.

TNA Kew KV2/1109, ROSTA.

TNA Kew KV2/1415, Klishko.

TNA KV2/1532, Undated Note by Major Ferguson on Information from Victor Fisher [*sic*].

TNA Kew KV2/1575 – 1584, Theodore and Andrew Rothstein.

TNA KV2/1655 G1, 'The British Socialist Party', 4 October 1916.

TNA Kew KV2/2317–2318, Edith Lunn.

TNA Kew KV2/2904, Mayskiy, Ivan Mikhailovich.

TNA Kew KV2/3331, Zinoviev.

TNA Kew KV3/17, 'Copy of a letter addressed to Mr. P. Miller', 1925. Letter No. 47. ARCOS Raid.

TNA Kew KV3/35, Note 19. ARCOS Raid.

TNA Kew KV3/35/7A, 'Documents Obtained From ARCOS Ltd'.

TNA Kew KV3/39, 'The Political background to the Houndsditch Murders and The Siege of Sydney Street'.

TNA Kew KV4/246, 'Extracts from Diary kept by M.I.(B)'.

TNA Kew KV4/246, 'Interview with Maisky', 8 May 1926.

TNA Kew KV4/246, 'Summary of Military Security Intelligence action in connection with the Civil Emergency', 1–18 April 1921.

TNA Kew KV4/282, 'Publication Entitled "Aspects Of The General Strike Of 1926" Issued By New Scotland Yard, June 1926. Foreign Influences on The Strike'.

TNA Kew MEPO38/72, ARCOS Raid.

TNA MUN 5/19/221.1/2, July 1915.

TNA WO 32/9302, MI7.

TNA WO32/10776, MI7.

TNA WO 106/6292, 'Conclusions of the Sub-Committee requested to consider how a secret service bureau could be established in Great Britain', 28 April 1909.

Wilfrid Scawen Blunt papers and correspondence, Fitzwilliam Museum Library, Cambridge.

Newspapers and Journals

Churchill, Winston, 'Zionism versus Bolshevism. A Struggle For The Soul Of The Jewish People'. *Illustrated Sunday Herald*, 8 June 1920.

Daily Herald.

Forward.

Free Russia.

Jewish World, 12 November 1919.

Justice.

Kommersant vlast', 'Zdes' lezhit Chicherin, zhertva sokrashchenii I chistok', 1 February 2010.

Kommunist.

Kommunisticheskii Internatsional, March 1920, April 1929.

Labour Leader.

Manchester Guardian. (Articles from Rothstein published in the *Manchester Guardian* included 'The Ukraine and its People'; 'The Disputed Baltic States'; 'The Turk Homeland'; 'The Bolshevik Proposals'; 'Adriatic Turkey. Allies Agreement with Ex-Tsar'; 'Bolsheviks and Class Struggle', 2, 5, 9, 11, 18, 23 January 1918, respectively.)

Nashe Slovo (Our Word).

Pall Mall Gazette.

Plebs Magazine.

Pravda.

Social-Democrat.

Soldat-Grazhdanin.

The Call.

The Challenge.

The Times.

To-Day.

To-Morrow: A Monthly Review.

Vanguard.

Workers Dreadnought.

Secondary Sources

Articles

Andrews, R.F (Andrew Rothstein), 'What Lenin said about the Jews', Marxist Internet Archive, 2008.

Barghoorn, Frederick C., 'Russian Radicals and the West European Revolutions of 1848', *The Review of Politics*, Vol. 11, No. 3 (July 1949).

Bloomfield, Jeffrey, 'The Rise and Fall of Basil Thomson, 1861–1939', *Journal of the Police History Society*, Vol 12 (1997).

Burke, David, 'Theodore Rothstein, Russian Émigré and British Socialist', in Slatter, John (ed.), *From The Other Shore. Russian Political Emigrants in Britain, 1880–1917* (London: Frank Cass).

C.P.C., 'The Land War in Ireland by Wilfrid Scawen Blunt', *The Irish Review (Dublin)*, Vol. 2, No. 22 (December 1912).

Crisp, Olga, 'The Russian Liberals and the 1906 Anglo-French Loan to Russia', *The Slavonic and East European Review*, Vol. 39 (June 1961).

Debo, Richard Kent, 'The Making of a Bolshevik: Goergii Chicherin in England, 1914–1918', *Slavic Review* 25 (1966).

Gorodetsky, Gabriel, 'The Other "Zinoviev Letters". New Light On The Mismanagement Of The Affair', Russian and East European Reseach Centre, Tel-Aviv University, 1976.

Henderson, Robert, 'The Free Russian Library in Whitechapel', in Beasley, Rebecca and Bullock, Philip Ross (eds), *Russia in Britain, 1880–1940: From Melodrama to Modernism* (Oxford University Press, 2013).

Hiley, Nicholas P., 'The Failure of British Espionage against Germany 1907–1914', *Historical Journal* 26, 4 (1983), pp. 867–89.

Hollingsworth, Barry, 'The Society of Friends of Russian Freedom: English Liberals and Russian Socialists, 1890–1917', *Oxford Slavonic Papers*, Vol. 3 (1970).

Hussey, L., 'Mr. Rothstein and the Soviet Union', *The New Reasoner*, Vol. 1, no. 1 (Summer 1957).

Johnson, Richard, J., '*Zagranichnaia agentura*: the Tsarist political police in Europe', *Journal of Contemporary History*, 6 (1971).

Long, James William, 'Organized protest against the 1906 Russian loan', *Cahiers du monde russe et sovietique*, Vol. 13, 13–1 (1972).

Maisky, I., 'Anglo-sovetskoye torgovoe soglashenie 1921 goda', *Voprosy Istorii*, No. 5, 1957.

McHugh, J. and Ripley, B.J., 'Russian Political Internees in First World War Britain: The Cases of Georgi Chicherin and Peter Petroff', *The Historical Journal*, Vol. 28, No. 3 (September 1985).

McIvor, Arthur, '"A Crusade for Capitalism": The Economic League, 1919–1939', *Journal of Contemporary History*, 23 (1988).

Neild, Keith, 'Theodore Rothstein', *Dictionary of Labour Biography*, Vol. VII, edited by Bellamy, Joyce and Saville, John (1984).

Partridge, Monica, 'Alexander Herzen and the English Press', *The Slavonic and East European Review*, Vol. 36, No. 87 (June 1958).

Porter, Bernard, 'The British Government And Political refugees, c. 1880–1914', in Slatter, John, *From The Other Shore, Russian Political Emigrants in Britain, 1880–1917* (London: Frank Cass, 1984).

Rothstein, Andrew, 'The Revolutionary Movement in Britain 1900–1921' (review), *Labour Monthly*, December 1969.

Rotshtein, Feodor, '*Pamyati odnovo pechal'nika Vostoka. Nekrolog o Wilfrid Scawen Blunt*', in *Novii Vostok*, No. 2 (1922).

Saunders, D.B., 'Stepniak and the London Emigration: Letters to Robert Spence Watson (1887–1890)', *Oxford Slavonic Papers* new series L3 (1980).

Senese, Donald, 'S. M. Stepniak-Kravchinskii and the National Front Against Autocracy', *Slavic Review* 34 (1975).

Slatter, John, 'Learning from Russia: The History of Soviets in Britain', *Labour History Review*, Vol. 61, No. 1, Spring 1996.

Wesker, Arnold, 'The Secret Reins "Centre 42"', *Encounter*, March 1962.

Williams, Carl, 'The Policing of Political Belief in Great Britain 1914–1918', http://.lse.ac.uk/CPNSS/pdf/DP_withCoverPages/DP58/DP58F.pdf.

Books

Altman, V.V., *Imperializm I borba rabochevo klassa. Sbornik statei patyati akademika F.A. Rotshteina* (Moskva, AN SSSR, 1961).

Andrew, Christopher, *The Defence of The Realm. The Authorized History of MI5* (London: Allen Lane, 2009).

———, *Secret Service* (London: Heinemann, 1985).

Armytage, W.H.G., *A. J. Mundella 1825–1897. The Liberal Background to The Labour Movement* (London: Ernest Benn Limited, 1951).

Baron, S.M., *Plekhanov, The Father of Russian Marxism* (Stanford, CA: Stanford University Press, 1963).

Beinin, Joel and Lockman, Zachary, *Workers on the Nile. Nationalism, Communism, Islam, and the Egyptian Working Class, 1882–1954.* (London: I.B.Tauris, 1988).

Bell, Tom, *John Maclean, a fighter for freedom* (Glasgow: Communist party, Scottish Committee, 1944).

———, *Pioneering Days* (London: Lawrence & Wishart, 1941).

Bennett, Gill, '*A most extraordinary and mysterious business': The Zinoviev Letter of 1924* (Foreign & Commonwealth Office, *Historians, LRD*, No. 14, February 1999).

———, *Churchill's Man of Mystery. Desmond Morton and the World of intelligence* (Abingdon: Routledge, 2007).

Berghahn, V.R., *Germany and the Approach of War in 1914* (London: St. Martin's Press, 1973).

Blunt, Wilfrid, *Land War in Ireland* (London: Stephen Swift & Co. Ltd., 1912).

———, *Married to a Single Life* (Salisbury: Michael Russell (Publishing) Ltd., 1983).

———, *My Diaries: being a personal narrative of events 1888–1914* (New York: Alfred A. Knopf, 1921).

———, *Secret History of the English Occupation of Egypt. Being a Personal Narrative of Events* (London: Alfred A. Knopf, 1922).

Branson, Noreen, *Poplarism 1919–1925. George Lansbury and the Councillors' Revolt* (London: Lawrence & Wishart, 1979).

Broido Vera, *Apostles Into Terrorists. Women and the Revolutionary Movement in the Russia of Alexander II* (New York: The Viking Press, 1977).

Brust, Harold, *I Guarded Kings* (New York: Hillman-Curl, Inc. New York, 1936).

Buchanan, Sir George, *My Mission to Russia and Other Diplomatic Memories* (London: Cassell and Company, 1923).

Bullock, Ian, *Romancing The Revolution. The Myth Of Soviet Democracy and the British Left* (Alberta: AU Press, Athabasca University 2011).

Burke, David, *The Lawn Road Flats. Spies, Writers and Artists* (Suffolk: The Boydell Press, 2014).

———, *The Spy Who Came In From The Co-op: Melita Norwood and the Ending of Cold War Espionage* (Suffolk: Boydell & Brewer, 2008).

Calhoun, Daniel F., *The United Front. The TUC and the Russians 1923–1928* (Cambridge: Cambridge University Press, 2009).

Carr, E.H., *Romantic Exiles* (Middlesex: Penguin Books Ltd., 1933).

———, *The Bolshevik Revolution 1917–1923* (London: MacMillan, 1953).

———, *A History of Soviet Russia. Socialism in One Country, 1924–1926* (London: MacMillan, 1950–1964).

———, *A History of Soviet Russia. Foundations of a Planned Economy, 1926–1928* (London: Macmillan, 1969).

Carter, Miranda, *Anthony Blunt, His Lives* (London: Pan, 2002).

Challinor, Raymond, *The Origins of British Bolshevism* (London: Croom Helm Ltd., 1977).

Chaqueri, Cosroe, *The Soviet Socialist Republic of Iran, 1920–21: Birth of the Trauma* (University of Pittsburgh Press, 1994).

Chester, Lewis, Fay, Stephen and Young, Hugo, *The Zinoviev Letter* (London: Heinemann, 1967).

Coates, W.P. and Kahan-Coates, Zelda, *A History of Anglo-Soviet Relations*. (London: Lawrence & Wishart, 1943).

Cohen, Stuart A., *English Zionists and British Jews: The Communal Politics of Anglo-Jewry, 1895–1920* (Princeton, New Jersey: University Press, 2014).

Cole G.D.H., *Socialist Thought. The Second International 1889–1914*, Part 1 (London: MacMillan, 1956).

Cole, G.D.H. and Postgate, Raymond, *The Common People* (London: Metheun & Co. Ltd. 1946).

Cole, Margaret, *Beatrice Webb* (London: Longmans, 1945).

Conrad, Joseph, *The Secret Agent* (London: Metheun, 1907).

———, *Under Western Eyes* (London: Meuthen, 1911).

Cook, Andrew, M. *MI5's First Spymaster* (London: The History Press, 2006).

Crick, Michael, *The History of the Social-Democratic Movement* (Keele University Press 1994).

Deacon, Richard, *A History of The Russian Secret Service* (London: Frederick Muller Ltd., 1972).

Debo, Richard Kent, *Survival and Consolidation: The Foreign Policy of Soviet Russia, 1918–1921* (Montreal: McGill – Queen's University Press).

Degras, Jane (ed.), *Soviet Documents on Foreign Policy* (Oxford: Oxford University Press, 1953).

———, *The Communist International 1919–1943, Volume 2, 1923–1928* (London: Frank Cass & Co. Ltd., 1971).

Dostoevsky, Fyodor, *The Idiot* (Harmondsworth, Middlesex: Penguin Books Ltd., 2004 [1868]).

Emsley, Clive, *The English Police: A Political and Social History* (London: Routledge, 1996).

Ewer, Monica, *Civil Liberties 1918* (1918).

Fatema, Nasrollah, *Diplomatic History of Persia, 1917–1923* (New York: Russell F. Moore, 1952).

Figes, Orlando, *People's Tragedy* (London: Pimlico, 1997).

Fischer, Fritz, *Germany's Aims in the First World War* (London: W.W. Norton & Company Ltd., 1967).

———, *War of Illusions. German policies from 1911–1914* (London: W.W. Norton & Company, 1975).

Fischer, Louis, *Men and Politics* (New York: Duell, Sloan and Pearce, 1941).

———, *Oil Imperialism. The International Struggle for Petroleum* (Westport, CT: Hyperion Press, 1926).

———, *The Life of Lenin* (London: Phoenix Press, 1964).

———, *The Soviets in World Affairs*, 2 vols (Princeton, NJ: Princeton University Press 1951 [1930]).

Fitch, Herbert, *Traitors Within* (London: Doubleday, 1933).

Gallacher, William G., *Revolt on the Clyde* (London: Lawrence & Wishart, 1949).

———, *Rolling of the Thunder* (London: Lawrence & Wishart, 1947).

———, *The Last Memoirs of William Gallacher* (London: Lawrence & Wishart, 1966).

Gilbert, Martin, *Winston S. Churchill, 1916–22*, Vol. IV (London: Rosetta Books, 1975).

Gilmour, David, *Curzon* (London: John Murray, 1994).

Glebov-Avilov, H., *Professional'nie Soyusi I gosudarstvo* (Moskva, 1924. c. 24).

Gleichen, Major-General Lord Edward, *A Guardsman's Memories* (Edinburgh and London: William Blackwood & Sons Ltd, 1932).

Gomme, Robert, *George Herbert Perris 1866–1920: The Life and Times of a Radical* (London: Peter Lang, 2003).

Gorney, Joseph, *The British Labour Movement and Zionism: 1917–1948* (London: Routledge, 2013).

Gorodetsky, Gabriel (ed.), *The Maisky Diaries. The Wartime Revelations Of Stalin's Ambassador In London* (London: Yale University Press, 2016).

Haslam, Jonathan, *Near and Distant Neighbours. A New History of Soviet Intelligence* (New York: Farrar, Straus And Giroux, 2015).

———, *Russia's Cold War: From the October Revolution to the Fall of the Wall* (New Haven, CT: Yale University Press, 2012).

———, *The Vices of Integrity. E.H. Carr, 1892–1982* (London: Verso, 1999).

Hastings, Patrick, *Autobiography* (London: Heinemann, 1948).

Heller, Joseph, *British Policy towards the Ottoman Empire, 1908–1914* (London: Psychology Press, 1983).

Hemming, Henry, *M: Maxwell Knight, MI5's Greatest Spymaster* (Preface Publishing, 2017).

Herzen, Alexander, *From the Other Shore* (Oxford: Oxford Paperbacks, 1979).

Hobson, J.A., *The War in South Africa. Its Causes and Effects* (London: Create Space Independent Publishing Platform, 2013 [1900]).

Hodgson, Earl W., *A Night with a Nihilist* (Cupar-Fife: Fifeshire Journal Office, 1886).

Holmes, Colin, *Anti-Semitism in British Society, 1876–1939* (London: Hodder & Stoughton, 1979).

Hopkirk, Peter, *On Secret Service East of Constantinople. The Plot To Bring Down The British Empire* (London: John Murray, 1984).

Hulse, J.W., *Revolutionists in London* (Oxford: Oxford University Press, 1970).

James, Henry, *The Princess Casamassima* (Harmondsworth, Middlesex: Penguin Books Ltd., 1987 [1886]).

Jefferys, James B., *The Story of The Engineers 1800–1945* (London: Lawrence & Wishart, 1945, 1970).

Jeffrey, Keith, *MI6. The History of The Secret Intelligence Service 1909–1949* (London: Bloomsbury, 2010).

Judd, Alan, *The Quest for C: Mansfield Cumming and the Founding of the Secret Service* (London: Harper Collins, 2000).

Kadish, Sharman, *Bolsheviks and British Jews* (London: Frank Cass, 1992).

Kendall, Walter, *The Revolutionary Movement in Britain, 1900–1921* (London: Wiedenfeld & Nicholson, 1969).

Kettle, Michael, *Russia and the Allies 1917–1920* (Minnesota: University of Minnesota Press, 1981).

Koss, Stephen, *The Pro-Boers: The Anatomy of an Anti-War Movement* (Chicago: University of Chicago Press, 1973).

Krupskaya, Nadezhda, *Memories of Lenin* (London: Lawrence & Wishart, 1970).

Lampert, E., *Studies in Rebellion* (London: Routledge and Kegan Paul, 1957).

Leggett, George, *Cheka: Lenin's Political Police* (Oxford: Oxford University Press, 1986).

Lenin, V.I., *Collected Works*, 4th edition, Vol. 44 (Moscow: Progress Publishers, 1964).

————, *The Collapse of the Second International*, translated by A. Sirnis (Glasgow: National Labour Press, 1918).

————, *Left-Wing Communism: An Infantile Disorder* (Moscow: Progress Publishers, 1964 [1920]).

————, 'Split or Decay', written between February/April 1916 but not published until 1931. Lenin, *Collected Works*, 4th edition, Vol. 22 (Moscow: Progress Publishers, 1964).

Lenz, J., *The Rise and Fall of the Second International* (New York: International Publishers, 1932).

Lineham, Thomas, *British Fascism, 1918–1939: Parties, Ideology and Culture* (Manchester: Manchester University Press, 2000).

Lloyd George, David, *War Memoirs of David Lloyd George*, Vol. 1 (London: Odhams Press Limited, 1938).

Lockhart, Sir Robert Bruce, *Memoirs of A British Agent. Being an Account Of The Author's Early Life In Many Lands And Of His Official Mission To Moscow in 1918* (Harmondsworth, Middlesex: Penguin Books Ltd., 1932).

Lutsky, Vladimir Borisovitch, *Modern History of the Arab Countries* (Moscow: Progress Publishers, 1969).

Macintyre, Stuart, *A Proletarian Science. Marxism in Britain 1917–1933* (Cambridge: Cambridge University Press, 1980).

Madeira, Victor, *Britannia and the Bear* (Suffolk: Boydell & Brewer, 2014).

Masterts, Anthony, *The Man Who Was M: Life of Charles Henry Maxwell Knight* (London: HarperCollins Publisher Ltd., 1986).

Men'shikov, L, *Okhrana I Revolyutsiya*. Chast' II, Vipusk I, 1898–1903 (Moscow, 1928).

Meynell, Francis, *My Lives* (London: The Bodley Head, 1971).

Mirfendereski, G., *A Diplomatic History of the Caspian Sea: Treaties, Diaries and Other Stories* (London: Palgrave MacMillan, 2001).

Montefiore, Simon Sebag, *Young Stalin* (London: Weidenfeld & Nicolson, 2004).

Mowat, R.B., *A History of European Diplomacy 1914–1925* (London: Edward Arnold & Co., 1927).

Nabokov, Vladimir, *Ordeal of a Diplomat* (London: Duckworth And Company, 1921).

Pearce, Brian and Woodehouse, Michael, *A History of Communism in Britain* (London: Bookmarks, 1969).

Pelling, Henry, *A Short History of the Labour Party* (London: Macmillan, 1968).

————, *The British Communist Party: A Historical Profile* (London: Adam and Charles Black, 1958).

————, *A History of British Trade Unionism* (London: MacMIllan, 1992).

Pollitt, Harry, *Serving My Time* (London: Lawrence & Wishart, 1940).

Pope, Arthur Upham, *Maxim Litvinov* (London: Martin Secker & Warburg Ltd., 1943).

Porter, Bernard, *Plots and Paranoia: The History of Political Espionage in Britain 1790–1988* (London: Routledge, 1989).

————, *The Origins of the Vigilant State* (London: Weidenfeld and Nicholson, 1987).

Rappoport, Helen, *Conspirator: Lenin in Exile* (New York: Perseus, 2010).

Reith, Charles, *A Short History of The British Police* (London: Oxford University Press, 1948).

————, *The Blind Eye of History: A Study of the Origins of the Present Police Era* (London: Patterson Smith Publishing, 1975 [1952]).

Rezun, Miron, *The Soviet Union and Iran: Soviet Policy in Iran from the Beginnings of the Pahlavi Dynasty Until the Soviet Invasion in 1941* (Boulder, CO: Westview Press, 1988).

Rogan, Eugene, *The Fall of the Ottomans. The Great War in the Middle East 1914–1920* (London: Allen Lane, 2015).

Rogers, Colin, *The Battle of Stepney. The Sidney Street Siege: Its Causes and Consequences* (London: Robert Hale Limited, 1981).

Rothstein, Andrew, *British Foreign Policy and its Critics 1830–1950* (London: Lawrence & Wishart, 1969).

———, *Lenin in Britain a communist party pamphlet* (Watford: Farleigh Press Ltd., 1970).

———, *The Soldiers' Strikes of 1919* (London: Palgrave MacMillan, 1980).

———, *The Soviet Constitution* (London: Labour Publishing Company, 1923).

———, *When Britain Invaded Soviet Russia: Consul Who Rebelled* (London: Pluto Press, 1979).

Rothstein, Theodore, *Egypt's Ruin. A Financial and Administrative Record*, with An Introduction by Wilfrid Scawen Blunt (London: A.C. Fifield, 1910).

Rumbelow, Donald, *The Houndsditch Murders and the Siege of Sydney Street* (London: The History Press, 1973).

Sabahi, Houshang, *British Policy In Persia, 1918–1925* (London: Routledge, 2015).

Scalapino, Robert A., *The Japanese Communist Movement, 1920–1966* (Berkeley and Los Angeles: University of California Press, 1967).

Schapiro, Leonard, *The Communist Party of the Soviet Union* (London: Eyre & Spottiswoode, 1970).

Schneer, J., *Ben Tillett* (London: Croom Helm, 1982).

Service, Robert, *A History of Twentieth-Century Russia* (Cambridge, MA: Harvard University Press, 1997).

———, *Lenin* (London: Macmillan, 2000).

———, *Spies and Commissars* (London: Pan, 2012).

Slatter, John, *From the Other Shore, Russian Political Emigrants in Britain, 1880–1917* (London: Frank Cass, 1984).

Smele, Jonathan (ed.), *The Russian Revolution and Civil War 1917–1921: An Annotated Bibliography* (London, Bloomsbury, 2006).

Smith, Stephen, *Russia in Revolution: An Empire in Crisis, 1890–1920* (Oxford: Oxford University Press, 2017).

Stepniak, Sergius, Volkhovskii, Feliks and Voynich, E.L., *Nihilism As It Is, Being Stepniak's Pamphlets Translated By E.L. Voynich, And Felix Volkhovsky's 'Claims Of The Russian Liberals'*, with an Introduction by Dr. R. Spence Watson (London: T. Fisher Unwin, n.d.).

Strang, William, *Home and Abroad* (London: Andre Deutsch, 1956).

Symons, Julian, *The General Strike* (London: The Cresset Press, 1959).

Tanner, Duncan, *Political Change and the Labour Party 1900–191* (Cambridge: Cambridge University Press, 1990).

Taratuta, E.A., *S. M. Stepniak-Kravchinski, Rossiya pod vlast'yu tsarei* (Moskva: Khudozh lit., 1973).

Taylor, A.J.P., *The Struggle for Mastery in Europe* (Oxford: Clarendon Press, 1954).

Thompson, Willie, *The Good Old Cause. British Communism 1920–1991* (London: Pluto Press, 1992).

Thomson, Basil, *Queer People* (London: Classic Reprint, Forgotten Books, 2012 [1922]).
———, *The Scene Changes* (London: Collins, 1939).
Thorpe, Andrew, *The British Communist Party and Moscow, 1920–1943* (Manchester: Manchester University Press, 2000).
Trotsky, Lev D., *History of the Russian Revolution* (1930, London: Haymarket Books, 2008).
———, *Where is Britain Going?* (1925, London: Socialist Labour League, 1960).
Tsuzuki, C., *Hyndman and British Socialism* (Oxford: Oxford University Press, 1961).
Ullman, Richard, *Anglo-Soviet Relations, 1917–1921* (Princeton, NJ: Princeton University Press), 3 vols: *Vol. 1 Intervention and the War*, 1961; *Vol. 2 Britain and the Russian Civil War, November 1918–February 1920*, 1968; *Vol. 3 The Anglo-Soviet Accord*, 1973.
Webb, Beatrice, *Diaries, 1924–1932* (London: Virago, new edition, 2002).
White, Joseph L., *Tom Mann* (Manchester: Manchester University Press, 1991).
White, Stephen, *Britain And The Bolshevik Revolution. A Study in the Politics of Diplomacy 1920–1924* (London: Macmillan Press: 1979).
Wilde, Oscar, *Lord Arthur Saville's Crime* (1891, London: Collins, 2003).
———, *Vera, or the Nihilists* (London: Collins, 2003 [1883]).
Woolf, Leonard, *Downhill All The Way: An Autobiography of the Years 1919–1939* (London: Harcourt Brace Jovanovich, 1960).
Zarnitskii, S. and Sergeyev, A., *Chicherin* (Moscow: Molodaia Cvardia, 1975).

Unpublished PhD Theses

Burke, David, 'Theodore Rothstein and Russian Political Emigre Influence on the British Labour Movement 1884–1920', unpublished PhD thesis, University of Greenwich, 1997.
Petersson, Fredrik, '"We Are neither Visionaries". Willi Munzenberg, the League Against Imperialism, and the Comintern, 1925–1933', unpublished PhD thesis, Abo Akademi University, 2013.
Rabinovitch, V., 'British Marxist Socialism and Trade Unionism: The Attitudes, Experiences and Activities of the Social-Democratic Federation 1884–1901', unpublished PhD thesis, University of Sussex, 1970.

Index

Plate 1   The 1848 Revolution in Paris. Public domain.

Plate 2   Alexander Herzen. Public domain.

Plate 3   Sergius Mikhailovitch Kravchinski, 'Stepniak'. Courtesy of the National Portrait Gallery.

Plate 4   Henry Hyndman. Courtesy of the National Portrait Gallery.

Plate 5   William Morris. Courtesy of the National Portrait Gallery.

Plate 6   Theodore Rothstein, circa 1920. Courtesy of David Burke.

Plate 7 Andrew Rothstein (right) walking with Harry Pollitt on their way to lay a wreath at Marx's grave for the annual commemoration 1956. Courtesy of the Marx Memorial Library.

Plate 8 An etching of Lenin published in the SLP's pamphlet *V. I. Lenin: Collapse of the Second International*, translated by A. Sirnis; the first portrait of Lenin published in Britain.

THE COLLAPSE OF
THE SECOND
INTERNATIONAL

BY
ULYANOV-LENIN.

TRANSLATED BY A. SIRNIS.

PUBLISHED BY
THE SOCIALIST LABOUR PRESS,
50, RENFREW STREET, GLASGOW.

Plate 9   Front cover of the SLP's *Collapse of the Second International*.

Plate 10   Vernon Kell. Public domain.

Plate 11   Basil Thomson. Courtesy of the National Portrait Gallery.

Plate 12   Grigori Zinoviev. Public domain.

Plate 13 Maxim Litvinov. Public domain.
Plate 14 Georgi Chicherin. Public domain.

Plate 15 General Strike 1926. Clockwise from left to right: Workers' demonstration; Oxford University student volunteers armed with wooden staves; Clashes between strikers and volunteer workers outside Kings Cross Station; Special Constables collecting their truncheons. Public domain.

Plate 16   Ivan Maisky. Courtesy of the National Portrait Gallery.

Plate 17   Mikhail Tomsky. Public domain.

Lightning Source UK Ltd.
Milton Keynes UK
UKHW022113070120
356523UK00007B/404/P

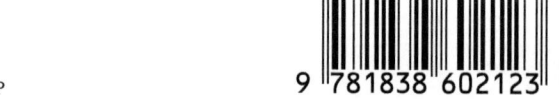